T3-BID-375

15—
ANATRO

Street Children of Cali

Lewis Aptekar

Duke
University Press
Durham
and London 1988

©1988 Duke University Press
All rights reserved
Printed in the United States of America
on acid-free paper ∞
Library of Congress Cataloging-in-Publication Data
Aptekar, Lewis.
Street children of Cali.
Bibliography: p.
Includes index.
1. Children, Vagrant—Colombia—Cali.   2. Homeless
youth—Colombia—Cali.   I. Title.
HV4537.A4A68   1988   362.7'044   87-34324
ISBN 0-8223-0834-7

*To the street children and
their benefactors*

Contents

Tables and Figures

Tables

Figures

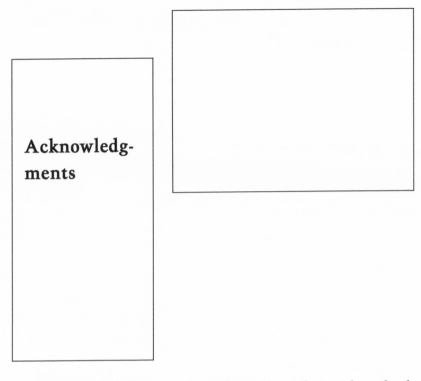

Acknowledgments

Many people helped me throughout the work. I wish to thank them all, and I do so by listing their names here, realizing that this is at best only a minor note in comparison with the magnitude of their help. I begin with the children at Bosconia and their friends, who delighted and saddened me throughout the work and afterward through my memories of them. I thank my students at the Universidad del Valle, whose help and friendship were invaluable. The Fulbright Commission in Colombia and Washington supported me well beyond financial contributions. My work in other countries in Latin America, much of which has been sponsored by Partners of the Americas, has provided the basis for many valuable friendships. I thank Peter Tacon, Ovidio Lopez, and others at Childhope and UNICEF who opened their doors to me.

The following scholars and writers, whom I list in alphabetical order, provided me with considerable emotional and intellectual help: Paul Ackerman, Marion Aptekar, Alan Boye, William Bruff, Kirk Felsman, Allen Menlo, Aaron Segal, Marshall Segall, Frank Schuster, Jr., Leslie Ullman, Thomas Whitby, and many others whose names I must omit due to space limitations.

I would also like to thank my colleagues at San Jose State University for supporting my efforts. Their contributions to my professional development have nourished me through to the end of the project.

Introduction

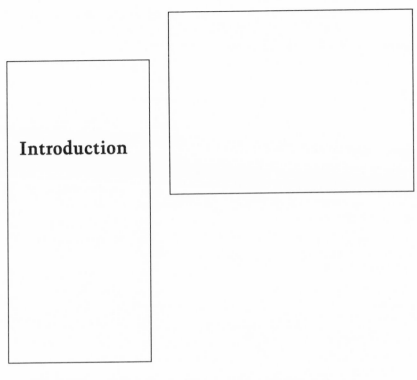

When I was a little boy, my parents explained about the hard times they were going through. Putting food on the table, I was told, was not a natural event like the change of seasons; it deserved respect. If we left carrots or broccoli on our plates, we heard the inevitable lines about all the kids in India who were starving and how hard Dad was working to provide for us. We were lectured about our responsibilities: we had to help around the house, do well in school, respect our grandparents, and, just as important, dress and keep ourselves clean. Looking back, I imagine these discussions were a way of keeping us kids in line, a way for our parents to define to us their own importance and our place. By the time we more or less internalized and assumed these demands—but before we could laugh at them—we had started school. And at school, like most North American children, we heard about the adventures of Huckleberry Finn. Huck was my first hero. By comparison to our timid dependencies, Huck, who didn't have to wash, dress up, listen to talks about being respectful, or do "nothin'" he didn't want to do, was indeed a heroic figure.

Working in Latin America over the past several years, I found it impossible to avoid these memories. There are so many children in the streets of Latin America who appear to be on their own, growing up without these early warnings and advice from their parents. Seeing them I often wondered what childhood would be like without parental authority. When I inquired about them in Colombia, as nearly all foreigners did, I was often told they were abandoned by their families and left to fend for themselves, an inevitable consequence of cruelty, poverty, and necessity. On other occasions they were described more menacingly as "dope addicts," prostitutes, and delinquents. However, when I talked to the street children, they smiled when speaking about their way of life. Neither the descriptions, which warranted pity, nor the judgmental descriptions, which implied delinquency, seemed to explain the total picture of these children. What was clear, however, was that a good part of the Colombian populace got vicarious enjoyment from these children. Something about them produced a kind of envy and longing in people who maintained a more "normal" way of life. This longing, I began to realize, was quite similar to the envy I once had for Huck Finn, whose lifestyle I had wished upon myself while eating my vegetables and doing as I was told.

In 1984 I was fortunate enough to be a Fulbright scholar in Colombia and to have the opportunity to look into the lives of the street children more systematically. On one of the first days of my study I observed a boy in the streets near the central market with half a cake in one hand. He weighed only fifty or sixty pounds. He was wearing very large pants that were rolled up three times to avoid dragging the cuffs on the ground. He was small enough that the pants were centered closer to his armpits than his waist. They were not ready-made pants, but appeared to be personally tailored by him, perhaps from an old piece of tarpaulin. He kept them on with a red bandana tied around his waist. He had no shirt or shoes. Over one shoulder lay his *cobija*, which is a standard item of clothing for street children. What separates a cobija from any other large piece of dirty cloth is its function: it is hung over a shoulder during the day and slept on at night. At this early stage of the study I came to feel that if I were asked to create an image of a child free to do as he wished, I couldn't do better than simply describe what I had seen in that downtown street. Here was a small child who seemed to go and come when and where he wanted, who ate only what struck his fancy, and who dressed as he wished. Was he like the boy I could have been, had I "lit out" like Huck?

As I was lost in thought about this possibility, I noticed that he began to suck one end of his cobija, and I was now forced to consider the difference between his street experience and his extreme youth. The cuddling of a treasured piece of blanket seemed to me to have more to do with the image of a pampered suburban child than a streetwise boy. It would be nearly a year later, when the study was almost completed, before I would understand the way in which this child, whom I came to know rather well, was at once a traveler beyond the known world of the majority of adult Colombian society, and also a small child. He was a cunning provocateur capable of outwitting the public to get what he needed and desired. But he was also not unlike more affluent children who needed the simple reassurance of a security blanket. By the end of the study I would comprehend that society's ambivalent reactions to street children were related to these paradoxical images.

Often throughout the study I felt as if I was in the company of mythical figures. Unlike the dying children of Africa whom I was reading about in the daily Colombian papers, these children were not starving. Nor did they seem to be like the emotionally injured "runaways" whom I had worked with in North America. I was intrigued and in part envious of them. Rather than seeing simply misery or delinquency I became aware of their play, their cunning ability, and their smiles. They produced powerful images that I did not understand at the time, but that nevertheless drew me as a fable might draw a child away from what is real toward what is mythical and of greater importance. My reactions to these children went beyond their immediate presence and came from deeper memories generated from my childhood recollections, from a time when I was still dependent on and beholden to my parents and yet wanting to flee from their authority.

I wanted to go beyond the reasons Colombian society gave for the phenomenon of these children, beyond such reasons as poverty, abusive parents, and rural-to-urban migrations. I sought to separate fact from fiction and to understand the mystery of these children. I wanted to know why I was so drawn to them and why I, like so many others, responded to them with an odd mixture of envy and disdain.

The study helped me know the boy in the marketplace, and he was only one of thousands whose lives could only be imagined. Collectively these children are called *gamines*. The word *gamine* means urchin in French and was first used in 1874 to explain the presence of an exceptional number of children on the streets (Ricaurte 1972, 9). Up until that time they were labeled *chinos de las calles* (*chino* is child in Quechua, the language of the Incas, and *calle* is a public street). For much of the latter part of the nineteenth century they were called *pilluelos* (little rascals or scamps). The descriptor *gamine* came into common usage when Meunier (1977), a French anthropologist who was fascinated by their apparent liberty, began to study them. Whatever the children are called, they are commonplace on the streets of Colombia and other Latin American cities. UNICEF estimated that in 1983 there were forty million children living on the streets in Latin American cities (Tacon 1981a, 1981b). Street children, although predominantly boys, are of both genders, range in age from six to sixteen, and spend a great deal of their time in public view. In Latin America today street children are a common sight, a part of everyday life that is unavoidable even to the most casual tourist. Their abundance poses interesting questions that are not addressed in the literature about them or discussed in everyday talk concerning them: How must parents feel when they have just asked their children to do some chore or take more responsibility when they know that they will encounter a group of street children who don't have to submit to these demands? And how do the children feel after being told to do yet another thing they don't want to do when they see so many children their own age playing freely in the streets?

In order to preserve a system of respect for parental authority and to permit an orderly transition between generations, Colombia society created ways to defend itself against these questions. The existence of so many street children could not simply be ignored. Street children affected the very fabric of family discipline and the ability of parents to enforce that discipline. In this interplay between the traditional family and the street children, changes occurred that eventually determined the identity of both. It was here that numbers and statistics lost much of their value and that an understanding of their way of life began to emerge.

As part of my Fulbright work I formed a research team with twelve graduate students in psychology from a public Colombian university, Universidad del Valle. Our first task was to get as close as possible to the children who were living outside of family and state control in order to gain their confidence and thus learn about their lives. We were willing to meet them on their turf, in spite of the admonition by many well-meaning people that this would be dangerous. We spent time with them as they ate, played, worked, and even slept so that we could share the variety of experiences they had as they moved around the city.

By volunteering to work in Bosconia, a program for street children that offered them something to eat and immediate medical attention, we were able to meet and become involved with many children. This program was housed in a large, vacant building in the *barrio* (neighborhood) of San Nicolas, in the city of Cali, the country's third-largest and fastest-growing urban area. Cali is located in the *departamento* (state) of El Valle. The fertile Cauca valley produces sugar cane and, in the higher regions, coffee.

El Valle is divided geographically and politically. On the western side of El Valle are the Pacific lowlands, a region of jungle and swamp that lacks roads and remains largely undeveloped. It was settled by descendants of African slaves who escaped from the Caribbean. Many people who live in this region still do not speak Spanish and retain their original African dialects and culture. The port of Buenaventura on the Pacific is something of an embarrassment to Colombians, not only because of the possibility of getting malaria and dengue (a flu-like sickness transmitted by mosquitos), but also because of the widespread corruption and crime that have characterized its existence since its opening to foreign trade. Colombians refer to it as the *mercado persa*, the Persian market.

The original Spanish conquistadores, in their search for El Dorado (the expectation of Indian gold), marched through the Cauca valley on their way to Quito, Ecuador. At its southern edge the valley meets the high Andes on the border with Ecuador. The ancient city of Popayan was founded near here in 1537, retaining its colonial character until its tragic demolition by an earthquake in 1982. Historically, the Indian peasants who farmed the high mountain valleys became financially dependent on the marketplace provided by their Spanish lords and spiritually dependent on the Catholic church. These institutions formed the people's attitudes toward the state and contributed to their concept of family structure.

Both the northern and eastern boundaries of the Cauca valley and the departamento del Valle have characteristics similar to the southern side. They are primarily agricultural centers, originally colonized by Spaniards and strongly influenced by the church, with the typical family and cultural influences of Latin American *mestizo* (a mixture of Indian and Spanish blood) life. This mixture of cultural and racial traditions has shaped society in the valley and profoundly affected its history.

The city of Cali, founded in 1536, has been the hub of urban life for the Cauca valley since transportation connected it with the port of Buenaventura and Bogotá. It is not only the political capital, but also the economic center. As the country began to industrialize, employment opportunities became available in major urban areas at the same time they were diminishing in the agricultural sectors. Cali, which began to produce, process, and package all the derivatives of sugar, was no exception. When its agricultural industry developed after World War II, there was a rapid influx of peasants from the rural areas in search of paying jobs. For the first time these peasants encountered a cash economy. People poured in not only from areas under the influence of Spanish and Catholic values, but also from sectors with African traditions.

The children we met in the barrio of San Nicolas were largely descendants of these migrants. Fortunately an Italian priest, Padre Nicolo, established the Bosconia program for street children. As part of Padre Nicolo's plan, children could enter Bosconia at will, eat one meal a day, get immediate medical attention if needed, do their laundry, find camaraderie among others like themselves, and, finally, leave when they wanted. However, they were not allowed to sleep in the facilities. They were permitted to spend the night or receive further assistance only if they asked admission to the Nicolo program. This meant that the children agreed to assume a series of responsibilities such as keeping themselves clean, going to school, and the like. Each time they solicited help they were asked to give more in terms of work and responsibility. Once the children committed themselves to the program and showed their willingness to continue their side of the bargain, they were allowed to move on to another building, Marcelina. There the program continued until they eventually graduated after several years of social and vocational training. The graduation ceremony stressed the fact that the children were leaving an aberrant life for the necessary and legitimate assumption of a moral one.

The children we met at Bosconia were essentially street children. Most of them came only for something to eat. Some stayed and joined the program, but the majority returned to the streets. At one time or another many of these children had been placed in detention by the state. Most of them had lived with adults other than their parents, often aunts, uncles, grandparents, or even friends of the family. However, more of them than we expected either lived with their parents intermittently or kept in contact with them. Nevertheless, the majority knew from a surprisingly early age the freedom and turmoil of life without parents or guardians.

Our work in Bosconia was a means of getting acquainted with the children who were actually living on the streets. Since all of them who were not in the program left after lunch, it was easy for us to walk out the door with them. We merely continued our conversations and stayed alongside them until we sensed they began to feel uncomfortable. As time went on, the conversations lasted longer and they began to show us their lives. Many had regular places to go, where they knew they could get food, a place to sleep, and find a community of playmates. After a few months we were able to divide up the city into different territories, and we walked these areas regularly, making contact with different *galladas* (certain groups of street children).

During our days at Bosconia we had children draw pictures, asking them to describe in their drawings where they went, what their families were like, and in general to show what went on in their past and present lives. As the idea of doing such drawings became more acceptable to them we asked them to draw

people, using the standard format for the Human Figure Drawing test. We also played organized games with them, observing
how they reacted to the frustrations of playing with rules and
regulations. We tutored others in reading and writing, noting
their questions and their academic skills. This helped us grasp
their cognitive abilities and development. Near the end of the
study we were able to administer fifty-six test protocols of the
Bender-Gestalt, the Kohs intelligence test, and the Human Figure Drawing test.

They often talked about their experiences and their fears of
being incarcerated. In order to get a more complete view of their
lives, we made plans for part of our research team to work in La
Sucre, the state's diagnostic center. Children were incarcerated
here for a variety of infractions, usually because of petty vandal-
ism or theft but sometimes because of more dangerous crimes
such as robbery or assault. The maximum stay at La Sucre was
sixty days, during which time the institution determined if the
children should be returned to the streets, to their guardians, or
placed in another institution for further confinement. Our data
collection here was similar to that in Bosconia. Soon we learned
that many children moved between the streets, Bosconia, La
Sucre, and back to the streets. When we missed children on the
streets for any period of time we most often encountered them in
La Sucre. In collecting data from several places we became aware
of their varied experiences, which helped us increase the depth of
our information about them.

Because we were also interested in understanding how people
perceived and reacted to the street children, we interviewed professional and nonprofessional workers at all the institutions
where we worked. I spent considerable time in the national library, reading past press releases in order to study the media's
portrayal of the children and their families. We reviewed the variety of documents that reported on attitudes toward the children.
This information and the professional literature were written in
Spanish. The translations in this text are my own.

Most of the children on the streets left home gradually, often at
their own will, and only after testing the waters of freedom in
stages. Many maintained contact with their families. They found
ways to become educated and to receive group support. Rather

than being pitiful victims, most were faring adequately, given their poor circumstances in an impoverished country. They found their own benefactors and maintained themselves emotionally and physically at least as well and often better than their counterparts who stayed at home. In short, the children were functioning much better than perceived by the public and presented by the press. Much of their behavior is appropriate, productive, and psychologically resilient, given their circumstances.

Much of what happened to them depended upon how they were perceived by the public. Their age, size, and demeanor created an image that contributed to the moral evaluations of the people who saw them. The results of this interplay were vital to the children's lives. For example, the younger children were viewed as "cute," but during their physical change into adolescence they came to be perceived as "delinquent." Two different psychological styles were characteristic of the small children. The first was the true gamine, who chose to leave home, having rejected the trade-off between childhood protection with family obligations for the freedom from authority with less security. The second style was the *chupagrueso*, who was more a victim of circumstances. Lacking the haughty independence of the gamines, chupagruesos had not made the clear-cut decision to leave their families and they learned to survive on the streets in a different fashion: by becoming servile to the powerful.

As the street children reached adolescence, they were perceived by the public as more menacing, and this forced changes in their lives. The chupagruesos tended to become marginal workers. The gamines moved either toward delinquency or toward a type of small-scale entrepreneurship. Three psychological reactions to postpuberty street life were apparent. First, the *desamparados* were those who were not coping. They made up about one-fourth of our sample. Second, the *sobrevivientes* were survivors who were coping; however the extent to which they were able to meet with success depended on the assistance they received in times of stress. This group was about one-third of our sample. And third, the *afortunados*, slightly more than 40 percent of the sample, were the fortunate ones who were making a successful adjustment to life and would continue to do so.

The children's behavior in groups gives us not only another aspect from which to view them, but also a context in which to see many of the misconceptions that society has of street children. We make distinctions between two kinds of groups: the *camada*, which is composed of two or three prepuberty street children who associate out of friendship, and the *gallada*, which is made up of many postpuberty children who associate together to conduct business.

Three "established" hypotheses for the causes of street children existed before we did our study. The first of these, which had its core in economics, stated that, as recent migrants from rural areas in search of work, the children were unskilled and therefore unable to compete for scarce employment. They were forced to work at an early age, or worse, were abandoned because there was no money to raise them. A second hypothesis concerned the internal dynamics of the family, which was said to have been headed by a frustrated and aggressive male stepfather and a wife victimized by his abuse. The tension eventually was transferred to the children, who were forced out of the home. The third hypothesis posited that the children lived in delinquent neighborhoods where the culture or values were not conducive to productive lives. However, these three hypotheses failed to take into account why the majority of children who were exposed to one or more of these conditions did not leave their families. The hypotheses also failed to explain why street children were perceived as being almost exclusively male. As the study shows, these hypotheses were ethnocentric assumptions made by the dominant social class, which felt itself in jeopardy from the presence of so many street children.

Colombian society is composed of two different family structures: the patriarchal Spanish family and the matriarchal African family. The former demands sons' obedience to their families while the latter, in order to strengthen their sons' independence, casts them out. The two family structures also have different relationships to their daughters.

The class and cultural differences of the two groups historically have brought them into conflict, and continue to do so. This conflict is exacerbated by the presence of street children. Street children have been perceived by the dominant patriarchal family as symbolic images of youth not obligated to follow adult demands, and thus they were viewed as threatening the "rights" of parents to demand obedience from their children. They were "symbolic images" in that society reacted to them beyond their mere presence; they became "examples" of possible, if not probable disorder to the established pattern of family and social class control. In good part this is why the children's abilities to cope and to fend for themselves were ignored by society while their lack of respect for authorities and their petty delinquency were exaggerated. The street children had unwillingly become a kind of weapon in the larger struggle between the disparate familial, cultural, and economic elements of Colombia.

In addition to these sociological and historical reasons for attitudes toward street children, there were other, more personal or psychological reasons that explained why people reacted to them as they did. Part of each person's emotional reaction to the street children could be explained in terms of the internal struggle between compliance with social norms in order to get societal status, and noncompliance, with concomitantly less security. The inevitable compromise, made as part of growing into adulthood, was felt by some adults to be fair, while others resented it. The particular attitude an individual had toward street children, that is, whether they were pitied, envied, or seen as threatening, depended on how that individual reacted to the compromise he himself had made.

Existing public and private programs for street children usually incorporate the prevailing, misinformed point of view about the children and thus often dwell on ways to help street children "adjust" to society. As a rule, programs for the children fail to note that there are a variety of children with different problems and assets and that several training approaches would be more appropriate than relying on one approach for all the children. Generally speaking, the programs train children to be obedient workers, usually emphasizing artisan skills. This fails to take into account the differences between those children who are simply poor and the many street children whose unique experiences give them good prospects to earn a living outside of the artisan class. It also ignores the importance of society's attitudes, which must ultimately be changed, with the help of the children themselves, so that the children and the society can live together more harmoniously.

1
Getting Acquainted with Fact and Fiction

First Impressions

Walking in El Centro through the semitropical heat of the midday sun on the Calle 13 I saw street vendors packed against each other as if from a desperate need to conserve space. The buses outnumbered the cars while the pedestrians mingled with the fumes and heat. The noise emanating from the continuous battle between vehicles and people conveyed an image of tumult following a tragedy. On the sidewalk one young man had partitioned off three square feet by setting up rosaries at the four boundaries. In the middle of this space he displayed in neatly formed lines a hundred or more inexpensive bracelets, rings, necklaces, and few foreign watches. At the union of the street with the sidewalk an elderly woman, dressed in black, sat on a wooden carton hawking numbers. Amid an onslaught of horns an old truck, its age and make beyond recognition, had stopped to unload its cargo of unmarked boxes. Next to it two boys carried half a pig, flies surrounding their faces.

El Centro, the downtown area, was typically where street children could be found. Vendors, shoppers, and street children mixed together in close quarters. El Centro is a place for strolling and shopping with one's family; there are many niches to meet various family needs. This block was part of my daily walking route.

Around the corner from Calle 13 lies La Ermita, the Spanish colonial church built in 1747 as an exact replica of Romanesque architecture. In front of La Ermita was a large metal box, wrapped and locked in an iron chain. A few pedestrians dropped coins in it, alms for the needy. As if in competition, an elderly and impoverished blind man sitting nearby held out his hand in the heavy air.

In the Plaza de Cacedo, the main plaza, book vendors had set up temporary stalls to sell used copies of paperbacks, posters of modern rock stars, and a variety of elderly religious paraphernalia. The authorities traditionally have allowed the deranged to speak here. One such man with a full beard, naked from the waist up, and painfully skinny, walked on the broken glass of a liquor bottle he had just smashed, while those who watched crossed themselves and gave him coins.

Over the Rio Cali, no more than a trickle of sewage, is the barrio of San Nicolas. Entering the barrio along Calle 20, the adobe homes, whitewashed in light shades of pastel blue and pink, seemed remarkably quiet in contrast to El Centro. Children played with wooden tops flung in gyrating circles by releasing wound string. Behind the open doors elderly women were preparing food while their husbands, huddled together over tables on the sidewalks, talked over bottles of *aguardiente*, the country's traditional sugar cane liquor. The plaza was filled with men, but no women. Crowded into small pockets of shade, they sat close together, talking about the work they didn't have and the government that wouldn't help them. One street away, and filling a square block, was the large Uniroyal factory, walled off from the street and silent. There was no way of telling that it operated twenty-four hours a day and was constantly filled with 250 workers.

One block farther down I waited in front of a two-story, faded-blue concrete building below a sign that read *Bosconia: El Futuro es Nuestro*, Bosconia: The Future Is Ours. I had agreed to meet Sylvia, one of the university students who would be working with me on this psychological and sociological study of the street children. Together we had already visited to the director of the Bosconia program, who had agreed to let us observe the events in Bosconia to see if it would be an appropriate place for us to conduct our study.

Entering the building was only possible with the permission of someone who had a key because the large iron grill that blocked off the interior was routinely locked. After passing through a short corridor we entered the main floor. A slab of concrete about sixty by fifty feet was used as a playing field, a hall for announcements, and a dining room. At one end of the concrete floor was the exposed latrine, a few empty holes in the cement floor. There were two pipes for showers, one with a showerhead. There was no hot water. Equally exposed at the other end was a cement ledge about three feet high and two feet wide running the length of the floor. Here and on the four long wooden benches facing the ledge a few feet away the children ate, occasionally listened to lectures from a variety of people who tried to get them to "give up the streets," and often slept in the middle of the day, laid out like casualties from a long forced march.

Stairways on the two other sides of the main floor led up to where other children slept. The "sleepers" were required to keep their cots clean and neatly made. The dormitories had been newly painted pale blue. There were about twelve beds in each of two large rooms. The beds were close together (less than four feet apart), but the space appeared ample because there was no storage for clothes or personal belongings. The children didn't have such items.

In the back of the building was a swimming pool with cloudy water the color of pea soup. Nowhere else in this otherwise austere place did the great incongruity between poverty and wealth, so common in this country, become more apparent. In their indifference to this irony the children never for a moment stopped their pursuit of pleasure. They enjoyed the refreshing respite from the heat of the day and the dirtiness of the night, jumping in the pool from every possible angle, swimming completely submerged, dunking each other, and splashing water so violently that it covered their broad smiles.

The kitchen was on the edge of the cement floor. It consisted of a gas stove, which was no more than a large metal box with two gas burners, and two twenty-gallon cauldrons for cooking made of old metal and scratched gray with countless washings. A large wooden table stood in the middle of the room. Lunch began when two children who had already been admitted to the first stage of the program (the "sleepers") began getting the meal ready to serve. At the appointed time they went into the kitchen where they were met by two other "sleepers" who were lifting the cauldrons off the stove with two large wooden poles. Each pole was about eight feet long and six inches in diameter. The servers lifted and carried the large cauldrons between the wooden poles, which they rested on their shoulders. Two to a vat they slowly, carefully, and with great pride carried them down the aisle made by the children sitting in two rows. A third "sleeper" began to ladle out the food to each of the waiting children sitting on the cement ledge or the wooden benches that faced it.

The meal consisted of a small piece of meat, plenty of yucca, rice and beans in modest amounts, shreds of beets, and pieces of banana. They drank fruit juice diluted enough to conceal the type of fruit. About fifty children assembled to eat lunch. Once they received their food they were free to leave the dining area, and many did. On the stairways small groups of children sat eating and talking. Larger groups sat congregated on the edge of the main floor, while others stayed on the ledges.

Several children eating on the benches in
Bosconia. In the foreground, the first boy has
traded for an extra plate of rice. The first boy in
the background is wearing his *cobija*. The children have also segregated themselves into two
groups: in the foreground are the *chupagruesos*
and in the background the *gamines*. The photograph portrays a sense of relaxation and camaraderie, and shows no evidence of fighting over
food or apparent starvation.

It wasn't long before we noticed that the lunch was quite different than we had anticipated. Although we were led to believe the
children were starving, they were in fact not begging to be served,
nor were they demanding food in a rampant or uncontrollable
melee. They were merely present. Most of them played with their
neighbors while waiting for the preliminary lines and announcements to be over. Others sat patiently, sucking their thumbs, as if
in contemplation. It was as if this respite from their street lives
had greater importance than the food they were waiting for.

Some other events, almost like rituals, also surprised us. These
events appeared as if they consistently occurred as frequently as
the daily lunch itself. One was the trading of food, which apparently had little to do with the demands of hunger or even the nutritional value of the food, but more with the relationships
among the traders themselves. Part of the reason why trading

flourished was that not all the children finished their food. There was not a tremendous among of excess food, but enough was left over so that different foodstuffs took on different values, and a currency was set up among the traders. The meat, for example, seemed to have the highest value and was rarely traded; the banana was also highly valued; the yucca was the first to be offered and the last to be accepted. The exchange of food involved a recognition of friendships and status ranks among the group. One of the larger boys, a subleader of a group of children, offered to trade a yucca to a smaller boy for a piece of meat. In itself this was an unthinkable business proposition, yet within the context of working out a broader arrangement, the offer had a different quality. When the smaller boy refused, it became apparent that he was rejecting the terms of an offer of entry into the older boy's group and was holding out for more status. To make his point clearer the older boy went down the row offering and finally finding someone to trade his meat for some yucca.

A second surprise was the ingenious use of materials for purposes other than they were designed for, but that made sense given the boys' poverty and vagabondism. Forks, spoons, and napkins were rare, thus leaving a void that opened up a kind of creative competition about what would suffice in their absence. The most common entry was the comb; easily taken from the back pocket and wiped on the pants leg, it was ready for service. This was the kind of easy substitution that won peer recognition. It also exhibited the kind of mentality that functions for the rest of us when we are camping in the wilderness and serves to make us feel self-assured and competent in an environment of sparse goods and services. It was not, as we had been led to believe, an example of their irrational behavior.

Another surprise was the emotional atmosphere at lunch. It was not rowdy or serious, but was a relaxed affair, in large part because a wide variety of behaviors were tolerated. The children supported each other; they were friendly, even gentlemanly in their own way and this, too, was not as we had been led to anticipate. The children were allowed to wander to any space and eat with whatever friend they chose. Perhaps this contributed to the relaxed atmosphere. There were no food fights.

Because of the heaviness of the food vats and the instability in carrying them, it was not surprising that food was occasionally spilled. Given the value of food in a country where so many people were obsessed with what their next meal might be, it was remarkable how well this situation was handled. On this occasion one of the vat carriers had been laughing, affecting his ability to keep the soup in the vat, thus ignoring his responsibility for an immediate moment of pleasure. As he was in clear violation of his status as a "sleeper" in the program, the leader on the floor, himself a graduate of the program and not much bigger than the offender, told the boy to leave the cauldron. He appointed another to take the offender's place and sent the wrongdoer to sit alone in the far corner of the room. The offender went and sat quietly, waiting until his banishment was finished, without interrupting the group. This seemed unusual because these children had been written and talked about as if they were delinquents with a short leash of control over a vast expanse of pent-up hostility. Working with children or adolescents who legitimately fit this indictment, one notices quickly that their ability to refrain from immediate pleasure or to set aside immediate gratification is severely reduced. For this type of child the capacity to accept discipline, particularly in front of peers, is nearly impossible, and the ability to control themselves while waiting is also nearly nonexistent. Yet in this short episode all those difficulties presented no problem. Even the ability of the group to refrain from adding fuel to the potential fire was sharply different from what one would expect from highly impulsive children and adolescents. Added to what we had already seen, we became keenly aware of the difference between the public's conception of these children and the reality.

When the children were not eating they were immersed in play on the cement floor, which they referred to as the "patio." The patio stayed remarkably busy, yet just as remarkably free of tension and fighting. A list of the various activities that we encountered on the patio on the first exploratory day illustrated the organization and control in the children's play. As we entered the patio we saw them playing soccer, basketball, and three or four other makeshift games. All of these games were going on simultaneously in the small space. As a basketball game was proceeding through the soccer match, a boy playing an ad hoc form of tag raced through both games, finding his way among the various activities as easily as if they were marked off in definite, patterned chalk lines. The players in all of the games allowed such easy penetration, continuing to play without so much as a gesture to the intruder.

We were able to see several incidents in which the children either helped each other directly or, through their ability to ignore potential problems, supported each other indirectly. A soccer game and a basketball game were the mainstays of the patio play. Yet the goals of the soccer field were no more than a few feet from the baskets, and the children played aggressively within and between each game without interfering with one another. One soccer player whose nickname was Muñoz (from the Spanish word for stump, because he did not have a leg below his knee) handled his metal crutch made from a welded piece of iron tube remarkably well. Though it would occasionally slip out from under him on the slippery floor, he ran so furiously that he and the others appeared oblivious of his handicap. Another boy was riding a makeshift cart with two small wheels. He pushed the cart with one leg on the ground to gain speed, then he would jump on it with both legs, gliding over the patio at the highest possible speed through the various games, which went on uninterrupted. Another disabled boy pulled his limp leg around with the assistance of his arm while he fought for the basketball. His handicap went unnoticed in the business of the game.

A couple of boys were sleeping on the benches. No one tried to wake them. A few others were huddled on the first step of the stairway—some of them sucking their thumbs—as they quietly watched the activities in front of them. Several others were talking and laughing. Two boys were in the showers. The two program leaders, called *educadores*, were talking to each other. Most of the children had shed their shirts and only a few were wearing shoes. This was laundry day, so many were wearing only their undershorts. Before lunch was called several of the children jumped into the showers. Shortly afterward one educador came to the middle of the floor with a large bundle of clean clothes, which he spilled in a big pile on the floor while the children flailed through them, sorting out their own. Within a couple of minutes, and without fighting, everyone was dressed in his own apparel.

After leaving Bosconia on that first day we stopped in a nearby restaurant to discuss how to proceed. We found ourselves talking about the discrepancy between what we had observed and what we had been told the children were like. This discrepancy was large enough that a question, and indeed a theme emerged that stayed with us throughout the study: Were we really seeing the children as they were in the streets, or were we in fact getting only a biased observation, only a glamorous impression of the more dastardly whole? Were the children as bad as we had been led to believe? We ran through our first impressions, noting all the healthy behavior we had seen: the informal yet mannerly way in which the children ate, the kindness they showed to the sleeping children, the tolerance for those sucking their thumbs, the integration of the handicapped into their play, the lack of hostility and fighting in their crowded quarters, the brisk but orderly manner in which each child was allowed to get his own clothes, their quiet talks on the sidelines, and the way the "sleeper" was able to refrain from impulsive anger after being punished in public. All of these were examples of healthy, nurturant behavior and certainly not evidence of widespread conduct or personality disorders. Their cognitive abilities in separating themselves in their various games in such a small space gave us some indication that their perceptual skills had not been ruined and that there was no widespread and obvious brain damage, as was suggested by reports of their alleged drug use. At lunch, the symbolic trading of food and the fact that many of them did not even finish what they were given suggested that they were not, as we had been told, starving. As we talked about these discrepancies, we reviewed our strategy for collecting data and realized that this would present more obstacles than we had anticipated.

Methodological Issues

Our methodology to obtain data was composed of several measures. Participant observational techniques were used to study the lives of the children in their natural setting. Three standardized tests were applied to gather quantitative data about the children. The Kohs Block Designs were used to assess their intelligence, the Bender-Gestalt to measure their ego functioning, and the Human Figure Drawing (HFD) to assess their neurological and emotional functioning. We examined a variety of secondary sources, such as newspaper articles, government and private organization reports, and research questionnaires to understand the rationale for the various hypotheses and programs that exist about and for the children. In order to help us understand our own and society's responses to the children, we analyzed our own subjective reactions by discussing our notes in the weekly debriefing sessions we held among ourselves.

Field studies in anthropology or sociology that rely on participant observational approaches to understand the lives of the subjects (including approaches that use the researcher's own reactions based on self-observations, as in the case of phenomenological research) yield data that have been critically labeled subjective. These data have often been contrasted with empirical psychological studies, which use experimental techniques and derive allegedly objective quantitative data. We believe, however, that our use of both the anthropologist's observational approach and the psychologist's empirical methods allowed us to obtain the most complete and accurate picture of Colombia's street children.

Our methods were determined in great part by three factors: (1) the cross-cultural nature of the study; (2) certain specific qualities of the children themselves; and (3) the importance of studying the children in a context that included how they interacted with, and were treated by, the society in which they lived. All three factors contributed to our choice of methods. In the end, what and whom we investigated led to our methodology and choice of methods.

The difficulties of getting social science information in a foreign culture have always presented technical problems (Triandis and Berry 1980; Segall 1983). One problem results from the practice of taking standardized tests out of the culture in which they were normed. Applying tests that have been normed in one culture and making comparisons with scores derived from a group in another culture yield speculative results. Although we sought instruments that were as valid as possible in the Colombian subculture in which we worked, there were no published local norms for any psychological tests. We were faced with either creating them—which would have been a time-consuming and expensive project beyond our resources—or rejecting the use of the tests altogether and thus giving up on this method of data collection. A third choice, the one we decided upon, was to use tests that have been shown to be the most valid, given the particular characteristics of our sample, the cross-cultural setting of the work, and the variables that we were interested in exploring. We used the Bender-Gestalt, Kohs, and Human Figure Drawing tests because they best fit this criterion (Anastasi 1982). We applied them so that the testing situation was kept as standardized as possible. The testing is discussed in more detail later in this chapter.

Another technical problem in cross-cultural social science research is that what the foreigner observes can be quite biased according to his own cultural point of view. How does the observer know that what he is perceiving has the same meaning to the actors? Peculiar idiosyncrasies, which determine the meaning of a statement or act, may lie beneath the surface and control its particular meaning, like the mass of submerged ice controls the movement of an iceberg. The naive scientist sees only the observable tip and postulates that there is nothing more to be seen. Fortunately, our research team was composed (with the exception of myself) entirely of Colombians. Our weekly meetings were used to discuss the data collected by each member and to offer possible connections between the data recorded in the prior week and the possible reasons why the actor behaved as he or she did. In this method we employed a cross-cultural "content analysis" (Brislin 1980, 395). This meant that our choice of categories for the collected data was determined by local "informants." Our research group was local not only from the standpoint of being Colombians, but also because many of them had experienced some form of street life as children.

In collecting cross-cultural data there are inevitably problems centered on the difficulties of getting accurate information in the foreign language of the host country. This was compounded in our case because the street children had developed their own argot. We were told that the children had their own secret code and that it would be very difficult for even native speakers of

Spanish to understand them, even if they were given the privilege
of being able to talk with them in their private idiom. Some researchers (Lemay 1975; Ricuarte 1972, 1977) have stated the relevance of the children's idiom as a means of self- and group
definition. This notoriety had even reached the press, and any
outsider was likely to encounter an obvious attempt on the part
of the children to make this linguistic difference a distinction
that was used to mark off the boundary between them and outsiders. After some time we found that they symbolically brought us
into their circles by offering us instruction in their argot. On
many occasions they wrote down some special words and their
meanings that helped orient us to their lives. Their argot had
great notoriety among those who were working with them, and
these people often shared the unusual words with us. We found
that their private language was not as private or as difficult to understand as we had been told. A glossary of their argot has been
included at the end of the book.

The above issues are only some of the general cross-cultural
problems that made our work of getting to know the children difficult. There were other problems more related to the particular
study of street children. Thus, the second factor that controlled
the manner in which we collected data was the children themselves. One of the difficulties in writing about street children is
not unlike the problem faced by those who choose to write about
the handicapped, the poor, or any group of people in the midst of
tragic or pitiful circumstances. The researcher can succumb easily to the quickly written and readily acceptable prose that describes these unfortunates in melodramatic terms, terms that
dwell upon their misery. By stating all of his subjects' problems
while ignoring their virtues, the researcher often inadvertently
falls prey to this distortion. In our case we had to be aware of the
tendency of many people to respond to us as heroes because we
had chosen, and were able to work with, a "dangerous" group.
Since these children were also described as pitiful victims, we had
to avoid consciously portraying ourselves as Good Samaritans. In
fact, we had to avoid either extreme if we were to reflect an accurate picture of the children. Only after discussing our own motives for the work in weekly debriefing sessions were we able to
understand how much like Good Samaritans or heroic healers we

wanted to be. At the beginning some of us believed that we were doing the work that no one else would do, either because they were not brave enough or because they were not socially conscious enough to give up their amenities to work in the trenches. Fortunately, this attitude was checked by the several ex–street children in our group; if not, it would have led us to portray the children as worse than they were, to emphasize their dangerous and pitiful qualities while ignoring their coping skills and strengths.

Conducive to a distortion in the other direction was the tendency to ignore their poverty and delinquency and make them heroic figures. If we had not checked this inclination we might have presented the children with "simple" or "small" problems, or showed them as successful adventurers against immense odds. We might have discounted any evidence of psychopathology and delinquency. Those in our group most eager to do this eventually talked about their lost opportunities to be street children. Through the discussions we were able to see that some members of the research team were trying to fill the void of these heroic and romantic characteristics in themselves. This overidentification with the children comes from the fairly typical kind of reaction that has made the literary figures of Huck Finn and Tom Sawyer so attractive, and helped us eventually to understand the ambivalent reactions of society toward the street children.

Given these two potential biases—becoming the savior of the pitiful or gaining power through the vicarious pleasure associated with turning the victim into a hero—we had to take considerable time debriefing our emotional reactions to the children. These biases were even more difficult to overcome because the public and international organizations formed to help the children were also involved in these distortions. The public wanted to hear not only about their miseries but also about their adventures, and reporters eager to sell copy followed their lead. The international organizations seeking attention from funding agencies were equally susceptible. In fact, most of the material published about street children was funded either by national social welfare agencies, which used the media to make their case for a piece of the financial pie, or by international organizations, from similar motives. Therefore, even though these groups were motivated by high ideals, they often contributed to the existing biases about the children and their problems.

Beltrán has remarked that "the acceptance of their histories as they give them to us, without verifying if they are true or not, is more than negligence or simple laziness, it has a more profound significance. As soon as we hear about their pitiful circumstance, the investigator relates them to his own past and they serve to fortify his delusional beliefs about them [the children]" (1969, 44–45). Since part of the focus in our study was the reactions, or as Beltrán says, "delusional beliefs" of the public and of professionals toward the children, we have not ignored this kind of error. When these subjective reactions of the observer became part of the descriptions of the children, as it often did in our debriefing sessions, we used this as data for our study. In a similar fashion we used all of the children's information, including their misinformation, because we believed it revealed something about them. Our task was to find out just what was revealed.

Getting accurate information from the children was difficult. Since they lived by their wits they had developed an extraordinary capacity to tell lies and to present themselves in ways that were either self-aggrandizing or self-effacing. Presenting false information about themselves was vital to their survival. I asked one boy how old he was, and in different situations his answer varied, depending on the advantage he would gain by being a certain age in a certain circumstance. Given the possibility of malnutrition, and therefore delayed physical growth, it was difficult to tell if his stated age of seven on one occasion was more accurate than his alleged age of fourteen on another. Since all the psychological tests we used are based on age norms, our problems in using the test data were compounded.

Not only had these children seen a lot of life, they had also seen a lot of investigators: some seeking research data and others looking for information that would be used for decisions that would affect their lives. By the time we did our study in 1984, the children were well seasoned as to what to expect and how to make appropriate impressions. They quickly developed ideas about how their information would be received and interpreted. They had learned early in their lives on the streets that the investigator wanted or needed to hear certain kinds of adventure stories or tragic events, and thus the children cultivated an ability to help the investigator get information that would be slanted to what the children perceived to be their own advantage.

The children's answers to other questions, such as "Why are you on the streets?" or "Why are you in this situation?" also depended on how they perceived that the information would or would not serve them. One boy told me he was in the state detention facility because his father beat him, while later the same day he told one of our female investigators that he was there because he was abandoned. To a potential benefactor on the streets, one boy said that he was nearly starving. Later the same day we observed him with a friend divvying up food that was so ample that, like pampered children, they chose what they wanted and discarded the less tasty.

This skill at manipulating information had become not only a mainstay of the children's work, but also a psychological way of defending and expressing themselves. In situations when the information being asked for was perceived by the children to have unimportant consequences, they used the occasion to make up stories whose main function was to make fun of the questioner. This not only allowed them an opportunity for getting back at a society that devalued them, but the falsified information also served to keep the interrogator at bay about the details of their actual lives. In many cases the children were purposely creating a secret code—a private language—and nothing is more effective in hiding the truth than the intelligent use of misinformation.

It was this highly practiced ability at observing their observers and learning how to manipulate information about themselves that helped us to understand the children in cross-cultural terms. A remarkable similarity exists between the street children and the nomadic entertainers Berland studied in Pakistan. Berland writes in his introduction,

Although I had anticipated their intercultural awareness to some degree, I was impressed early in my field work with the fact that the subjects of my investigation were extremely curious and knowledgeable about the very phenomena I was there to investigate among them—the nature of individual and group differences in behavior. From experience in my own culture and in previous research among sedentary populations in the Pacific and Asia, I had observed stereotyped humor, knowledge, and curiosity about other people, but never to the extent that I found expressed among these nomadic entertainers. . . . the professional entertainer must be particularly sensitive to perceptual and social cues from an audience. Certainly these peripatetic performers recognized that flexible social skills across a wide range of ecocultural contexts were as vital to their survival as individual mastery of the numerous perceptual-motor activities associated with their entertainment routines. (Berland 1982, 4–5)

To begin to view the street children in the context of nomadic entertainers is to begin to understand their need for accurate perceptions of others and their skills at manipulating information. We had some grave doubts about the accuracy of some of the Colombian literature about the children since the most common form of gathering information about street children was to write questionnaires without standardizing either the questions or administration, and worse, merely accepting the answers as if they were facts. Thus Granados (1976), for example, merely asked children the leading question why they "abandoned" their homes. Only 4.5 percent said they left because they wanted to, while more than 75 percent answered in a manner that might elicit pity. These results, as we shall soon see, are quite different from our data.

Originally we attempted to understand the children in their natural living environment—the streets. As we proceeded to collect data we learned that it was necessary to realize that the children lived not just in "the streets," but in particular streets that had their own history and cultural context. Since we noted that society's reaction to them, which did not take place in a vacuum but included the children's responses to adults, was influencing their self-concepts and how they lived, we needed to understand this interaction. Therefore the study focused on the nature of childhood as it is controlled by the pressing needs of the adult community to define its boundaries and privileges.

We encountered one other persistent problem in our methodology. As demonstrated by the examples that opened this chapter, we found that our observations were often contradictory to what we had been told by the public and also to material published by national and international organizations established to help the children. Working as best we could to separate fact from fiction, we were able to get two kinds of data directly from the children: first, the field notes, which were based on participant observational data over nine months, and second, quantitative data obtained through the battery of three standardized tests we administered. The combination of quantitative data and qualitative data helped us make educated hypotheses about the discrepancies that existed. The children's IQS, which were said to be high by some observers and low by others, were assessed by the Kohs Block Designs. The extent of their neurological impairment, which was hypothesized by some to be grave as a consequence of their alleged drug abuse and/or poor nutrition, was assessed with the Human Figure Drawings (HFD). Their emotional health was considered by many observers to be poor, given their poverty and their alleged lack of family stability and love. On the other hand, others wrote about their liberty and adventures as if they were heroes. We obtained a general measure of their psychological health or ego strength with the Bender-Gestalt and HFD tests.

Choosing the Psychological Tests

The Kohs Block Design intelligence test, the Bender-Gestalt test, and the Human Figure Drawing test were administered to fifty-six children. The children whom we tested were all in Bosconia, but were at one time or another during our stay in the field incarcerated in La Sucre, the state's diagnostic center. All of the tests were administered individually by the author with the help of two Colombian psychologists who were participating in the project.

There were several requirements for the standardized tests that we used. First, they had to be of some interest to the children and fairly easy to administer since the children would not sit for long testing sessions. Second, the tests had to be geared toward nonreaders; otherwise we would have reduced the sample size and biased the selection of the subjects since only 40 percent of our sample could read and the majority of these children were older. We chose the three standardized tests because they fulfilled these requirements. They were also the most accurate in the cross-cultural context for the variables we were exploring (Anastasi 1982). Although there were no published local norms for these tests, they all had been used in Colombia and they were the ones that Colombian psychologists were most familiar with.

We chose the Kohs Block Design intelligence tests to measure the children's intelligence because of the lack of written material in it and because it was designed for cross-cultural use. "The special value of the block-design test lies in the fact that valid results may be obtained independently of the 'language factor'" (Kohs 1923, 235). Since the test has no verbal component and was administered by Colombian psychologists, we were able to reduce the bias produced by differences in language. We presented the explanation for the directions to the children in words comparable to the standard procedure in English. The blocks were presented to the children in individual administrations according to the directions of Kohs (1923). A sample problem was given to the children and demonstrated by the administrator. The child had to construct it accurately before the remainder of the blocks were presented. After three consecutive failures the testing was discontinued.

We have assumed that the perceptions of the presented stimuli, the blocks in the test, were comparable to the normative sample in the United States. This assumption has been tested in several cross-cultural contexts. Deregowski (1972) and Jahoda (1956) have reported that the stimuli are perceived differently in non-Western cultures but similarly in a variety of Western cultures.

The Kohs Block Design test was constructed as a measure of overall (g-factor) intelligence, which was the measure that we were most interested in since tests that simply reflected schooling and reading skills would have underrepresented the children's abilities to function intelligently on the streets. Nevertheless, the correlation between the Kohs test and the Stanford Binet was reported by Kohs to be .84 (Kohs 1923). Budoff and Corman (1974) have reported that the Kohs scores were significantly correlated with Wechsler Intelligence Scale for Children (wisc) Verbal and Performance scores in a group of minority North American adolescents. They also report that, in their sample, race and social class were not related to Kohs scores. Although there has not been a great deal of cross-cultural research relevant to our sample, there is ample reason to believe that the Kohs is a reasonable measure of the children's general intellectual functioning.

The Bender-Gestalt test was employed to measure the overall emotional health of the children. We chose it because it has proved to be a valuable tool in cross-cultural personality research. Tolar and Brannigan state in their review of the cross-cultural use of the Bender that "while it is difficult, if not impossible, to assess the abilities of the members of an ethnic culture apart from the achievements prized by that culture, the Bender stands up well as a cross-cultural assessment tool" (1980, 26). The authors also studied the application of the Bender in a variety of cross-cultural measures of personality and concluded that "the Bender-Gestalt performance is quite unaffected by cultural factors" (1980, 61). Although they caution against the use of the test as a means to make individual diagnoses (a caution we have adhered to), they claim it does have value as a method of separating group differences. When comparing the Bender with other cross-cultural personality measures such as the Rorschach inkblot test, the House-Tree-Person test, the Thematic Apperception test and the Minnesota Multiphasic Personality Inventory (MMPI), "the Bender-Gestalt was found to be second inaccuracy of diagnostic judgment" (1980, 170). Only the MMPI was better, but this would have been inappropriate given the age and lack of reading skills of our children. Using the Bender in situations where language or culture is possibly a biasing factor was suggested by Hutt, who reported that the "performance [on the Bender] is largely independent of these factors" (1985, 113).

Golden (1979) lists many advantages to the use of the Bender that were of particular concern to us. "It can be used as a buffer or warm-up test as it is not threatening to most patients and may be enjoyable to many. It is useful as a supplementary technique which provides a good source of nonverbal material more reliable than many other projective techniques. It provides information otherwise difficult to obtain from uneducated or culturally deprived individuals. It is a useful measure of emotional states when the person otherwise denies problems. It is sensitive to malingering" (Golden 1979, 142).

We utilized the Human Figure Drawings to assess the children's emotional and neurological functioning. There are several attractive reasons to use this test: drawings are not mediated by language, the test is easy to administer, and drawing is nearly a universally interesting task for children. Margaret Mead (1954) considered drawings to be an efficient manner to assess children's personality in cross-cultural contexts. Gardiner used drawings to study cultural values of Thai children and concluded his study with the following assessment of this technique as a cross-cultural tool: "It can be used with equal ease in any group from the most primitive to the most highly advanced without encountering the familiar difficulties of translation or adaptation common to many other research techniques. The task is intrinsically interesting to most children and instructions can be communicated with a minimum of three words—'draw,' 'man' and 'woman'" (1974, 129).

There are, however, more problems with the use of this test in cross-cultural contexts than originally foreseen by its authors, who developed it as a culture-free measure. Koppitz (1984), whose system we used to score the drawings, reviewed the literature concerning the effects of culture on the HFD and concluded by stating that there are both cultural differences and cross-cultural similarities. Although several studies indicate that drawings are reflective of the cultural differences of the drawers (Harris 1963; Laosa, Swartz, and Diaz-Guerrero 1974; Dennis 1966; Gardiner 1974), the studies taken as a whole are difficult to interpret because they often assess different variables and use different scoring systems. Some of these studies assessed developmental differences while others assessed intelligence. We deal with neither of these here because we have used the test for other purposes. Swenson (1968) and Roback (1968) point out that only global, not individual items are reliable. We adhered to their advice and did not use the test to make individual diagnoses.

Since cultures that differ widely from the original North American sample have been studied, the range of differences between cultures is important to consider. As Holtzman points out, "for most cultures, the drawing techniques and story-telling methods are quite suitable although their equivalence cross-culturally speaking may be difficult to achieve" (1980, 268).

However, he speaks of overcoming some of these problems with the Koppitz system of scoring, which we used. "The Draw-a-Person Test is also likely to have a fairly wide range of cross-cultural equivalence, and Koppitz's scale of emotional stability looks promising as a quantitative score" (Holtzman 1980, 269).

In examining studies that were conducted on cultures similar to Colombia's, we found some important information. Koppitz and de Moreau (1968) compared the emotional indicators of Mexican and North American children. They found, as reported by Koppitz (1984, 71), that the "majority of the HFDS of the Mexican and U.S. boys and girls did not differ markedly from each other." Koppitz and Casullo (1983) compared Argentine and U.S. children on emotional indicators and found that there were cultural differences. They suggest that these differences represent the fact that drawings are of a particular time and place. As we began to score points for the degree of psychopathology based on the drawings of the normative sample in the United States, we noticed that our children who admired bravado and lack of respect for state authorities (as illustrated by their drawing many guerrillas and figures with guns) received more points on the scale of psychopathology, based on the Koppitz system, than might have been appropriate given their subcultural values. Inasmuch as we have no normative group comparable to these children, we cannot be secure in making a statement about how they compare on these dimensions. Given this possibly inconsistent equivalence of scoring between cultures we used our results carefully, combining them with the Bender score when we made use of them in sorting children into groups. This will become clearer when we discuss how we defined the characteristics of the subgroups in the sample.

The standard on the HFD necessary for validity between cultures is dependent on how the results will be used. The HFD was originally developed by Machover (1949) to assess individual personalities, while we used the HFD to indicate differences between groups of children in our study. "The kind of measurement required for individual reliability and validity is of a higher, more stringent order than the kind needed when only group trends are of interest. An instrument that may have unsatisfactory reliability for individual measurement can still be used effectively

where differences in cultures or large groups are the main concern" (Holtzman 1980, 268). Thus we included the results cau-
tiously to make comparisons between the groups of children.

Although we favored the use of a complete multitest single-
trait approach (assessing a single characteristic with more than
one standardized psychological test), the variety of methodological problems already discussed made this difficult under the circumstances we faced. Nevertheless, we dealt with this problem
by getting *two* measures of emotional functioning, from the
Bender-Gestalt and the Human Figure Drawings, and two measures of neurological functioning, by assuming that the results of
the Kohs Block Designs and the Human Figure Drawings over-
lapped. As we have seen, there is ample evidence to support the
use of these tests and the conclusions we have drawn from them.
We were also able to support our conclusions from the tests by
supplementing them with other kinds of data.

Triangulating the Data Collection

In addition to the quantitative data from the tests of the children,
we also obtained qualitative information. We supplemented our
standardized tests with participant observational notes so that
we could triangulate our data (Campbell 1961). By using more
than one method of data collection we hoped to reduce some of
the bias in each method. By having more than one person observe
the children we hoped to eliminate some of the biases inherent in
any one observer. And by collecting observations in more than
one situation we were able to reduce the bias of our observations.
We also increased our scope of information by examining the variety of secondary sources that we have mentioned. Thus,
through these multiple, heterogeneous measures, all of which focused on how the children lived their lives, we were able to avoid
many of the methodological problems that a single view of them
would have produced.

We made a heuristic plan to analyze the qualitative data. This
data included information from secondary sources, such as government documents, newspaper reports, and observations of

people's reactions when they were confronted with street children, and our own reactions to them as discussed in our weekly debriefing sessions. I have also included my own reactions to the children. We used this data to make logical arguments to help us disprove or collaborate existing theories. Validity with this process resides in the confidence the reader can have that the investigator has been thorough and has dealt coherently with the data so as to make the refutations of certain hypotheses and the acceptance of others easily understood and logically coherent (Kvale 1986).

Two sampling problems exist with qualitative data: How representative is the sample of subjects to the focus of the study? and How representative is the research situation or the place the data was collected? We chose Bosconia because it was a place where street children went without being obliged to do so. This gave us the opportunity to see how they lived when they were free to live as they pleased. To avoid the sampling bias produced by the situational factors of time and place, we also collected data in a place where they were incarcerated, La Sucre, the state diagnostic center. The children remained in La Sucre for a maximum of sixty days but most commonly for much less time. We noted that children commonly drifted from the streets to Bosconia, to La Sucre, and back to the streets. The same sample of children was often, at different times, in all three places and we observed them in all three locations. This helped us to ensure that our sampling bias was minimal.

We agreed with a criticism of quantitative psychology, that the artificial nature of the laboratory produces results that are not likely to be reproduced in the more complex social reality of the "real world," and we dealt with this by gathering a variety of both qualitative and quantitative data. We did not abandon the choice to study the children in their natural habitat, although this made it nearly impossible to have the type of control over our data collection that a laboratory would have provided. We counteracted this problem with the methodology of triangulation. Thus, the children were studied by applying standardized tests, observing them in different situations, and evaluating what we and others thought and said about them. We hope that this study lays the foundation for a more controlled exploration of the children that will test specific hypotheses about them. This would help in using the limited available funds more advantageously.

After collecting the data we were ready to generate some hypotheses about the children. We substantiated our hypotheses in two ways. First, we backed them up with our triangulated data, and second, we looked for rival explanations that did not go along with one of our hypotheses. Each time we encountered a rival explanation we examined possible alternatives in order to see if they could be substantiated or refuted by our data. To the extent that we were able to refute the rival hypotheses, our own became stronger. This form of validation is referred to as "communicative validity" (Kvale 1986). "The investigator puts his cards on the table for the reader, emphasizing the presentation of the results through documentation and argumentation" (Kvale 1986, 33).

Characteristics of the Sample

The children included in the sample had to be known to the research team in Bosconia for at least six weeks in order to be eligible subjects. When these children entered La Sucre for diagnosis we chose them for our test battery. We used this procedure for two reasons. First, since we were interested in studying children who were living on the streets, we used the criterion of knowing them at Bosconia as evidence that they were indeed street children. And we were able to eliminate the confusion of roles that we might have expected from them if we tried to test them while we were being their "friends" in Bosconia.

The actual administration of the tests was in La Sucre for several reasons, the most important of which was that in Bosconia we were their friends, not their examiners. They always associated examinations with people who were not trying to help them but to adjudicate them. Bosconia, because it was a place to play, was inappropriate for testing. In La Sucre, where testing was commonplace, we were able to use our friendship to instill trust. Because of this they preferred to have us, rather than an unknown member of the agency, test them.

Table 1 Age of Subjects in Sample (N = 56)

Age	Frequency	Percent	Cumulative percent
7	3	5.4	5.4
8	4	7.1	12.5
9	3	5.4	17.9
10	9	16.1	34.0
11	5	8.9	42.9
12	11	19.6	62.5
13	11	19.6	82.1
14	4	7.1	89.2
15	3	5.4	94.6
16	2	3.6	98.2
17	1	1.8	100.0
Total	56	100.0	

Mean age = 11.60
Median = 12.00
Mode = 12.00

Our sample included fifty-six male children who ranged in age from seven to seventeen, with an average age of 11.6 years. Table 1 shows the age distribution of all the children. Twelve and a half percent of our sample were below nine, 30 percent were between nine and eleven, 46 percent were between twelve and fourteen, and 10.8 percent were above fourteen.

Téllez's (1976) sample of street children was somewhat different. He reported that 24.5 percent of his sample was below twelve. This was much less than our 43 percent. The majority of his sample was between twelve and fourteen (58.2 percent), which was comparable to our group. The samples of Lopez and Lopez (1964) and Rotter (1967) were older, but both studies included only children over the age of ten. Our sample is quite comparable in age with that of Felsman (1981a, 1981b), whose work has the most recent figures. He shows 28 percent of children (ours was 17.9 percent) were below nine, 40 percent between ten and twelve (ours was 44.6 percent), and 24 percent between thirteen and sixteen (ours was 35.7 percent). It is difficult to determine from these figures if the ages of the children on the streets had changed between 1964 and 1984. First, two of the samples did not include children below ten. Second, there have been no studies that have tried systematically to get a random sample. And third, the actual ages of the children are difficult to determine since many do not have birth certificates and there is little reliability in their reported ages. The information about the ages of our sample came from the official documents at La Sucre, not from the information that the children gave us while they were on the streets.

Another factor may have contributed to the age differences in the studies mentioned above. For the last twenty years Colombia has been in a period of economic growth. This means that if children in the latter part of this twenty-year period were doing poorly in school and were receiving abuse at home, they would have a better possibility of getting some kind of an income away from home than they did twenty years ago. With this situation there is reason to believe that there would be an absolute increase in the number of children on the streets, and that more of the total number would be younger since the economy has been improving (Interamerican Development Bank 1987). Younger children also have more opportunities.

La Sucre also listed the places of birth for the children in our sample. Thirty-seven (66 percent) were born in the state of Cauca, where Cali is the capital. Another 10 percent were born in adjacent states, leaving only 18 percent of the children as migrants from distant regions of the country. In Felsman's (1981a) study in Cali 56 percent of the core sample were from Cali. Téllez (1976), who conducted his study in Bogotá, reported that 41 percent were born in Bogotá and another 25 percent in adjacent states. Thus, it appears that the majority of street children were born and lived locally, in spite of the fact that they often traveled a great deal to other parts of the country for diversion. These data are also reflected in the information about internal migration from Mohan (1980), who reports that the great majority of migration within the country is from the rural zones to the nearest urban area.

We have some official information, which came from La Sucre, about the family situations of the children in our sample. Nine of the fifty-six children (16 percent) had no known family to contact. Five children (9 percent) were under the care of at least one grandparent. The remaining forty-two children (75 percent) had at least one parent whom they claimed could be contacted, although La Sucre reported that it was often difficult to locate them. Felsman (1981a) reported that nearly three quarters of the children did not have their biological father in the home when they left, but that 84 percent had their biological mother at home. This is comparable to our sample. The Téllez (1976) data illustrated a slightly different, but comparable, situation. In his Bogotá sample 15.4 percent had no known family, which was nearly identical to our sample. He indicated that 52.7 percent of his sample had parents who were separated and 39.1 percent had parents who lived together. In all three samples the family situations were comparable. The children, as a rule, knew their parents, but if they lived at home it was most often with their mothers, who were separated from their biological fathers. Only a very small percentage of the children did not know any family member.

The most common reason given in the La Sucre records for the children being on the streets was financial (48 percent), and the second was abuse (32 percent). This was different from the Téllez questionnaire data, where 52.7 percent of the children said they left home because they were hit by their parents (1976, 16). Only 5.5 percent of the children in his questionnaire said they were on the streets because of economic reasons. The differences here are probably related to the manner in which the data were collected. Our information comes from the official statistics obtained when the parents were being interviewed and the fate of their children's incarceration was being ascertained, while Téllez's information came from direct questions to the children. As noted earlier, given the characteristics of the children, direct solicitation of information from them through questionnaires yielded highly suspect information.

The records from La Sucre gave us some information about the amount of time spent on the streets. Two children had been abandoned at a very early age, and three others had records indicating that they were badly abused before age ten. Another child had a mother in prison. For the most part the children drifted in and out of street life, and the amount of time on the street between the time we tested them and the last record of incarceration was usually less than a year. Felsman (1981a) reported that 44 percent of his sample had spent less than a year on the streets. Téllez (1976) stated that 41.8 percent of his sample had been on the streets for a year or less. They both reported that about 20 percent of the children were on the streets for at least two years. The data from these two samples are consistent with each other and with our information. Most of the younger children in our sample were not on the streets for longer than a year. They moved between the streets and being in an institution or with their families or guardians. There was, however, a group of older children who had been on the streets for longer periods of time, some of them for over two years and a few for as many as five years.

Table 2 illustrates the range of IQs for the whole sample. This range was from 40 to 115, with a mean of 88.38. This is a positively skewed distribution, with only four of fifty-five (one score was eliminated) children scoring below 70, the cutoff score for the definition of mentally retarded. Thus, 7 percent of the sample scored in the mentally retarded range. However, two of these four children had IQs of 69, nearly in the normal range, and thus 7 percent is a high figure. Excluding these two children, whose scores were within the margin of error, we have 3.6 percent in the retarded range. The American Association on Mental Deficiency uses not only the IQ scores but also the social adaptability of children for criteria of mental retardation; thus, these scores are only assessing one aspect of intelligence. The children's social skills were often well ahead of their counterparts who stayed at home, and thus there is reason to suspect that both 7 percent and 3.6 percent are high figures.

The frequency distribution for intelligence, excluding persons with brain damage, approximates the normal distribution. We would therefore expect that about 2.3 percent of children should have been in the mentally retarded category and about 84 percent should have an IQ of 85 or greater. Sixty-nine percent of the sample had IQs above 85, the normal cutoff for average intelligence. Our sample was slightly below the average for the general population. Yet, our results are remarkably above those reported by Beltrán (1969). He reported on a sample of 263 children to whom

Table 2 Kohs Block Design IQ Test

IQ score	Frequency	Percent	Cumulative percent
40	1	1.8	1.8
60	1	1.8	3.6
69	2	3.6	7.2
75	1	1.8	9.0
76	2	3.6	12.6
77	1	1.8	14.4
78	2	3.6	18.0
79	1	1.8	19.8
80	1	1.8	21.6
81	1	1.8	23.4
82	1	1.8	25.2
84	3	5.5	30.7
85	4	7.3	38.0
86	4	7.3	45.3
89	3	5.5	50.8
90	3	5.5	56.3
91	1	1.8	58.1
92	2	3.6	61.7
93	2	3.6	65.3
94	3	5.5	70.8
95	3	5.5	76.3
96	1	1.8	78.1
97	1	1.8	79.9
98	3	5.5	85.4
101	2	3.6	89.0
105	3	5.5	94.5
107	1	1.8	96.3
114	1	1.8	98.1
115	1	1.8	99.9
Total	55	100.0	

Mean = 88.38
Median = 89.00
Standard error = 1.71

were administered "the usual intelligence tests." Twenty-six percent of the children were mentally retarded and only 22.06 percent
of average or above-average intelligence. It is difficult to determine
why our sample scored higher than Beltrán's group, inasmuch as he
gives no data about the tests he used or how the children were
tested. But, as we shall see in the narrative, the social skills pos-
sessed by the children in our sample lead us to assume that our sample is functioning intellectually well within the boundaries of
adaptability, given their subcultural and societal norms.

There are many reasons why our sample should have low
scores. Many siblings, nonintact or one-parent families, and low
socioeconomic status are associated with low academic aptitude
(Anastasi 1982). These were characteristic of our sample. In addition, Téllez (1976) reported in his sample of street children that
less than one-half of the fathers and about one-third of the mothers were literate, and on the average their parents had only three
years of schooling. Pineda and her colleagues reported that in the
cities of Bogotá, Medellín, and Cartagena, "almost 100 percent of
the mothers of children who they labeled as street children were
illiterate" (1978, 169). They also estimated that in their sample of
children "nearly 80 percent of them were without any schooling"
(1978, 170).

Broman, Nichols, and Kennedy (1975), in a longitudinal study of
early developmental factors that lowered the IQS of a racial and socioeconomic cross-section of North American children, illustrated
that three factors emerged that accounted for most of the variance
of future intellectual capacity: the mother's educational level, the
weight of the children between four months and four years, and the
rate of growth in motor development. In Ochoa's (1979) investigation for SENA, the national government health organization, she
points out that 63 percent of the Colombian children were suffering
from some malnutrition. De Galán (1981) says that 60 percent of
the infant population has malnutrition and 78 percent suffer from
lack of proteins. Felsman (1981a) reports that in Cali the infant
mortality rate is 92 per 1,000, compared to 16 per 1,000 in New
York. De Galán, two years later, says that "Colombia registers the
highest rate of infant mortality in the world with 97 in one thousand" (1981, 67). With poor nutrition comes low weight and increased chance of delayed motor development. Added to this is the

low educational level of the children's mothers, showing that all three factors are present for low intellectual skills.

As Nerlove and Roberts (1975) mention in their study of the Guatemalan "street" children, there are many "natural indicators" of intelligence. These authors measured the complexity of the tests that the children in their study performed in their daily lives, such as the degree of self-managed, nonsupervised activities, their abilities to initiate and complete tasks, their social awareness of people, and their knowledge of their natural environment, which included their ability to move around at considerable distances away from home and the neighborhood. These abilities were also common characteristics of our sample and speak of a kind of intelligence that involves competence in the local subculture. These types of skills illustrate that the children were acting even more intelligently than their test scores revealed, even though these scores are remarkably high given their circumstances. We conclude that the way they were living on the streets, the demands that the streets made on them, and the advanced development because of these demands actually accelerated, rather than retarded their intellectual skills.

We used the Bender-Gestalt to measure the children's ego functioning. Although many scoring systems have been used for the Bender, we chose the Pascal-Suttell method for several reasons. One of the early criticisms of the Bender was that there was no good quantitative scoring system. The Pascal-Suttell method has overcome this problem, and does so with age groups that are comparable to the ones in our sample. Another reason we chose this scoring method is that the measure of interjudge reliability is strong, ranging from .90 (Pascal and Suttell 1951) to .99 (Story 1960).

The authors claim that this system provides a measure of general emotional functioning. Hutt reviews the literature on the Bender-Gestalt and says that, "although some contradictory findings have been published, these conclusions by Pascal and Suttell have stood the test of research quite well; as a rough measure of severity of general psychopathology the scale has demonstrated validity" (Hutt 1985, 31).

The scoring of the Bender-Gestalt and the Human Figure Drawing tests was done by two independent Colombian psychologists with experience in scoring projective tests for children.

The tests were rated separately and the scorers did not know which tests belonged to whom. Neither of the psychologists knew the children or were informed about the study. They worked together to establish their interrater reliability by scoring sample protocols not in the study. When there were differences in the raters' scores the text was consulted to determine the expert's rating and then a decision was made as to the proper score. This process was repeated until the raters were able to rate three consecutive figures with 100 percent agreement between themselves and the text. Then they rated the test protocols separately. When there were discrepancies they discussed them and came to a mutual agreement.

We wanted to segregate the sample into groups based on different levels of emotional functioning. The Bender is not considered valid for making individual diagnoses and it was not used in individual cases, but the test does separate group differences. "In support of their contention that the score (on the Bender Gestalt) may be used as a measure of degree of psychopathology, Pascal and Suttell present data to show that there are progressive and significant differences in mean scores between the normal group and the neurotic and the psychotic" (Hutt 1985, 31).

Pascal and Suttell give cutoff scores for different functioning abilities. "With T scores of 50 and below we can be fairly confident that the subject does not need psychiatric help. Whereas, between 50 and 70 we are in a transitional state and those subjects would seem, therefore, suspect" (1951, 36). Subjects with scores over 70 are in need of psychiatric help. Note that the lower the score the better the overall ego functioning of the child. Table 3 illustrates the scores on the Bender for the whole sample, which ranged from 12 to 161 with a mean of 60.43. It can be seen that 48 percent (twenty-seven) of the sample scored 50 or below, 25 percent (fourteen) were in the transitional category, and 27 percent of the fifty-six children scored over 70.

As was the case with IQ scores, the Bender scores are better than expected. There were many reasons why our children could have shown more psychopathology on their scores. In spite of the fact that they had lived on the streets for at least three months, that they had been incarcerated at least once, that many had been abused, that most came from homes without two parents and

Table 3 Bender-Gestalt Scale Scores

Bender score	Frequency	Percent
0–50	27	48
51–70	14	25
71 and above	15	27
Total	56	100.0

Mean = 60.42
Median = 51.50
Standard error = 4.56

some had no homes, and that they lived in the lowest socioeconomic stratum of their society, only 27 percent had Bender scores that were within the pathological range, while half of them showed good ego strength. Many authors (as well as public opinion) have said that the children were either pitiful and in need of psychological help or that they were delinquent drug abusers and should therefore be in poor mental health. Others have claimed that they are adventurers, describing them in nearly heroic terms. The results from our data lie somewhere in between. We found that in their peer relations on the streets they had developed many coping mechanisms that we think accounted for the fact that their Bender scores were quite good. We shall return to this point later.

The Human Figure Drawings (HFD) were scored by the method of Koppitz (1968) for neurological and emotional indicators. We wanted to ascertain the degree to which the children were neurologically damaged due to their alleged drug abuse and also to get another measure of their emotional functioning. A rating system was devised with the same two psychologists working to get 100 percent interrater reliability, then scoring the tests separately and coming together to discuss discrepancies. Following the Koppitz procedure, the children were asked to draw one whole person. Koppitz based her assessment of the HFD on Sullivan's interpersonal psychology. The child's drawing represents "his attitudes toward himself and toward significant others in his life" (Koppitz

1968, 3). The HFD is *not* a "portrait of the child's basic and enduring personality traits nor is it an image of the child's appearance. Instead, it is believed that the HFDS reflect the child's current stage of mental development and his attitudes and concerns of the given moment. . . . The HFD is regarded here as a portrait of the inner child of the moment" (Koppitz 1968, 4). Since the emotional indicators (EI) are not related to the child's age, they reduced the influence of age and gave us a measure that reflected the children's "anxieties, concerns and attitudes" (Koppitz 1968, 35).

The drawings were used to differentiate between children with and without emotional problems. "When a HFD shows none of the 30 Emotional Indicators, then it seems likely that the child is free from serious emotional problems. The presence of only one Emotional Indicator on a HFD appears to be inconclusive and is not necessarily a sign of emotional disturbance. . . . However, two or more Emotional Indicators on a HFD are highly suggestive of emotional problems and unsatisfactory interpersonal relationships" (Koppitz 1968, 42). Emotional indicators on the Draw-a-Person test are listed in table 4. The average for the whole sample was 2.7, the median was 2.0. The results show that 27 percent (fifteen) of the children had zero or one EI, 24 percent (thirteen) had two EIS, and 49 percent (twenty-seven) had three or more EIS.

Using Kendall's Tau, we ascertained the correlation between the immediate emotional status, as judged by the HFD, with the more permanent emotional health or ego functioning, derived from the score on the Bender. They were not significantly correlated ($p = .128$). We can assume that the two tests are measuring—as they were devised to do—two different types of emotional conditions: the Bender is more of a trait test and the HFD is more of a state test. There were more signs of emotional distress on the HFD than on the Bender. Only 27 percent of the children showed no emotional problems on the HFD, while nearly 50 percent showed no ego problems on the Bender. This might have been an artifact of the testing situation inasmuch as the children were tested while they were in La Sucre. Being both incarcerated and waiting to see where they might be sent increased their anxiety, which is more likely to be reflected on the HFD, since it assesses immediate emotional conditions, than on the Bender, which is a test of more permanent ego functioning. Also, since

Table 4 Koppitz Human Figure Drawing, Emotional Indicators

Emotional indicators	Frequency	Percent	Cumulative percent
0	5	9.1	9.1
1	10	18.2	27.3
2	13	24.0	51.3
3	9	16.0	67.3
4	10	18.2	85.5
5	4	7.3	92.8
6	2	3.6	96.4
7	2	3.6	100.0
Total	55	100.0	

Mean = 2.70
Median = 2.00
Standard error = .239

the children drew many pictures of very masculine, aggressive males, the result of their enviable relationship to the guerrillas, these were scored, perhaps inaccurately, as emotional indicators. Given their coping skills, which are discussed later, we will see that they possess more emotional strength than the HFDS suggest.

Table 5 illustrates the neurological indicators (NI) on the HFD. As Koppitz says, "There seems to be a consensus among clinicians that some drawings have an 'organic' quality and some signs on the HFDS tend to be frequently associated with neurological impairment. However, the experts also agree that it is not possible to diagnose brain injury or Minimal Brain Damage (MBD) solely from HFDS. Drawings can be helpful, nevertheless, in pointing to the possible presence of brain pathology in a youth, and to the need for further investigation" (Koppitz 1984, 59). We did not use this measure to diagnose any particular child, but to obtain a measure of the sample's scores and then to break down these scores between different age groups. Our intent was to get an overall measure of organicity to see if either malnutrition or drugs caused brain damage. Thus, the NIS were used to measure group differences because they "seem to point to possible neurological

Table 5 Koppitz Human Figure Drawing, Neurological
Indicators

Neurological indicators	Frequency	Percent	Cumulative percent
0	6	10.7	10.7
1	8	14.3	25.0
2	8	14.3	39.3
3	17	30.4	69.7
4	6	10.7	80.4
5	5	8.9	89.3
6	4	7.1	96.4
7	1	1.8	98.2
8	1	1.8	100.0
Total	56	100.0	

Mean = 2.91
Median = 3.00
Standard error = .253

involvement even though the Organic Signs cannot be used by themselves to diagnose brain pathology" (Koppitz 1984, 60).

Since it is not possible to separate emotional problems from neurological indicators on the HFD, and therefore to make a differential diagnosis between emotional and neurological problems based solely on the HFD, we were unable to make this distinction. Indeed, the Kendall's Tau correlation indicates that the EIS and the NIS were significantly correlated ($p = .038$) and thus acting in accordance with the fact that the test cannot distinguish between the two groups. This significant correlation also means that the number of NIS was inflated because they were not independent of the EIS. As noted earlier, there is evidence to assume that the EIS were also inflated, making the NIS even higher.

In comparing children with and without diagnosed neurological impairment it was "shown that the chances are 5:1 that a young adolescent may suffer from neurological malfunctioning if his or her HFD reveals two or more Organic Signs" (Koppitz 1984, 64). Zero or one NI does not imply that the child has neurological impairment. Table 5 shows that 25 percent (fourteen) of the sample had zero or one NI. Fourteen percent (eight) had two NIS, and 60 percent (thirty-four) of the children had three or more NIS. The mean was 2.9 and the median and mode were 3. The NIS indicated the most pathology of all the test measures. However, there are reasons to suggest that we should temper these results. First, there is the confounding factor with the EIS, and second, the impairment suggested by the test results was not so great as to reduce their intellectual or emotional functioning as expressed on the IQ and Bender tests. Their work and play in the streets also illustrated a good deal of cognitive development and mastery of skills that would have been reduced with neurological impairment. Thus, we used the NIS with caution when we examined the effects of drugs and malnutrition on the children.

Table 6 illustrates the means and standard deviations for age and the four measures for the whole sample. We divided the whole sample into three age groups: prepuberty (younger than twelve years old), transitional (twelve year olds), and postpuberty (over twelve). There are two prepuberty groups and three postpuberty groups. Their scores on the tests are presented in the forthcoming sections, where we give examples of each of the five groups and present them as case histories in the narrative. Each case history provides a psychological profile that includes examples of the child's HFD, his Bender, and a narrative description of his life in the streets. This will help in understanding the different types of street children and the personal reactions they have toward the streets.

Some Problems with Defining "Street Children"

The term "street children," when used routinely by the public, and even by most professionals, implied that the children had been abruptly left by their families, and indeed they were often referred to as "abandoned." Both terms assumed that they had no other place to live but on the streets. We found that this was rarely the case. Instead, the usual course of events was for the children to leave their homes first for a short period of time, then

Table 6 Means and Standard Deviations on All Variables for
All Children

Variable	Cases	Mean	Standard deviation
Age	56	11.60	2.37
Bender	56	60.42	34.17
Kohs IQ	55	88.38	12.6
HFD-EI	55	2.70	1.7
HFD-NI	56	2.91	1.8

slowly to increase the amount of time spent away from home
(Felsman 1981b; Pineda et al. 1978). While establishing themselves as independent from their families, the children would
come into contact with one of the nonstate institutions such as
Bosconia, where they would receive food, companionship, and
instruction through informal channels about life on the streets.
During this initial period of time they often returned home, left
again, and moved in and out of places like Bosconia. Some children moved away from home and immediately joined other children who were living on the streets. Most often they stayed with
children on the streets for a time and later returned to their
homes. Then they began the cycle anew.

For many of them this cycle continued and escalated. Depending on their behavior and the demands placed upon them by the
community and the police, the next step usually involved getting
picked up by a representative of the state and moved into a diagnostic center like La Sucre. Here, after a maximum of sixty days,
the majority were returned to their parents or guardians and the
cycle continued. Others were moved up a level in the state's cus-
todial care, usually to a "home" like La Casa de Menores de
Ospina, where they were detained for a few months. Only a few
went to places like this, mainly because the great number of children and the limited sources of income at the disposal of the state
made any further commitment cost-prohibitive. Thus, even
those who were mandated for incarceration had only short stays
and before long returned to the streets.

As the following quote by a street child suggests, it is necessary to understand that street children rarely lived permanently in the streets and were only occasionally abandoned in the sense of having no place to go. It was more likely that they were living between a variety of public and private places, including their homes and the streets, and that each place had for them some advantages and disadvantages.

Between living in the house and in the streets and in the institution, the best is in the institution, because here I get food and clothes. What happens is that at times one gets bored; one gets bored at times in any place. For me, I always have this circle, or better said, I go to an institution and I go to the streets and I return home. What I like about the institutions is that they dress a person, the worst is that it is very small. The best of life on the streets is that a person can stay with the gallada [a group of street children]; that is delightful, but the worst is that there are people who beat up on a person. What is bad about the home is that parents beat us up. What is good about the home is the food and the place to sleep. The food is better in the institution where a person has a bed; in the home there are many to a bed and a person can hardly fit. I don't know where I will end up. I leave from the house and I go to the street and then I come to the institution, and then I leave from there—this is my street life. (Muñoz and Pachón 1980, 95)

In addition to their continual movement between home, the streets, and a variety of programs, these children also found private benefactors. The relationship between street children and benefactors was firmly established in the culture and it indicated not only an important source of help that was often overlooked by the people who tried to serve them but also suggested why many children who appeared abandoned were not without contacts and assistance. The initiation of the benefactor relationship usually started when a child, through his own suggestion and manipulation of circumstances, convinced an adult that he could be of value. One child, Pedro, was able to do this by sleeping at the edge of the garage of a wealthy family. Since he never left to sleep in another place, the family could not help but deal with him. Finally Pedro suggested to them that they might be robbed and needed his protection. Eventually, and in large part because of his friendly manner (which did not quite touch the level of intimidation), they allowed him to sleep inside the garage. Pedro began doing a few errands and slowly became part of their group of workers, which in turn gave him more amenities such as food and a "place."

Another kind of benefactor relationship might begin when an adult wanted to help an "abandoned" child. In effect the adult temporarily adopted him. There were many motives for this, including political reasons. For example, one couple we knew already had four children, but their political orientation toward social justice made them feel compelled to offer assistance and care to a street child. There is a tradition in Colombia of children being given as gifts, *regalitos*, to relatives or even close friends of the family. Many children were brought up by their grandparents, by their uncles or aunts, or simply by friends of the parents who were more economically able to care for them. Several children in our study were living as regalitos.

Other adults became benefactors for personal reasons. Jorge, who lost his younger brother to typhus, routinely gave shelter to Arturo, a street child, because Arturo reminded him of his brother. Alarico, another adult who became a benefactor, was himself a street boy before being taken in by a family who helped him find work, which eventually allowed him to marry and start his own family. Word of Alarico's generosity got around so that many of the children in Bosconia knew that if they needed a place to spend the night or some food Alarico could be easily persuaded to come to their aid. Like the children's other living arrangements, these benefactor relationships were generally not stable and came and went for a variety of reasons: because the child was ready to seek another adventure, because of abuse, or because circumstances changed on either side.

Thus, three salient facts came from our observations. First, the children most often had a home with an adult whom they knew; second, they were often in contact with their families; and third, rather than being children of the streets, or abandoned children, they could, moving from place to place, be more appropriately called child vagabonds, or *niños vagos*.

Whether they were on the streets out of necessity or from

Some *trabajadores jóvenes* were merely supplementing income for their families in rather traditional ways, vending inexpensive items. In some cases they were closely supervised and often did work comparable to North American children selling newspapers.

choice was not as easy to determine as the description "abandoned children" or "street children" implied. One problem with the use of the term "street child," which reflected on the difficulty of determining how many of them there were, arose when they were seen with other poor children. In appearance and in what they did during the day they were not much different from many child workers, *trabajadores jóvenes*. Trabajadores jóvenes are children who are poor, live at home, and begin to work at a young age instead of attending school. Both street children and trabajadores jóvenes spent their days looking for ways to make money or to secure goods. Initiation of both groups into the economy could begin at quite an early age. Both groups of children worked at a variety of similar tasks, which often involved finding something cheap in one place that could be traded more dearly in another locale, contracting their services to someone who was

Trabajadores jóvenes often began street life at a very young age. It was not uncommon for these children to choose street life over the kind of enforced servitude portrayed here.

willing to pay them, or offering their services in exchange for barter. Being poor, child workers looked as ragged as the proverbial street children just as some street children looked like the rather average poor worker. Our experience indicated that it was quite likely that the children moved between the two groups easily and often. Since the two groups were so similar in background and life-styles, whether the outcome of this early adult status resulted in their becoming street children or trabajadores jóvenes was, at this age, impossible to discern.

The simple application of the term street child blurred the fact that many children who were doing the same things as the street children, and looking about as poorly groomed, were in fact returning to their intact and loving families at the end of each day. In the daytime it was particularly difficult to discern one group from the other, and we have no doubt that much of the previous research that refers to the numbers of street children has made the mistake of counting noses during the normal adult hours of work.

This well-dressed young adolescent with his out-stretched hand was singing a Mexican *ranchera*, a song of melancholy romance. His niche seemed to be somewhere between that of street children, who routinely perform in exchange for alms, and that of child workers, who assume a more traditional place in the child economy.

Inasmuch as the term street children is applied to many children who have a variety of different circumstances and characteristics, it tends erroneously to block them all together into a single mass of children who share a series of common histories and problems, while it fails to take into account their differences.

When we briefly defined street children in the Introduction, we noted that they are of both genders. But at first we saw almost all males, and the children at Bosconia were about 95 percent boys. There were state and private programs for girls, and girls had better opportunities to establish benefactor relationships. The private institutions for girls were generally run by nuns, and the philosophies of these institutions were different from those for boys. The institutions for girls tried to change character, while the ones for boys tried to build vocational commitment and skills. Gender differences will be discussed in detail later. For now, we can say that the girls on the streets are not put into the category of street children. They are given a different niche, one that is more often associated with prostitution.

There was a good deal of confusion about what was meant by the terms "street children" and "abandoned children," revealing the difficulties not only of ascertaining the nature of their lives, but also of establishing a reasonably accurate count. For example, the Instituto Colombiano Bienestar Familiar (ICBSF) conducted a demographic study in 1975. In it they estimated "that the city of Bogotá has produced in the neighborhood of 130,000 *gamines* [the name refers to all street children]" (Pineda et al. 1978, 243). This is about 3.9 percent of the three and a half million people in Bogotá. In 1973 Díaz published an article in *Education Hoy*, a national periodical, giving a figure of 3,000 street children in Bogotá (Díaz 1973). This amounts to about one-tenth of one percent of the total population, which is considerably smaller than the 3.9 percent suggested by the ICBSF. In a 1976 article, "The Census of Gamines," published in *El Tiempo* (1976, 22) (one of the two leading Bogotá daily newspapers), it was estimated that about 60,000 street children were in the city. Gutiérrez, the author of a definitive study on street children (1972b) and a national expert on the topic, claimed that there were about 5,000. The mayor of Bogotá, who from 1968 to 1980 was responsible for supplying the official statistics, said there were no more than about 2,000 in 1980. The commander of the police, Hernando Herras, claimed that many of the statistics have been exaggerated and that "there appears to be a gamine population in Bogotá that is not less than 6,000 and not more than 12,000" (de Mantilla 1980, 460).

According to the 1976 census (Jaramillo 1976), out of twenty-eight million Colombians, 41 percent are below fifteen years of age and 70 percent of the country's population is considered to be poor. Jaramillo defined poor as not having the basic elements for a dignified life. This meant that in the country there were nearly 8 million poor children and in Bogotá, assuming a population of 3.5 million, there were about 1.3 million poor children. Even taking the highest figure of street children used by the ICBSF (130,000), this indicates that only one in ten poor children are considered street children. These statistics not only show that there is not much reliability in the estimates of the numbers of street children, but they also pose a very important question: inasmuch as poverty is given as the major reason for the existence of street children, why is it that only one in ten poor children becomes a street child? Something more, something beyond poverty per se must be involved. We will explore this in detail later.

It is obvious from this discussion that the seemingly factual material provided a less-than-accurate description of who the children were, what kinds of lives they were living, and how many of them there were. The "terms" applied to these children had more than descriptive qualities—they also carried emotive meanings. The easy acceptance of the term "street children" covered up the tension evoked by connecting the two words. Children do not belong in the streets, and the words used together made it quite clear that the children who were referred to under this rubric were out of place. Children belong in the home, and if they are not there then either they or their families are problematic. The term "street children" was no longer used as a way of describing or identifying a particular group of children in need of help. Instead, the terms "street children" and "abandoned children" obscured an accurate description of the children's lives and that of their families by being less than accurate about who the children were, where they came from, and the nature of their unique problems. The terms "street child" and "abandoned child" came from a particular society and had a political tone whose use suggested action or remedy, while at the same time it justified the power needed to carry out those remedies.

In fact, there were many street children and many variations in where they lived, what they did, and what kinds of skills or problems they had. What characterized this diverse group of children is that they lived in a society that had allocated certain rights and privileges to childhood. Above all else, the street children were, in one way or another, outside the accepted role of childhood. Some had chosen this and others had been forced into it. There is one very salient fact: being a "street child" had only partially to do with the children's characteristics. How they were perceived and consequently treated by the society in which they lived also contributed to defining each of them. It is in this interaction between Colombian society and the street children that a great part of the definition of street children can be understood. Although our descriptions in this chapter reveal some of the characteristics of the children, street children cannot be defined solely by these characteristics because they are shared with other children like child workers.

Even from the point of view of the society that labeled the street children, variations beyond the children's characteristics determined whether or not they carried that label. As street children got clean clothes or became less obvious to the world at large by receding from prankish acts, they became in their own terms *amando*, or conformists, and thus no longer street children. From the perspective of the children, one definitive characteristic was a nonconformist attitude toward society. When Colombian parents want to insult their own children they call them gamines, to indicate that their children need to straighten out and become less libertine. The most affluent families fear the idea of their own children becoming street children, indicating that the street child is a national reference point. The label indicates not just an impoverished condition, but a style of life that includes disrespect to authority and to family.

Street children can be defined as an aberration of childhood in a particular society with a particular point of view about childhood, but this cannot really be comprehended until we can understand the interactions between the children and the society in which they live. In chapters 2 through 4 the children's lives and how they are treated by society will become more clear. Then, in chapter 5, a case will be built to demonstrate why society treats these children in a particular way.

2
The Prepuberty Children: Taking Advantage of Being Little

The importance of the ways that society's reactions to street children influenced the children's lives was illustrated dramatically when they reached puberty. Street children often created their own work with a style of daring mischief. Thus, when a driver entered his car he would be met by an innocent-looking offender who, with a bright smile, offered for a few cents to clean the car windows he had just dirtied. Muñoz and Pachón commented on how the public responded to children who did this based on their size. "If a bigger child did the same thing, it might be considered a violent attack on the liberty of the citizen, but the little kids are able to get away with it. Initially, these acts are received with a gesture of sympathy or even reacted to lovingly. Nevertheless, after awhile the same acts by larger children are received more negatively and responded to with a hostile yell, 'Don't wash my window. You dirtied it. Get the hell out of here!'" (Muñoz and Pachón 1980, 55).

The "cute" image changed to a perception of older children as thugs. They were treated accordingly, with the nature of their street life inevitably and profoundly altered as a result. Given these circumstances a surprising phenomenon existed. The smaller children were often more economically productive than the older ones and this often changed the normal developmental sequence. Adolescence, a period for learning to adapt to and accept adult standards, was greatly compressed, and young children often had much more power over their older colleagues than expected, making them at times more like adults than their older companions.

The smallest children benefited the most from contact with adults. In size many appeared like they should still be very dependent on their mothers for their basic needs of shelter and food. These little ones weighed less than fifty or sixty pounds and were no taller than the tables at restaurants where they were often seen successfully getting *sobres* (leftovers) from the plates of the patrons. Because they looked so small and young they stood out against the large "real world" in which they apparently roamed without supervision. Thus, the smallest children produced a form of cognitive dissonance in many adults. As this theory proposes, a person in a dissonant state experiences two conflicting beliefs and thus feels compelled to change his opinion about one because of the tension of holding two incompatible attitudes (Festinger 1965). In this case the observer's concepts of a child as innocent and in need of a family for protection, and a child who is capable of producing a self-sustaining livelihood are incongruent, particularly so when the child is so small. When the public reacted to these small children by using such adjectives as "cute" and "adorable," they were overemphasizing one aspect of these children's character, the one most congruent with their concept of a small child. It was psychologically easier to grant to these little children the status of children (i.e., dependent, in need of protection, and helpless), no matter how independent they may have been, than to change one's concept of childhood. This was why small children were paid for cleaning the very windows they had just dirtied. When the older children did the same thing, however, there was no dissonance and the reactions of the drivers were in line with their concept of how adolescents should be treated.

One day in Marcelina a group of boys was watching intently as a potential patron was showing some photos of her trip to the north coast. As they were crowding very close to her, a staff member pushed them back to a safer distance, but one small boy stayed nearby while she and I began to discuss her plans for contributing to the program. She began to tell me how cute the child looked, how smart and how wonderfully adorable, not realizing that he was at that very same time picking her pocket. One of my colleagues and I saw the incident, looked at each other, and without thinking we both smiled.

Other incidents pointed out the differences between how older and younger children were perceived. It was common in Bosconia, for example, to shave children's heads, presumably because they had lice. At first it was surprising to us that the small children did not protest this treatment but merely submitted to it like lambs being shorn. But their new appearance added to their cuteness, which in turn made them economically more viable. When the older boys were shaved they either protested or sulked. Their new appearance inevitably meant economic hardship because they appeared more thuglike, less trustworthy, and better avoided.

One day I left Bosconia following two little boys about seven years old. They were walking with their arms over each other's shoulders with an easy, childlike gait, in harmony with each other. One of them had two gym shoes tied together by their laces and slung over his shoulder. He was wearing a pair of green shorts over his longer blue jeans. His belt was a white cord, hanging down from his waist to his knees. In the heat of the day they both walked barefoot, their shirts tied around their waists. They appeared as comfortable in the streets as if they were relaxing in their living room after a long day of work. As I watched them I was flooded with memories of being free, of being boyish. The image of Huck Finn down by the river resurfaced in my mind.

As I continued my daily route I saw Enrique farther down the street. He was a fourteen-year-old boy, a regular at Bosconia, old enough to have a mustache. He was carrying a plastic sack over his shoulder with his belongings in it. His untucked shirt was too small, so tight against his chest and shoulders that there was a rip in the seam under one arm. As I got closer I could see the wet marks from his sweat across his chest and under his arms. As soon as we had seen one another, and in spite of the fact that we knew each other, my first reaction was of fright, tensing myself against a possible intrusion. With his adultlike body he appeared thuggish, down-and-out, and potentially dangerous.

These differing social perceptions changed the lives of the children. The larger children were more likely to be suspected of committing delinquent acts. They rarely received alms through pity. Without being able to beg or rely on being "cute," they were forced to develop delinquent work habits to survive. The smaller children were more reliable in bringing in food and money, and thus often became the providers for their larger peers. This gave the smaller children a larger claim to power among their friends in their galladas. Other authors have corroborated this finding (Beltrán 1969; Téllez 1976; Néron 1953). "The role of the smallest ones, of the *chichiguas*, has a value radically different than the rest of the members [of the gallada]. The little ones receive special attention because generally they are the most productive in begging and the ones who are last suspected by adults of being in delinquent activities" (Gutiérrez 1972a, 199). The smaller children learned quickly that they were capable of generating income for survival. This brought them prestige and safety among the older members of the gallada.

On the other hand, smaller children were more naive in the ways of the street, their cognitive development was less mature, and they had less emotional capacity to deal with the harshness of street life than their older counterparts. These facts tempered their advantage with their older friends in the galladas. In their social world the smaller children were taking on roles associated with different ages. This pointed out the necessity of seeing the phenomena of street life in a developmental perspective. With respect to their development the smaller children were living a kind of schizophrenic existence. Among their peers they were often given the status of elders, or more appropriately, of providers. But because of their ages of six, seven, eight, and nine, they often had a hard time carrying this emotional load. In contrast to being adultlike in their peer groups, they were treated as cute little children by society. Being away from home at an early age, they were living a premature adolescence. The relevance of this complex developmental status surfaced around an important and commonly overlooked aspect to street life: the night.

One nine-year-old boy in the sample said that he always had bad dreams at night: "People are going to kill me, they are pursuing me, either waiting to shoot me or obliging me to do things." This paranoid dream had some basis in reality since street children could be persecuted by the police and other adults. This fate was particularly likely late at night, when their persecutors were freer to act without fear of reprisals and when the children, particularly if they were small, were the most vulnerable. In explaining this vulnerability, another small boy in the sample said, "This is why I am afraid of the night. It scares me to see things. When I see men that are stopped together talking I start to think that they might try to kill me or to take advantage of me."

Seeing children sleeping during the day was one of the most common sights in the institutions where we collected data. We rarely saw any of them suddenly (even if jokingly) awakened by their friends. Sleeping during the day for these children was just the opposite of what it was for a child in the mainstream culture. Mainstream children would be in school and would be made fun of for falling asleep during the day. The street children in our study, particularly if they were young, knew that the nights would be long, and that when and how they would sleep would be problematic. The few hours or even minutes of catnapping they were able to catch in the protected shelter of the programs like Bosconia were treated by others as one respects the rest of a soldier in a momentary respite from active duty.

Another problem of the night was that street children, particularly the younger ones, were less protected against whatever emotional traumas they lived with, either from their earlier lives with their families or from the recent process of breaking away from them. These fears were easier to suppress during their active days. Thus several of the small children reported night terrors and nightmares, and more than once we saw mattresses drying, the result of the younger children urinating in their beds. When this happened in Bosconia they were not teased; instead, the educadores helped them change their sheets without comment, as parents in more normal family situations would have done. Some children told us that part of the reason they inhaled gasoline, paint, or other inhalants, or drank alcohol was that it helped them sleep at night. Gutiérrez (1972a) reports that drug use in his sample was primarily the result of trying to ease the fears of the night.

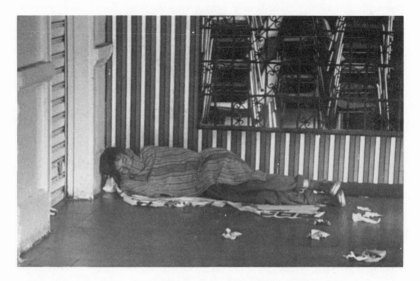

The night posed several problems for the children. Not the least of these was the psychological distress from their past that appeared in their dreams. This was particularly difficult since no one was around at night to comfort them.

On several occasions we were able to visit the children at night as they were settling into their sleeping places. This in itself was rare because they did not, as a rule, reveal to more than a friend or two where they slept. For the children nothing could be more hazardous than to be awakened by a hostile force. We were told more than once that it was better to be cold than to be vulnerable to a possible invader who might accost them and take their belongings or actually hurt them. The major complaint of the children who were exposed to the elements and without the emotional or physical warmth of a guardian was their fear of having their sleep interrupted. Many of the smallest children would make pitiful comparisons between themselves and other children who had the amenities of family life.

The first night on the streets for a six, seven, or eight year old was considered by them as an initiation rite comparable in importance and fear to an adolescent's passage into adulthood. One eight-year-old boy said, "The first night in the streets was very difficult. I felt very sad, but I was also very angry at everyone. I imagined how other kids, who live with rich families, have everything. I felt I had nothing and that to be like them would be impossible. I was hateful toward them and everything. Then I slept and dreamt of returning to be born again as equal to the rest of the children."

This small child's fear of the night poignantly illustrates one of the most significant problems in adapting to being on the streets—the turmoil street life created in the developmental sequence. First, there was little middle ground between young childhood and early adulthood. Adolescence as we normally conceive of it, as a time of learning to be an adult and accept responsibilities, was nearly missing. Second, the common assumption that young children are helpless and gain independence as they grow older was in many respects turned upside down. It was evident that the smallest children suffered as they became street children, but they also learned that they had certain powers denied to the older ones. Their success as providers was in itself so contrary to the traditional family's view of "children" that the public, rather than accept the ramifications of this paradox, preferred to grant the smallest children a kind of pardon for their mistakes. Ironically, this allowed them the very freedom that was so difficult for the public to accept. While the smaller children received extra leniency, the older ones were put on a tighter chain. As soon as the public was no longer lenient (which was at the time the children no longer appeared cute), the children were treated as adults. The leeway that adolescents normally receive was absent. The severity of the attitude toward those who were older made it more difficult for them to continue in their established way of dealing with the streets. Instead of being able to do what they had learned as small children, they either had to rely on their younger friends to support them or adopt a delinquent life-style.

Up to this point we have been viewing the children as if through a rather weak microscope, seeing them as members of age groups. As we turn to a more powerful lens we will note that there are considerable differences between the children in each age group. The above material oriented us to the disorderly psychological development that the public's reaction demanded of all of them. There were, however, some common ways in which specific children responded to these demands.

Among the children who did not yet appear to have reached puberty there were two reactions to life on the streets. The Spanish word *chiquitos*, which means little ones, will be used to refer to the entire prepuberty group. The two different prepuberty subgroups will be called *gamines* and *chupagruesos*. Generally speaking, the gamines chose to leave home, while the chupagruesos were abandoned or forced to leave. On the streets the gamines acted with haughtiness and independence; the chupagruesos were more timid and attached themselves to the more powerful for protection and advice. The two groups differed in their emotional reactions to street life. The gamines enjoyed and displayed their freedom, while the chupagruesos often regressed or became depressed. The two subgroups are defined in more detail later both with respect to their reasons for leaving home and the ways in which they responded to being on the streets.

Table 7 shows the descriptive statistics for all the prepuberty children. It is presented here as an overview of the chiquitos' characteristics. Table 8 demonstrates how the prepuberty groups were divided into the two different subgroups. We supplemented our participant observational information with data from La Sucre and used the following formula to subdivide the prepuberty group.

To be put into the gamine subcategory the children had to have the following characteristics: they had to be under twelve years of age; the Bender score had to be less than or equal to 60, *or* both the NIS and EIS had to be less than two. Only those children who had these scores and reported to us that they had chosen to leave their home were put into the gamine subgroup. This information about leaving home had to be comparable to the information that was supplied by La Sucre. If they met these criteria we assumed that these children, as characterized by their test scores, were emotionally and neurologically healthy. Their IQ had to be greater than 85 so that we could assume their intelligence to be average or above average. We chose these scores because 60 on the Bender was the halfway point between 50, which indicated good ego strength, and 70, which indicated emotional problems on the Pascal-Suttell scoring system. EI and NI scores of zero or one were used because these are the cutoff points for emotional and neuro-

Table 7 Means and Standard Deviations on All Variables for Prepuberty Children

Variable	N	Mean	Standard deviation
Age	24	9.37	1.34
Bender	24	78.04	39.65
Kohs IQ	24	89.56	13.83
HFD-EI	24	3.12	2.05
HFD-NI	24	3.70	1.83

logical problems using the Koppitz scoring method. Note that lower indicators on the HFD and Bender indicate less pathology, or better mental health. This system of grouping gave us confidence that the gamines were emotionally, intellectually, and neurologically within the nonpathological norms. The prepuberty children who did not meet the test scores criteria or the criterion of leaving the home voluntarily were put into the chupagrueso category.

Table 8 shows the results of the Kruskal-Wallis ANOVA for the gamines and the chupagruesos. Forty-five percent (eleven) of the twenty-four prepuberty children were gamines. The gamines functioned significantly better than the chupagruesos with respect to their IQs (p = .006), their Benders (p = .0004), and their NIS (p = .003). Their EIS, although not significantly different, were in the direction of being better. These scores helped us to assert that there were differences between the two groups' abilities to function. Before testing, the children were asked their reasons for leaving home. These responses were compared with the data from La Sucre. Those children who indicated they made a choice to leave home and whose information was corroborated with that from La Sucre were compared with those who left home for other reasons. Fifteen of the twenty-four prepuberty children, or nearly 62 percent had chosen to leave home. Eleven of these fifteen met the criteria for the gamine category.

Table 8 Prepuberty Children

Variable	Gamines (N = 11)		Chupagruesos (N = 13)	
	Mean	Standard deviation	Mean	Standard deviation
Age	10.27	.467	8.61	1.38
IQ[a]	96.81	8.48	82.91	14.71
Bender[b]	46.83	12.229	102.92	37.73
EI	2.72	2.37	3.46	1.76
NI[c]	2.63	1.50	4.61	1.60

a. Results of the ANOVA (N = 22, df = 1,21, F ratio = 7.50, F probability = .012) indicate that the samples differ significantly on their IQ scores.

b. Results of the ANOVA (N = 22, df = 1,21, F ratio = 20.77, F probability = .0002) indicate that the samples differ significantly on their Bender scores.

c. Results of the Kruskal-Wallis test (N = 24, df = 1, H' = 8.72) indicate that the samples differ significantly on their NI scores: p ≤ .005.

Los Gamines

One characteristic emerged as a central feature for gamines. As one boy said in Spanish, "gamines are *ser firme*." The literal translation of this is "to be firm," but the verb to be takes two forms in Spanish, *ser* and *estar*. *Ser* refers to long-lasting personal characteristics. Thus, one doesn't say what one *does* for a living, but what one *is* for a living. When a child used the verb *ser*, he was saying that his central self was firmly opposed to what he perceived as illegitimate authority, whatever the personal costs of that opposition might be. As Padre Nicolo said of the gamines: "In his background is the attitude of choosing between a total misery without liberty and a partial misery with liberty. He has opted for the second" (Nicolo 1981, 424). As young children gamines had chosen to leave their homes, the most dependable thing they had known. They fought hard to maintain themselves on the streets against considerable odds and they did so in a way that kept them independent. They felt beholden to no one. For the sake of not surrendering their freedom to those they did not personally respect they often paid dearly.

Thus, the gamines are children who are at once a threat to the family's claim of authority and possessors of prized freedom. They can be characterized as independent, cunning, and even mischievous. They have adopted an attitude about themselves that has been described in Spanish as *altivez*, best translated as haughty. This type of child is evident in nearly all myths and fantasies of eternal childhood. At various times he is perceived as heroic, tragic, enviable, or disgusting. The very existence of the gamines questions something that is considered sacrosanct and beyond inquiry: To be dependent on one's family or guardian is the only way to live between the ages of approximately six and fifteen. Their abilities and their success on the streets make them likely targets of parents who fear their own children might wish to live outside the accepted notions of childhood.

I first met Antonio in the video arcade off the Plaza de Cacedo, where children congregated to play the video machines. He was with his friend Roberto. Without any money of their own, these two boys were observing the play of others. On this day I decided to play. I arranged my position so that I was near the machine where Roberto and Antonio had been huddled watching. They continued to enjoy the game vicariously, and when I finished I made eye contact with them. This gave them an opportunity to ask for some change, which I offered them. Roberto took it without even a moment of further acknowledgment. After taking my money they became engaged in the tangle of the line by staking out and defending their positions with poking jabs, athletic karate kicks, and alternative gestures of feigned hostility and smiling faces. Roberto, who was not much taller than the window of the game display, exchanged his shoes, at least for the moment, with a shoeshine boy for the use of a box to stand on. Antonio was wearing two pairs of pants. Evidently his excited mood prompted him to bargain because he exchanged his outer pair for about a dozen cigarettes, increasing the air of festivity.

It was part of our plan for collecting information to pursue informal contacts where the children were immersed in their regular places doing the things that they normally did, so I continued to frequent this arcade at the same time each day and to cultivate interchanges with the two boys. I would go and play, they would watch, and I would give them enough money to play a game. By the end of two weeks I was able to connect my giving them money with a few words of conversation. More than a month passed by when, to our mutual surprise, they wandered into Bosconia. Seeing that I was part of the routine there, that other children talked with me, and that I was with our Colombian researchers, they assumed that I was not up to something dastardly and that I would not take advantage of them by asking them to do something for me or turning them in to the police. In the next month or so we became more friendly. Even so, they dealt with me only as long as I would or could be helpful to them. Routinely during this period of time, whenever we encountered each other in Bosconia, at the arcade, or on the streets during my daily walks, they would come up to me and shake my hand, say hello and then rather quickly leave to go and play with their friends or carry on their business. Each day that I saw them I got this cursory hello.

I did not see them for a few weeks and then one morning, while I was having breakfast at an outdoor café, they were there with their cursory hello. They accepted my offer of breakfast in spite of, or perhaps because of, the disapproving eyes of the other patrons. They had just come back from a kind of vacation to the north coast. They had been, via the help of a friendly truck driver, visiting Antonio's mother and enjoying themselves. I ordered them a couple of breakfast rolls and they each ate one quickly and put the other in their pockets. They were off after a few minutes. Once again a few weeks went by when I didn't see them until one day in La Sucre, where they rushed up to me to give me a larger-than-usual hello. Because they were in captivity their quick smiles and sense of joy were now subdued and they seemed more eager to talk. They said they were there "for nothing"; the institution said it was for vagrancy. With no place to go and with little to do, we had the longest of our conversations. I was able to talk to them about what they had been doing, even about where they came from and what they did on the streets.

Figure 1 Antonio's Human Figure Drawing
(age = 11, IQ = 91, HFD-EI = 2, HFD-NI= 1)

Figures 1 and 2 show Antonio's HFD and Bender. He was described in his chart at La Sucre as being "aggressive, impulsive, and emotionally immature." Antonio was the oldest of five children, the son of a well-to-do man of Spanish descent. The next two children were by another man, and the last two children were born after his mother separated from this common-law husband. Antonio began to spend more time away from home because the men his mother was involved with took all the money that he earned. By the time he was eight he was spending more time on the streets than at home. After being away from home for two weeks he told his mother that he was going to Bogotá with a friend. They set out on this journey over his mother's objections but did not get very far because they were picked up by the authorities and taken to La Sucre. His mother and aunt went down to pick him up. For a time he stayed with his aunt, a working mother with five children and without a husband, but he left her house for long periods on the streets. He continued to play with other children in the streets and we often saw him at Bosconia.

Antonio's HFD shows an image that is a combination of a self-assertive adolescent and a child's figure. There is both a sense of frailty and animation. The heavy, dark hair, exaggerated collar around the neck, and the prominent belt buckle bring the observer's eye toward the stumplike feet which, without toes, appear to be unsturdy, unable to carry the weight of the body. The dangling cigarette, cavalierly held between the smiling lips, suggests humor and perhaps a knowledge of pleasure beyond his years. The figure, which stands facing the observer, and the enlarged head with a fully drawn face are bold, but the feet which must carry this boldness and the hands which must turn the boldness into reality are without form, incapable of performing.

Like his HFD, his Bender score is also in the healthy range and shows a similar variation. The figures are well drawn and accurate beyond his chronological age. Placed in the upper corner of the page they suggest boldness, but in the use of only part of the space provided, also a lack of self-assuredness. His IQ is 91, which is within the normal range, but not as high as his social skills suggest he is capable of performing. His single NI suggested no neurological dysfunction. Perhaps he had some learning disability for, in spite of his IQ and social dexterity, he did not read. What characterized him most in our conversations was his mastery and enjoyment of street life. He was angry at his mother but he liked his aunt, although he felt that she was overprotective. He was even ready to give her some of the money that he earned on the streets. What he wanted was more freedom to come and go as he pleased.

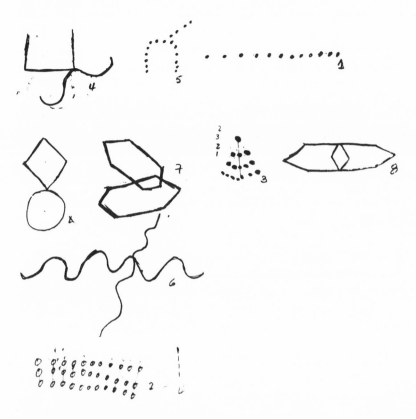

Figure 2 Antonio's Bender (B = 34)

After Antonio was released he continued to spend time on the streets, joining his friend Roberto and resuming where they had left off. In the next couple of months I established a friendship with the two boys that allowed me to know more about their routines. I was able to construct a sense of their life on the streets. They had made an arrangement with Pedro, a *vigilante* (any man who is hired by one or more households to serve as night guard from potential robbers), to spend the nights in a quiet corner of one of his buildings in exchange for bringing him cigarettes, food and, occasionally, liquor. They would return to this locale every night and begin afresh from there every morning. With their knowledge I followed them at a distance for the better part of a day. Upon leaving home they walked over to El Centro, where the early market was still open. On their way they passed through the major park, where they paused for a few minutes to watch a storyteller who, after talking about the mysteries of women in the Amazon, passed around his hat for money. By offering to do this for him they were able to earn a few pesos. Moving on, they stood very close to a fruit vendor, neither leaving nor asking for anything. They eventually were given a piece of pineapple, which they ate quickly, and they walked on. They stopped to study a woman holding a cage from which she sold brightly colored parakeets. Seeing an older woman trying to move a heavy box across the street, they offered to help her and in exchange she gave them a few more pesos.

A few blocks later they stopped at the El Paradiso restaurant, where they went each morning to exchange washing the front sidewalk with a hose (which they also used for washing themselves) for leftover food, sobres, from the previous night. Antonio put the plastic bag of sobres over his shoulder and they went to a quiet side street, sat down in the shade, and emptied the food, which was lumped together in a mass about the size of a small pillow. Using the plastic bag as their table setting, they began separating the good from the chaff. They ate the few pieces of leftover meat, most of which was still connected to the bones, before throwing the bones as close to a tree as possible in a makeshift contest. Dessert was a conglomerate of sweets that was molded together in an indiscriminate mass that they ate not just with their fingers but with their whole hands as they laughed loudly. The major part of the mound of food was still left, about two pounds of bread and yucca. Putting this back in the bag, they took it a few blocks to where they knew a blind man who used a corner for begging and other business activities. In exchange for their leftovers, now the sobres of the blind man, they received a few pesos and a couple of cigarettes.

Walking past the movie house on their way to the bus stop, they saw that a new Mexican cowboy movie was playing. They got on the bus that was going to the cemetery and asked the driver to let them ride for free so that they might ask for food, since, they said, they were starving. Not knowing these boys, and having no benefactor relationship with them, he told them they would have to pay. But in order to avoid problems he gave them a quick nod, a subliminal assurance that they could ask for money while riding. On the bus Roberto put on a pitiful expression and began to sing soulfully about the difficulties of having a sick mother whom he was trying to support. The song concluded with "could you give my mother a few pesos so she could go to the doctor?" He got a few pesos, enough to pay for their ride to the cemetery. Meanwhile Antonio lodged himself in the exit well, standing in the way of exiting passengers, offering them his hand so that they might climb down more easily. Most of the passengers ignored him, some were indignant and made comments to the bus driver, a few found his scheme amusing and gave him a peso.

At the cemetery the two boys met a few older friends and gave some of the bus money to them in exchange for a ladder, which they carried over to an area where relatives were visiting a loved one's grave. As it was nearly impossible to place wreaths on the higher grave sites, Roberto and Antonio rented out the use of the ladder. By early afternoon the two boys had returned the ladder to their friends and the four of them smoked a couple of cigarettes, which they hung from their mouths demonstrating their natural and easy manner of being "cool." They practiced a game of drooling, letting the spit go as far down their chins as possible until the ultimate moment, when they withdrew it without allowing any of the saliva to fall off. After an hour or so the four of them headed back to El Centro, where people were beginning to gather after the afternoon siesta. The traffic was quite thick, and the boys got off their bus when it became bogged down in congestion. Upon exiting they immediately began a game of tag, running in between cars whose drivers were sounding horns as a way of demanding, rather unsuccessfully, that the traffic move more quickly. Two of the older boys, with Antonio behind them, had evidently worked out a way to get some money. They spotted a car with a single passenger and an open window. One of the older boys pounded his fist on the passenger side of the car. The loud noise startled the woman driver, who had mistakenly left her window open in the midday heat. While the woman's attention was distracted to the side of the car where the noise was coming from, the other, older boy had slipped over to the driver's side, reached into her car, and grabbed her shopping bag. Then all four of them ran under the bridge, where they discovered that what they had stolen was only a few pieces of cloth. On their way to Bosconia for the four o'clock afternoon lunch they passed a street vendor and exchanged the material for a dozen cigarettes and a few pesos. When they arrived at Bosconia they greeted their friends with playful swatting slaps across their backs. A few times their exuberance exceeded the acceptable pain level of their friends and they received snarls and punches as ritualistic reprisals in return.

At play in Bosconia, they began a game of soccer in which Antonio assumed the position of goalie. Soon he was bored and began a conversation with a friend. He told the friend about the exploits of the day and the friend told him about the new movie. Meanwhile a game of tag ensued and Antonio left the conversation and joined in, running wildly after another boy. As the soccer game continued, Antonio decided to leave the tag and resume his role as goalie, only to arrive in time to be met by a bigger boy, who plunged into the goal head first. Antonio, apparently feeling taken advantage of, put on his tough face and started to fight with the older boy. The older boy ignored him and continued playing, whereupon Antonio went back to the game of tag.

All the children assembled for their late afternoon lunch: yucca, rice, and a few small pieces of tough meat that they had to eat with both hands. As they all sat eating their food, they discussed what they had done during the day, exaggerating their income and the level of danger to achieve it. Many of the boys made plans to go to the movie that night. At this point the educador began to make a speech to the boys about how they shouldn't just come to Bosconia to get free food and a place to socialize, but that they should "get with the program, begin to think about making something of themselves and their lives and start acting more responsibly." As if in reply to any prepackaged program designed to "help street children," Antonio and Roberto gulped down the last bit of food and walked out the door arm in arm.

At the corner they exchanged some cigarettes for a bottle of Coke, which they shared, drinking it in a matter of moments. Being the first to arrive at the arcade, they spent some of their money on a few video games. By the time they finished, some other boys had come over from Bosconia and they all left for the movie. Roberto and Antonio got an early place in the line, which soon began to get considerably longer. While Roberto waited, Antonio went to the end and began telling a young couple that they wouldn't get in unless they moved up to where Roberto was waiting. Since the request was not too unusual in Colombia, the couple agreed to pay the tax of a few pesos. The boys tried to do this again, but without success. Spending the rest of their money, they entered the theater and took seats in the first row. During the movie they made loud catcalls of appreciation, laughing, clapping their hands, and whistling each time someone was killed or when a disadvantaged person gained back his land from the government.

After the show ended they searched the place for refuse. They found only a few cigarette butts, which they smoked as they walked out of the theater. By now it was evening and they walked down the *sexta* (Sixth Avenue, an avenue of fashionable shops and restaurants), where they were looked upon with disdain by the middle-class shoppers. The boys' disordered and disheveled appearance was perceived as threatening by the diners enjoying their meals in open-air restaurants only a few feet away from the streets. After receiving some menacing looks and rude comments from people, they stopped on a side street where a rather young, affluent couple was dining. When the boys asked for food the couple tried to ignore them. The two boys sensed that they were intruding on a special occasion for the couple and so were insistent, thinking that they were likely to be paid to leave the diners alone. Finally, the man told them in a loud voice to leave. When they didn't he called the waiter for help. He told the boys half-heartedly to go. They went across the street, maintaining subliminal eye contact with the diners, who were losing the pleasure of the occasion. Sensing this, the waiter took the opportunity to ascertain whether the customers were willing to pay an additional *propina*, or tip, for the extra service of a quiet, undisturbed dinner. The waiter, not getting a clear answer to his obtuse, but nevertheless definite question to the patrons, disappeared for the moment inside the restaurant. The two boys, merely engaging in their normal style of work, were able to sense the outcome of this interchange between the patrons and the waiter and came back to the outdoor table. While

Roberto approached the woman from one side and asked once again for something to eat, Antonio came from the other direction and grabbed a piece of meat from the man's plate. Running and laughing, they receded into the darkened street. They carried the piece of meat in Roberto's pocket and returned to Pedro, the vigilante. They gave him part of it as they tiredly entered their vacant corner, which they called their "home." Putting their cobijas (blankets) over themselves, they spent the few minutes before falling asleep planning, not much differently than other eleven year olds, what they would do tomorrow.

Los Chupagruesos

The name *chupagrueso* comes from the Spanish verb *chupar*, which means to absorb through sucking, as a sponge absorbs water. In certain rural places in the Andean countries of South America it is applied to plants, and idiomatically to people, who stick to their hosts like leeches, living at the host's expense. The preadolescent children we refer to as chupagruesos seek out and attach themselves to the powerful children and adults in their circles, doing whatever is necessary to gain their favor. Since in much of Latin America the economy relies on who one knows (having *palanca*, as they say in Colombia), this attitude of the chupagruesos is also common in the larger society. It is despised by the gamines. They would never earn their living or define their own power by their associations with people, or by using palanca instead of their own wits. Where the gamine defines himself independent of others, the chupagrueso sees himself in relation to others.

As shown in table 8, the chupagruesos were significantly in poorer mental health, less intelligent, and more likely to have indications of neurological impairments than the gamines. They were also significantly younger. To be in the chupagrueso category the children had to indicate that they had not chosen to leave home. This information had to be corroborated from the records in La Sucre. Of the twenty-four prepuberty children, fifteen had chosen to leave home. Of those fifteen, only eleven met the testing criteria for the gamines. Thus, four of them were put into the chupagrueso group. Of the remaining nine, five said they were abandoned, two said they were living with non–blood relatives, and two said they left home because they had to. On the test scores the chupagruesos either had Bender scores over 70, two or more NIS and EIS, or IQS under 85.

When I met Luiz at Bosconia he looked like many of the children I would routinely pass on the streets shining shoes, selling newspapers, or vending fruits. He wore dark-colored, khaki-style pants, was quite clean, and dressed well. In short, he appeared like any other polite ten-year-old Colombian boy.

Figures 3 and 4 illustrate Luiz's HFD and Bender. The social information that was given to us in La Sucre described Luiz as "immature, dependent, and with pent-up hostility." He was the youngest of six children. His father left home when he was five and he had not seen or heard from him since. His chart indicated that he had a pattern of getting into peer relations with older children who took advantage of him. The most startling image in his HFD is the fact that the drawing has shortened arms and no hands, as if the child is unable to "get a handle on things." The large, circular belt buckle drawn over widely placed legs suggests vulnerability in a symbolically prominent place. On the lower side of the head is an elongated neck, on the upper side is a skimpy patch of hair. Together they make the head appear precarious, an impression that is reinforced by a smile on the face that has no depth, no joy. The whole figure is immaturely drawn. There is no indication of pleasurable experience, only of insecurity. The three EIS on the HFD are in the pathological range, as is his 72 on the Bender. His IQ of 89 is within the normal range.

After an unusually short introductory period he was quite talkative about his past and shared the following story with me. He started going to school but he was always angry at his teachers. He did badly in school. "I didn't see what sense school made." He was afraid of his parents, but he was also afraid to leave them and become a "gamine," a term he used pejoratively. At age seven he got a job carrying boxes from a factory to the delivery trucks. He described his boss as "very mean" and said he was treated badly by him. "I was scared of him, but I was also afraid of not bringing home money to my parents." At about this time he met a woman

Figure 3 Luiz's Human Figure Drawing
(age = 10, IQ = 82, HFD-EI = 3, HFD-NI = 3)

who was selling sunglasses and who said he could help her. She
would give him food and sometimes money. "She was very
friendly and so I started working with her. I had to arrange all of
the glasses on a table and make them look very neat. I had to sell
them at good prices so she could make a profit and have enough
left over to pay me. Sometimes I had to go home hungry and without money. At these times my mother would be very angry at me
for leaving the other job. Sometimes she would punish me, but if I
pleaded with her and told her I just couldn't work for that man in
the factory she would let me go to bed hungry but without hurting me. I pretended that I wasn't hungry when I got to bed and I
felt better."

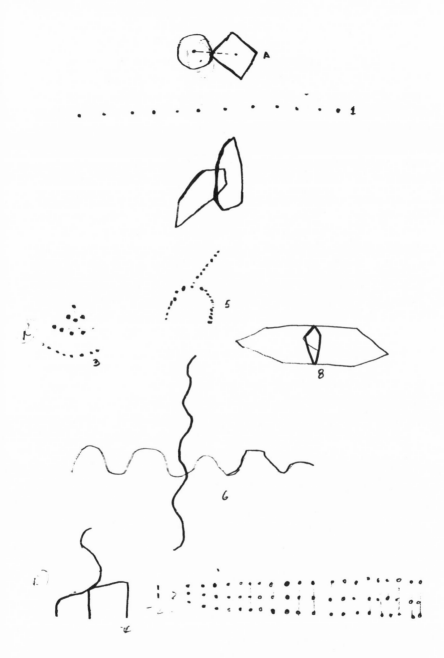

Figure 4 Luiz's Bender (B = 72)

During the time he was working with this woman, he would
have coffee and bread in the morning and then go out to sell the
sunglasses. If he couldn't sell them he wouldn't get food for
lunch and the woman would make him beg for money before she
would let him go home. "This is when I started to go to Bosconia
because I could get food and there was a lot of other kids to play
with. When I arrived at Bosconia I was able to take a shower and
get clean. I really liked that. I could get my clothes washed and I
liked that, too. But I had to be careful about washing my clothes
because the older ones would steal them and then I wouldn't be
able to get them back. But I guess it is pretty good anyway. I
played a lot with the older kids and I learned a lot about being on
the streets."

After a while he started going with Natacio and Miguel to sell
cigarettes and candy. They were working for a man whom he referred to as "El Señor." El Señor gave them cigarettes and candy to
sell. At the end of the day El Señor gave them some money, "a lot
less than what we sold them for, but it was better than nothing
and we thought that one day we could buy our own cigarettes . . .
only El Señor told us that it is safer to work for him."

Musing over his life, he said he hoped to become a "sleeper" in
Bosconia. He was willing to go back to school because without
doing this he couldn't sleep at Bosconia. He wanted to learn to become a carpenter.

I guess it will depend if Ricardo [the educador] likes me. I do
what he asks because I don't want to get him mad at me. The
other day I cut my finger while I was playing basketball and
there was a lot of blood. I was afraid that something awful had
happened. They took me to the infirmary and the other boys
came and they told me that I wasn't hurt too badly so I went
back to play. But, I was thinking that if I was hurt I wouldn't be
able to go to school and Ricardo would be mad at me and I
would have to leave Bosconia and go back to selling glasses or
working for that man who made me work all the time and
didn't give me any money or food.

Before he went to Bosconia he stayed with the gallada of Calle
31. He described the group as having six members, four older

boys and two smaller ones, of which he was one. He liked being with the bigger ones because

> they kept us safe from the police and although they made me get up early in the morning when it was still very cold to go and ask for money so they could eat, they at least shared the food with me. At times I was very hungry when I was with the gallada. Alvaro [the biggest boy] told me to keep asking people for money, that I should tell them how hungry I was. I kept on doing this, but when I didn't get any money he wouldn't give me any food and everyone in the gallada made fun of me. Sometimes I had to fight with the older boys just to get a place to sleep or to stay warm. And, because they were so much bigger than me I couldn't win, but I still had to fight with them. I didn't want to fight because I liked them, but I had to do something to get some food and get in out of the cold. Sometimes Alvaro would tell the others to stop fighting with me and I was happy when he did this.

In the time he spent with the gallada he went to a meat store early in the morning and helped Fredrico clean meat, and then Fredrico would give him some of the leftovers. He said he ate some of it and took the rest back to the gallada so they would be good to him. In the middle of the day he would work with Alvaro on the buses. He would sing a *ranchera* (a soulful Mexican song) and ask for money while Alvaro waited on the back of the bus. When they got off he would give Alvaro some of the money he had earned singing and together they would go to the bakery and buy some bread. Sometimes, if Tomás (a worker in the bakery) was not there they would steal the bread. But this was dangerous because Tomás, he said, hated them. When he saw them coming he took out his broom and "tried to kill us."

Luiz also described his best friend, Carlos, a vigilante who reminded him of his father. Carlos had grown up in a family like his. Luiz hardly knew his father and his *padrastro* (stepfather) was "very mean to me." Carlos let Luiz stay with him during the day, when the owners of the house he guarded were gone. Carlos would tell him stories about how he had traveled all around Colombia. Luiz had never left Cali, but hoped that when he was older he could join the army and see a lot of the country. Not only would Carlos share extra food with him, he would sometimes give him money to buy cigarettes or aguardiente. "Once he let me drink the aguardiente and I got drunk with him and his friends. I remember dancing in the streets while they were singing. I got so drunk that I fell down. One day I went back to the house to see Carlos and he was gone. I don't know where he went, but I miss him."

Jorge was his best friend in the gallada. He allowed Luiz to help him shine shoes by sending Luiz to get polishing rags. "I took them back to Jorge and he let me sniff the polish, which made me feel dizzy, but I liked to smell it because it helped me forget how hard it is to live on the streets." Jorge also instructed Luiz how to ask for money from strangers. "He said that I had to tell them how sick my mother was and how hungry I was. He helped me practice to say this so I could get money from people. He showed me where he leaves his shoe box at night and once we went together to practice asking for money and he showed me how to make a face that looked sad."

Once Luiz went into a market with Jorge and saw a man selling watches. Jorge told him that he should try to get one of the watches from him. They would then sell the watch for money so that they could go to the movies and eat what they wanted. Jorge set the stage for the crime: Luiz would walk behind the man who was selling the watches and Jorge would walk in front of him and get his attention. Luiz would have time to pull one of the watches off the stand and run. "On that day I was very scared, but I thought that if Jorge said we could do it, we could. I wanted to be able to eat all I wanted and see the movies. So we went over there and Jorge walked in front of the man and stepped on his foot and the man started to yell at Jorge and I started to take the watch from his stand, but he saw me and when I tried to run away he grabbed me by my arm and called the police. They took me to La Sucre."

At La Sucre he was told by the bigger boys that he would have to share his food with them or they would take all of it. During the day he played tag and watched television, which he said he liked to do, but "at night I was really lonely. All we had to do was go to bed and a lot of the kids yelled while they were sleeping. Sometimes I got scared at what I dreamt about." His sister and her husband came to visit him, but they left right after they got there. "I prayed that when I got out they would let me go to their house." He said he was afraid of having to go back to the gallada and sleep on the streets where it was cold, and where he never knew if someone was going to hurt him, or if the police would come and take him away to a jail like La Sucre.

After he got out of La Sucre he did stay with his sister and her husband. At first this worked out adequately. He began going with his stepfather to El Centro. While the stepfather was selling shoes on the street, Luiz was told to go into the crowds and beg for money. Luiz said he was afraid to do this because the police might take him back to La Sucre. But he knew that he had to follow his stepfather's orders or he would have to leave his sister's house.

As the situation at his sister's house deteriorated he began to move around the city with the children he had met at Bosconia and La Sucre. An older boy from La Sucre who sold newspapers would give Luiz some papers to sell and Luiz, after paying the boy his share, would take the bus to the Unicentro, the newest shopping center in town. When he was on the bus he would tell people that he was poor, that his mother was sick, and that he had to have money for her to get better. This would earn him a few pesos. He went to the Unicentro because he liked seeing the wealthy people and what they bought. "Once I got enough money to get a pastry like the rich people eat. It was still warm. Sometimes I went to the back of the bakery and I told the people that I was starving and I had to have something to eat and they gave me some bread, which I liked to eat."

Reflecting on his sense of being an exile, Luiz said, "I guess I'd rather be in Bosconia if they will let me in, because there at least I have the chance to go to school and learn something that will help me get work. If I stay at my sister's I have to work all the time and I can't go to school. Besides my padrastro wants me to leave because I can't bring him enough money. If I go back to the gallada I am afraid something awful will happen to me. I think I like Bosconia the best."

What will happen to Luiz in the future? As he talked, he often reminisced in a way that was clearly different from the manner in which gamines recalled their past. The gamines did so in a way that indicated self-aggrandizement, attempting to make a favorable impression. Luiz's comments were full of fear and doubts, expressing a longing for some peace in an otherwise troubled existence. As compared with Roberto and Antonio, the two gamines, Luiz did not enjoy street life. He was smart enough to realize that the rough knocks of street life were not for him. Intermingled in all his talk was a sense of fear and personal self-doubt. He made continual comparisons between his situation and that of others: the gamines were much more independent, the wealthy children didn't have to face the turmoils that had befallen him. Like Job, Luiz asked in the midst of his personal misfortunes the timeworn question: Why me?

Simply by asking this question, Luiz, and the other chupagruesos, demonstrated a capacity for depression, anger, and guilt—ingredients alien to the gamines. The chupagruesos were preparing to fit into society, most likely as *obreros*, working-class people. Their characteristic submission to others would be helpful when it came time to take orders and follow the directives of their eventual bosses.

This same dichotomy is evident in the life stories told to Muñoz and Palacios (1980) by child workers. Children assuming the chupagrueso role, even though they came from the same sociological situations as the gamines, were quite different in outlook. They were more eager to please adults, more likely to see themselves as pitiful or abused, and less mischievous and independent.

It is likely that Luiz will accept his future position as an obrero, but he may well be exploited by those who employ him since he has learned to do the bidding of those more powerful than himself. However, it is also possible that his anger at himself and his place in society may emerge when he becomes a father and assumes a similar role to that of his padrastro, who forced him to leave his sister's home and begin street life. As he grows older and becomes one of the bigger children in a gallada, he might well do the same kind of exploiting of smaller children that he has portrayed as being so painful to him.

The concerns faced by chupagruesos are dramatically different than those faced by gamines. When the chupagruesos reach puberty their problems are more related to gaining independence than losing it; to increasing self-respect rather than having to trim down excessive self-perceptions; and to learning to live with their fears and lift their depression rather than to curtail, as the gamines must, their grandiosity.

In their attempts to work through the transition from chiquitos to older street children, there is a dialectical tension between the chupagruesos and the gamines. The gamines use the chupagruesos as a mirror to reflect not who they are, but who they do not want to be or become. The chupagruesos look on gamines as the kind of people they would like to be. Not only did the gamines appear much more independent and less self-doubting, they also enjoyed their independence. On the test scores they were significantly brighter and showed better emotional functioning and less neurological impairment than the chupagruesos.

The two groups developed psychologically much differently. At first they stayed together while playing, but soon a differentiation occurred between them that illustrated some of these differences. Since the chiquitos were good at eliciting alms, they were eventually asked to offer their services to the older children. The smaller children who began to respond to this demand compromised their liberty and became dependent on the larger boys. Those who demonstrated their will, even if it meant a fight against odds of winning, were establishing themselves as independent. Thus, the young street children were tested early in their street lives to determine whether they would associate with the gamine subgroup or the chupagruesos.

A pattern soon emerged that became rather hard to change. The demands put upon the chupagruesos by the *jefes* (bosses) of the groups made it extremely difficult for them to seek their independence. In their relationships with other street children the chupagruesos began to form sado-masochistic connections with the larger boys, which often resulted in depression or regression to immature behavior. This in turn led to a submissive life-style.

It was the chupagrueso children who returned to their deprived homes, found abusive benefactors, or became ill-treated child workers. However, the lack of independence and haughtiness that made them unacceptable to the gamines was helpful to them in getting along with the more common forms of exploitative day labor that characterized many lower-class workers.

There was a code of ethics among the chiquitos who were begging for alms or receiving money based on their cuteness that demonstrated this dichotomy between gamine and chupagrueso. If the *attitude* assumed when one went asking for money was defiant and contained a certain amount of disdain for the person being asked to give something, it was gaminelike. When the chupagruesos solicited money they implored the person's pity. Although both groups might use the same line, asking for money to alleviate their misery or that of their family, the approach was quite different. The gamine's approach contained a sense of drama and cunning, an element of play or revenge, while that of the chupagrueso lacked these elements.

In Bettelheim's book on the psychological importance of fairy tales, he discusses a universal motif of children interacting with adults. This motif features a giant in conflict with an ordinary child, who through wit overpowers the giant. "This theme is common to all cultures in some form, since children everywhere fear and chafe under the power that adults have over them. . . . Children know that short of doing adults' bidding, they have only one way to be safe from adult wrath: through outwitting them" (1976, 28). It was through wit and cunning that the gamines expressed their anger and learned to cope with their situations, while the chupagruesos prevented themselves from expressing their wrath, often reacting more neurotically, even if this submission was more socially acceptable.

Although all the chiquitos eventually lost the value associated with being perceived as cute, the problems faced by the two groups as they approached adolescence were quite different. Our study indicated that there were almost no possibilities for the gamine facing puberty. To continue with petty robbery and cunning mischief, to acquire worse habits such as assaulting pedestrians on the streets or committing more serious forms of robbery are inappropriate to *gaminismo*. The reason for this is that these alternatives do not fulfill the requirements of the universal motif that Bettleheim ascribes to the importance of children outwitting adults. With the increased experience and skill that age brought, the same acts of mischievousness that once were thrilling became degrading. They no longer tested the integrity of the child's intelligence and ability. Escalating petty mischievousness into delinquent acts led to associations with gangs and the friendships and customs that belonged to the delinquent world. The ethos of this subculture of delinquency was not outwitting authority, but crime for wealth or power. The motives of the children in the two worlds were different.

Thus, the same acts that allowed the gamines to feel good about themselves as small children no longer gave them the same satisfaction as adolescents. If they merely repeated what they did as smaller children they could not get the sense of competence about themselves essential to being a gamine. The gamines, as they grew older, were compelled by their perceptions of themselves as haughty provocateurs to give up small-scale mischief and become either full-scale delinquents or find a way to live outside the mainstream of the larger society.

Thus, gaminismo is a developmental stage that faces a nearly inevitable end as the child reaches puberty. The best and only way to maintain a form of gaminismo is to choose a type of livelihood that will be true to the gaminelike spirit, that will, in Ericksonian terms, seek to promote and not change their identity. Adolescence for gamines was a particularly difficult time because they had to give up so many of the acts that had brought them mastery and pleasure. The only way to maintain their hard-won sense of independence was to hide their haughtiness and accept poverty without giving it up, a task that was not easy to accomplish. Having made one important life decision—to leave home at a time when most children are fully dependent on the decisions of their families—the gamines were forced to make another vital decision. One avenue that some took was to become small-scale entrepreneurs, vagabonds. If they couldn't do this they changed careers, eventually becoming criminals or going against their grain to accept a worker's life of servility; that is, to become chupagruesic. By choosing the role of entrepreneurial vagabond they could roam the city, looking to buy something cheap in one place in order to try to resell it in another place. In this way they could maintain their street life and friendships. This would allow them to be outside the mainstream of the working class, to refrain from being beholden to anyone's palanca for finding work, and to avoid being under the authority of a jefe. They could stay, under these circumstances, true to their sense of gamine identity and keep the integrity that they had fought to establish. Chupagruesos had fewer choices to make at puberty. Since they had not chosen to leave home, and had been forced to accept an intolerable situation, they lived with great emotional turmoil. As they approached adolescence they were much more in the grasp of what little society had to offer and they had little capacity to reject this offering.

By definition both gamines and chupagruesos have to be small and young because society reacts to their physical growth in an adverse way. Their biggest enemy, then, is not the police, as is usually assumed, but their growing age and size; for once they reach a certain physical maturity they can no longer be cute. They move from being street children to being street people. This change occurs sometime after the age of twelve, when they reach the physical qualities of adulthood.

At the same time that chiquitos are growing into puberty, the community's reactions to them are changing: they are beginning to be perceived as thugs instead of thieves. Coming of age in the Colombian streets is a far cry from that in Samoa, where adolescence is considered to be, at least from Margaret Mead's perception, a time of extreme happiness with an opportunity to discover one's own identity in a tranquil way. Street children at adolescence have crossed the boundaries into thuggery, with little opportunity for adolescent self-indulgence and little time to learn what their adult identities might be. As their youthful bodies begin to be perceived as adultlike, the pity or vicarious pleasure they might have produced in the public changes. They are no longer allowed to be children. As the chiquitos become adolescents, the tightrope they have been walking between sustenance and destruction, between being functional or criminal, is drawn tighter, and the fall, if there is to be one, becomes much larger.

3
Street Life
for the
Adolescents

For both gamines and chupagruesos, a key element determining how well they are able to make the adjustment to adulthood is their skill at making and taking advantage of "connections." As in most societies that have very few opportunities, what often determines whether or not someone will find work is what is known in Colombia as palanca—friends in powerful positions who can and will help the anonymous job-seeker become someone, become "known." In fact, a good test of an adolescent's readiness to assume adult life is his capacity to endure the tribulations of locating, courting, and securing sufficient palanca to obtain and maintain work. This is particularly difficult for street children, whose connections with important people are quite minimal. They remain anonymous and in poverty unless they create their own palanca. The families of the more affluent Colombian adolescents assume the task of making connections for their children as part of their family duties. They actually compete among themselves to see how well they can "place" their children. Ironically, in Colombian society, as in most of Latin America, the importance of family connections works at the expense of the general populace and acts as a deterrent to adolescents entering society without a family to help them.

Elaborate mechanisms in all social strata of Colombia make the family the main cultural identity and the key agent in defining self-identity. In cases where families cannot care for their children, there is a system of appointing a friend as a potential ally against unforeseen disaster. This is called *compadrazgo*. It is common practice to appoint a special non-family member, known as the *comadre* or *compadre* (literally, the co-mother and co-father), who assumes a commitment to help the "adopted" child. This commitment is one of the most sacred between friends. The compadrazgo relationship begins at birth with church services and continues with community and church support throughout life. Unfortunately, this relationship increases the disadvantage for street children, who are without extended family or close family friends and thus are unable to take advantage of the palanca that compadrazgo brings.

The degree and manner in which the *jóvenes* (the Spanish word for young adults, which is used here as a generic term to refer to all postpuberty street children) were successful in finding their place in the adult society depended as much on how they were able to create their own palanca and thus overcome the great disadvantage of not having access to family help as it did on how they were able to function in meeting normal adolescent demands placed on them by adult society. Given that the postpuberty children in the study sample were without the help of family palanca and lived in a society that opened doors into adult employment through family channels, these children had to demonstrate great energy if they were to assume adult responsibilities.

In order to be sure that the children labeled as postpuberty had indeed physically reached adolescence, the twelve year olds, representing an age that was on the border between pre- and postpuberty, were placed in a separate category, the transitionals. There were eleven transitional children. All their scores were between those of the pre- and postpuberty groups with the exception of their IQs, which were higher, but not significantly so, than

Table 9 Means and Standard Deviations on All Variables for Postpuberty Children

Variable	N	Mean	Standard deviation
Age	21	13.95	1.24
Bender	21	46.19	25.84
Kohs IQ	21	84.57	13.21
HFD-EI	21	2.30	1.38
HFD-NI	21	2.09	1.61

the other two age groups. With this exception, all measures of this transitional group were between the poorer-scoring younger children and the better-scoring older children.

Table 9 gives the descriptive statistics for the twenty-one children in the postpuberty group. Their average age was nearly fourteen. The average Bender (46.19) was below the cutoff for pathology, although the standard deviation was quite large, indicating a range of emotional functioning. The eis and nis averaged more than two and thus fell above the cutoff for pathology. However, the standard deviation was large enough to suggest a spread of functioning. Given these differences the postpuberty group was divided into three different categories according to their overall ability to function. This distinction was made using the following criteria.

To be in the best category the children had to have zero or one ni *and* zero or one ei, *or* they had to have a Bender of less than 50. In addition, they had to have an iq over 85. As was the case for the prepuberty children, these scores were chosen because they are the cutoff points for healthy functioning and normal intelligence. This group was called the *afortunados*, the fortunate ones. Regardless of their iq scores, if the eis *and* nis were three or greater *or* the Bender was 70 or above, the cutoff points for pathology, the children were placed in the lowest-functioning category. This group was called the *desamparados*, the forsaken or deserted ones. The remaining children were placed in the middle group, the *sobrevivientes*, or survivors.

Table 10 Postpuberty Children

	Afortunados (N = 9)		Sobrevivientes (N = 7)		Desamparados (N = 5)	
Variable	Mean	Standard deviation	Mean	Standard deviation	Mean	Standard deviation
Age	13.77	1.09	13.71	1.11	14.60	1.67
IQ[a]	93.66	6.55	83.14	3.38	70.20	17.93
Bender[b]	29.66	10.57	48.28	16.96	73.00	34.12
EI	1.55	1.13	2.66	1.63	3.20	.83
NI	1.55	1.66	1.85	1.46	3.40	1.14

a. Results of the ANOVA (N = 21, df = 2, 18, F ratio = 9.49, F probability = .0015) and the Tukey HSD procedure indicate that the *afortunados* and the *desamparados* differ significantly on their IQ scores: p $\leq$ .05.

b. Results of the ANOVA (N = 21, df = 2,18, F ratio = 7.52, F probability = .0042) and the Tukey HSD procedure indicate that the *afortunados* and the *desamparados* differ significantly on their Bender scores: p $\leq$ .05.

Table 10 illustrates the three levels of functioning in the postpuberty group: those who were without pathology on the test results and were coping (afortunados); those who were able to cope with help (sobrevivientes); and those whose scores were pathological and who were in need of continued help (desamparados). Nearly 43 percent of the jóvenes were in the best category, while nearly 24 percent were functioning far below them on all scores. We computed the Kruskal-Wallis ANOVA and used the Tukey HSD post hoc procedure to see which dimensions were statistically significant between the three postpuberty groups. Both the Bender and IQ scores were significantly different between the best- and worst-functioning groups. Both the NIS and the EIS decreased between the three groups as predicted, but they did not reach a level of significance. The differences between the three postpuberty groups of children, particularly since the ages of the three groups were nearly identical, illustrated that there was a great deal of diversity between the children in their teen years.

Of the three groups of jóvenes, los desamparados, the "forsaken" children, were often physically and emotionally in crisis and barely able to care for themselves. They were unable to find others to care for them and had little motivation to assume adult roles. Since they looked poor and down-and-out and were no longer little children, they were perceived as derelicts and avoided like the proverbial skid-row bum. If they were to rise above this status they would need concerted effort and care, not just periodic assistance. Table 10 indicates that this group included 23.8 percent of the jóvenes. Their IQs were low—on the verge of being classified as retarded—their EIS and NIS were in the pathological category, and their Bender scores were above the score that indicates pathology.

The second group, one-third of the postpuberty sample, was los sobrevivientes, the survivors. They were coping, but it took all the psychic energy they had, leaving little for further development. When under duress they showed obvious signs of depression or demonstrated other types of adjustment disorders, including aggressive behavior. Their ability to prosper or to find work varied over time. When they were functioning well they were motivated to achieve, to work, to take care of themselves, and to find others to help them, but in times of stress they lost their abilities. Unfortunately, it was at these very times that society shunned them because their looks portrayed their distress. With periodic forms of assistance, particularly at those stressful times, they would be able to maintain their shaky stake in adulthood, and possibly even improve. Their scores, which fell between those of the other two groups, were considerably better than the desamparados' and showed that they had some emotional and intellectual strengths. Their IQs were above the retarded range, their Bender scores and their NIS were slightly below the area of concern, while their EIS were in the pathological range.

The third group, los afortunados, the fortunate ones, represented 42.9 percent of the sample. They were successfully making the transition into adulthood. When they were given the opportunities to get ahead, to get a foot in the door, they took advantage of the help. They seemed likely to become satisfied and productive adults in the larger society. Some might choose to live outside of the mainstream, but in so doing they would not be likely to create havoc for themselves or those around them. Their appearance was not much different from their counterparts in the same social class. They may even have appeared more mature and ready to occupy adulthood than others of the same age.

Given their histories they scored remarkably well on the test battery. On the average their Bender scores were less than 30, which is well within the normal population. Likewise, their IQs averaged nearly 94 and their HFDS were not pathological. To lump these children in with the desamparados when planning or executing programs would be of little value, as they appeared ready to move ahead with their lives and leave behind whatever tragedies they had known.

Before discussing the characteristics of each group it must be stressed that although they are presented as separate entities, they were in fact fluid categories. Many children moved in and out of the middle sobreviviente group into one of the other two postpuberty groups. This was particularly true during the change into adolesence. The data suggested that the movement from one postpuberty group to the other depended on several factors. These factors included their relationships to their homes, which changed as they became adolescents; the extent and quality of their friendships with pre- and postpuberty street children; their self-concept and desire to become adultlike; the amount of support they got from peers, extended family, benefactors, or private or public institutions; the way they "looked" and were perceived by the public; and finally, and very important, their luck.

As I have mentioned, society gave little tolerance to street children as they began to reach puberty. When these children made mistakes in learning the ways of adult society they received fairly serious sanctions. Many of the children were unable to comprehend what the demands of adult life might be for them, and often did not know if they in fact wanted to take on adult responsibilities. These children moved between the three categories of jóvenes and alternated between the pre- and postpuberty stages. Given these problems it was expected that the stress of puberty would bring out the worst in the children and that they would, at least during this transitional time, be less tolerant and more abusive to their younger friends. This, however, was not the case; in fact they often supported each other.

Many times the patio at Bosconia appeared like an infirmary for injured soldiers. Cuts, scratches, injured ankles and feet, and more serious wounds were commonplace. Children slept on the benches while others huddled together to discuss plans or reminisce about past episodes. Some children made crutches and staffs to support themselves, as if they were tired soldiers after a long day's battle. Other children, well beyond the appropriate age, sucked their thumbs as if resuming, after battle, their proper child identities. Such sights often produced this disturbing image of children and war—soldiers barely old enough to have facial hair already wounded by battle. This image of being simultaneously young in age and old in experience was what kept our thoughts on the developmental irregularities of these children. Associating with children who were seasoned so early often confused us, making it difficult to know how to act toward them; and they often surprised us when we saw how they acted toward each other. By the time they reached puberty they carried the weight of elder statesmen with respect to many chiquitos. As we began to understand this role we became less surprised at how they were able to help the younger ones, in spite of their own obvious problems. Since they were becoming the "officers," they began assuming the responsibility of aiding the "enlisted," which helped them cope with their own problems.

Nevertheless, the transitional children's cognitive and emotional capacity to understand their situation was not up to the task of being officers. For example, after seeing him wear one shoe for days, I asked Eduardo, a twelve year old, why he didn't take the other one off, store it, and go barefoot like so many of the others. His response was that having one shoe "was twice as good as having none," because, he said, "I have less chance of hurting my feet." Although this was quite important to him, as running was a part of his survival skills, it also represented a manner of thinking and coping that befitted the mind of a much younger child. For nearly two months another twelve-year-old boy appeared barefoot and in the same outfit: a T-shirt, white cotton pants cut off at the knee, and with an inch-wide leather band around his ankle. When asked about his ankle band, he said that two months before he was almost hit by a car. A friend of his told him to wear the ankle band as a way of giving thanks to fate for not being hurt. He had decided to continue wearing it for protection against bad fortune. I saw Carlos, another boy on the verge of entering puberty, leaving Bosconia for the night with his cobija slung over his shoulder like a cape, his chest bulging with

Bosconia often provided a respite for some very tired children. This close-up of a few postpuberty street children gives a sense of the strains of their daily life and the value of relaxing in safety. The boy staring into space is Enrique. He and the boy on his right are *desamparados*. In the front is a *sobreviviente*.

something under his T-shirt. When I asked him what he had hidden, he revealed a full roll of toilet paper and replied, "I am always prepared."

After seeing many injuries we began to notice that when the chiquitos and adolescents were hurt, the jóvenes found ways to help them. The younger ones received their attention with enjoyment, giving in to their elders with good will. On one occasion Miguel, a boy of about twelve, was playing roughly with his elders and received a cut on his head that, though minor, produced a lot of blood. He sheepishly let himself be taken by four jóvenes to the section of Bosconia that was called the infirmary, no more than a quiet room off the main corridor with a couple of bottles of disinfectant, a few Band-Aids, and an old, unmarked, and disused bottle of antibiotic. There he lay on his back like a puppy, quiet and subdued, his eyes tracing the broken lines of plaster on the ceiling while, distressed but nevertheless content, he received the attention of his older compatriots. When it became obvious that his cut was more bloody than serious the attention subsided and they all went back to the floor. He then continued moving between episodes, fighting for his position in each activity, being the tough recruit that his preparation for life on the streets demanded.

One day at Bosconia I saw Eduardo, a boy of twelve and a regular there for several months, leaning against a pillar, almost completely covered in a new body cast. Only his stomach was not covered with plaster. A new white T-shirt made him appear to be a human sculpture of white on white. The only visible parts above his neck were his eyes, the tip of his nose, and, through a small slit barely large enough to allow for eating, his mouth. Because of the weight of this massive cast he was unable to move, and he needed to be lifted from his resting place by two helpers. He walked like a robot, each movement disjointed and deliberate. It was obvious that he was in a great deal of pain, yet he seemed happier than we had ever seen him. Everyone went up to him to see how he was and ask what had happened. He had been run over by a car while trying to *linchar*.

Linchando is a game played by many street children. It involves grabbing hold of the back bumper of an automobile or bus and staying on the bumper to enjoy the ride as long as possible. The game itself brought great delight to the children. Once, on a major thoroughfare, I saw a boy riding on the bumper of a car smiling the kind of deep smile that brings envy to adults who can only remember such pleasure. Linchando was used by the jóvenes as a kind of exercise to teach the children in transition some of the skills necessary for street life: daring, physical dexterity, and a haughty and public display of disregard for authority. This time there was an accident, and Eduardo had fractured his spine. His confinement in the bulky cast was clearly distressing, not only to him but to everyone, as it was a poignant reminder of the perils of their lives. Yet often over the next six weeks we were to see Eduardo leaning against the same pillar, ironically happy as he received the various grimaces and humorous reproofs from the others.

Injuries, particularly when they were visible, became events in the public domain, a testimony to commonly shared problems and adventures. This allowed friendships to form beyond immediate subgroups of companions and afforded an opportunity for the injured ones to relax their public pose, giving them a momentary reprieve from having to perform beyond their years. Their injuries gave them the opportunity to receive the attention that was normally due to children their chronological age.

This process was sanctioned only under certain definite, yet unspoken rules. The chiquitos were in many respects like recruits who needed to understand that there were rules to be learned, poses to be adopted, and an attitude to be maintained. It was the job of the jóvenes to teach these skills to the chiquitos, and if necessary to enforce them. On one occasion an obviously chupagruesic chiquito in a game of impromptu tag was regressing to infantile behavior. Rather than running, he was skipping, acting more from a need to get attention than trying to display commitment to the task of exercising physical skills. At one point, in a meager attempt to escape, he twisted his ankle and overreacted with tears and bodily grimaces. He was left alone, being neither stoic enough about the pain nor deserving the respect given to a valiant injury. Guarding against a too easily assumed regression to a younger status is one of the jobs that jóvenes have assumed because it helps them feel important and thus helps them cope with their own problems. They have learned remarkable skills of diagnosis and know which injuries are serious and which are of minor importance, and therefore what status the injured child should receive. As a kind of balance to all that had been denied them in the past, through this coping mechanism they created ways to dole out affection, concern, and attention. Both the injured and their caretakers knew when this attention was deserved and both were able to enjoy the ritual surrounding this protective device of helping and being helped. The nurturance that came from these events helped many of them to cope. Through this process the children were able to experience their own form of palanca and thus limit the pain they felt when they made comparisons between themselves and children who were better placed with respect to family support. It also helped the children in transition to puberty to avoid the lower status that regressing into a more dependent state would have given them, and it gave the helpers an assurance that they were indeed no longer chiquitos, but full-fledged soldiers, capable of taking care of their recruits.

The Forlorn, the Unfortunate, and the Survivors

In spite of the ways they helped each other cope with the new problems encountered in leaving the more benign status of chiquitos and assuming the growing pains of the transitionals, there were many children among the jóvenes who did not have the emotional energy to deal with these changes. Several episodes that occurred during the months that we knew Enrique, a fourteen year old, will demonstrate how the desamparados lived.

Figures 5 and 6 show Enrique's HFD and Bender. From the short social history that was given by La Sucre it was ascertained that Enrique was given to the state by his mother and stepfather, who said they did not have the financial resources to feed him. At the insistence of the authorities he would occasionally be returned to his family, who would reluctantly take him, but in short order he would rejoin his friends on the streets. For the previous two years Enrique's worst problem had been his bizarre thinking. His thoughts raced together and were nearly impossible to follow. At these times he could not sleep and was very irritable. At other times he was lethargic and could not muster the energy to take care of himself.

The state reported that he was "aggressive, had precocious sexual fantasies, and was often engaged in autoeroticism." This is evident in his HFD, which depicts an overly developed masculine image, complete with a large Nazi belt buckle. With the exception of the hands, which are mysteriously missing, as if they might be tucked inside the man's trousers, the drawing is grandiose. The unusually long, feminine hair, particularly since it is affixed to such a masculine image, is indicative of Enrique's sexual confusion. His IQ is 81.

Figure 5 Enrique's Human Figure Drawing
(age = 14, IQ = 81, HFD-EI = 3, HFD-NI = 3)

The first time I saw Enrique was in Bosconia. Instead of trousers he was wearing a piece of leather fastened on like a skirt by a rope around his waist. He later told me it had come from the rubbish of a leather tanner. He was barefoot and shirtless. From his mouth hung a cigarette. His demeanor and appearance made his smile appear menacing. His eyes, when not darting away to avoid my contact, almost always appeared glazed. He talked to me

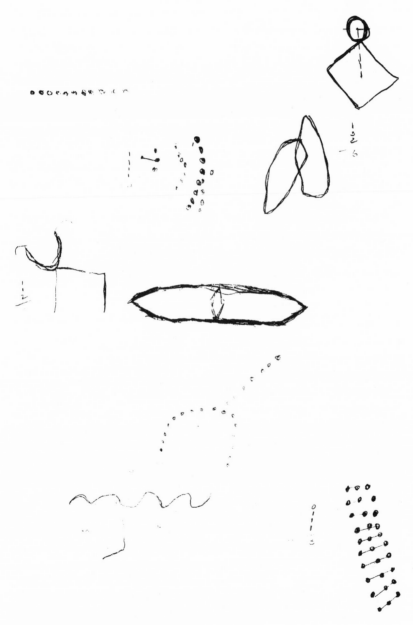

Figure 6 Enrique's Bender (B = 78)

about his plans for the day, which included walking over to La Sucre to thank all the people there for helping him. On his way he was going to buy them all presents. I said this would be difficult because he didn't have any money. In rapid speech that seemed to come from his mouth as if pushed through a narrow channel, he explained that he would be able to get all the money he wanted because no one would turn him down when he asked for money. I chose to accompany him in order to see how he might accomplish this with his rather bizarre costume. He stopped every pedestrian he encountered and talked with them about several unrelated topics, never pausing for a breath, much less making the necessary transitions. Some of the people laughed and left, others left quickly, but a few, amused by what must have appeared an incredible sight, gave him some pesos.

Two weeks later I saw Enrique for the first time on the streets, walking with several smaller children in the unlikely place of the Avenida Sexta, the very fashionable street commonly used by strollers for window shopping. I was walking with my wife, whom he had not yet met. All the children appeared to be in a state of great animation, running and joking loudly and generally drawing a great deal of attention to themselves. As soon as we recognized each other I immediately felt concerned about how my wife and I were going to be treated. Would he take advantage of my previous relationship to him? As he approached, leaving his friends behind, I feared that he might be too out of touch with reality to be reckoned with easily. To my surprise, however, he recognized and greeted me in a friendly fashion. We even talked briefly about Bosconia. I introduced him to my wife and he greeted her politely. He then asked me for some money, which I gave him, and he thanked me and returned to his companions. A few days later he came up to me in Bosconia and thanked me again.

About a month later the whole group from Bosconia went over to a large park to have an outdoor evening songfest. We watched the children arrive in a large, open-sided truck and walked over to meet them. Enrique's immediate response was to disrobe down to his underpants and, with a loud yell, run straight for the public fountain only a few short yards from a busy main thoroughfare. Without hesitation he plunged directly in the spouting water and pretended to bathe. Then, dripping wet, he returned to the group.

Part of the reason for the songfest was the visit of a distinguished person from UNICEF, whom the authorities at Bosconia wanted to impress. When the visitor addressed the group with a pep talk, Enrique interrupted him and began to give advice, which was difficult to follow, about how to run programs for street children. Everyone laughed at him but this didn't stop him from continuing. As we began to sing songs we sat down in a large circle. Enrique could not keep himself from pacing around and talking to every passerby. Most of them tried to get away as he told them about Bosconia and his plans for his life, and gave them suggestions about how to live their lives. When a couple of boys tried to get him back into the group he started to fight them. Finally, he disappeared into the night.

The next day I was surprised to see him sitting very peacefully in Bosconia, with many friends around him inquiring about a large gash on his back that he had received the previous night. His back had been stitched and was bandaged. He described being in a fight, holding a large stick in his hand that he used to support himself, like a sage holding court to whomever would listen to his wise tales.

After listening a while the children went on with their business and we took the opportunity to ask Enrique to draw a picture of the city as he saw it, of where he went and what he did. He did so with eagerness and complete absorption. His picture was brightly colored and full of natural scenes of birds and trees, yet the setting was urban. Talking about that contrast, he described himself as an itinerant on the streets, but nevertheless one who was always aware of the birds and flowers. He said, "they remind me of a peaceful life." Later the same day the educador told me that when Enrique got his stitches the doctor gave him some type of psychotropic medicine, probably to treat his hypomanic behavior, which helped explain the difference between his behavior at the songfest and his calm manner when drawing.

A week later at Bosconia Enrique was in a slump. He said he couldn't get any money and his gallada had left him. When I left him to talk to some of the others he fell asleep. After lunch was served he didn't want to leave, but because he was not a "sleeper" the educador insisted, and he walked out alone. I went with him. After a few blocks we sat down in the park. I bought him a couple of rolls from the bakery and as he began to eat them he started to cry. Last week, he said, he went home to see if his mother would take him back. He couldn't understand why she wouldn't. He blamed himself and started to get angry. Then he told me about how he had fought with two members in his gallada, one of whom was half his size. This boy was hurt badly enough that he had to go to the hospital. Enrique described himself as a devil. When I tried to inquire about the cause of the fight he got angry with me and I left him there alone.

It appeared that when not under some personal stress or exposed to a potentially volatile situation Enrique was somewhat capable of being polite and taking care of himself, but otherwise he was either dangerously close to exaggerated eccentricity or overly self-deprecatory. At times he could not restrain his anger. He was almost always too easily attracted to acts that could lead to his demise. He was homeless, had no supervision, and was without palanca. His physical size, his looks, and the way he dressed predisposed him to appear like a thug. With plenty of supervision, including medical pharmacology, he might have been able to control his emotions better and possibly make a successful attempt into at least a periodic well-being.

Muñoz, who was introduced in chapter 1, was the nickname given to one of the jóvenes who years ago had lost his leg. He was a fourteen-year-old boy in very good health—even with his handicap—and coping adequately. He serves as a good example of a sobreviviente. His ancestry was African, his skin pitch black. His crutch was an old welded piece of steel tubing too short for him, so that when he stood he leaned to one side. His one foot was always bare. He had a way of melting into places on the floor that no one else would ever use. In this pose I would see him on his belly, his two arms supporting his torso to allow him to twist his head perpendicular to his body in order to observe an event. In repose he would sit in a small space, cross-legged, his crutch under his legless side. When he played, his ability to move around with the aid of his too-short crutch reminded me of a predatory animal, camouflaged with tranquil dignity in a background of shaded spots, but with the ability to pounce into activity at any moment.

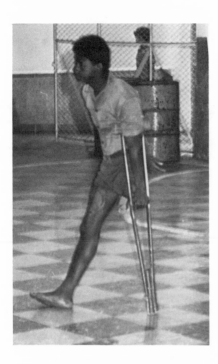

Muñoz with his makeshift crutch and the scar from the car accident on his good leg. He always maintained his dignity, even if it meant that he had to give the extra effort at getting along in the world of the less handicapped. His spirit was up to the task but his disability often brought him many moments of sad contemplation.

Figures 7 and 8 show Muñoz's HFD and Bender. The social history from La Sucre indicated that he never knew his father, who left his mother before he was born. When he was six his mother remarried. At first he lived with his new family, during which time he was forced to bring home a daily amount of money. He began to spend more time on the streets and gave up school. His two older sisters left home to live with relatives, then his older brother joined friends on the streets and was rarely at home. Between his older brother's friends and the children he met while working, he spent less and less time at home. Muñoz befriended one boy he met on the streets, who took him to his home, where Muñoz stayed for a time. His mother was upset about this and persuaded a friend to help her take care of Muñoz. Then his mother left town with her husband and for the next two years Muñoz was raised by this *madre de crianza*, a nonrelated woman who took on the responsibility of parenting. Most of the information about Muñoz was given by her when she went to La Sucre

Figure 7 Muñoz's Human Figure Drawing
(age = 14, IQ = 81, HFD-EI = 2, HFD-NI = 2)

to obtain his release. She reported that at age twelve he was run
over by a car and lost his leg. For a while his mother visited him
but then she returned to her new home and his madre de crianza
nursed him through the tragedy for the next twelve months. At
this time her own mother became sick and she had to leave and
take care of her. Muñoz then began to live more permanently on
the streets.

La Sucre reported that Muñoz was ambivalent toward adults.
He either became overly attached or rejected them. He was "shy
and avoided people and situations that he perceived as dangerous." His HFD portrays a sad image. Only the head of a man stares
mournfully, through large, vacant eyes without pupils. He did
not draw the man's body, as if he wanted to dismiss the part that
must have been the most important to him. The masklike appearance of the blank stare suggests that inside this head are thoughts
that do not want to be made public. The long, narrow, downward

mouth is clamped shut. The ears are empty, anchored too closely to a neck drawn like a tree trunk. The image is that of a person who is already seeing too much and doesn't want to hear anything else. Certainly the person in Muñoz's drawing does not have the physical characteristics of Muñoz. Muñoz's Bender is not pathological, but it is also not entirely within the normal range. Nearly all the lines are reinforced to make them bold, as if to be sure they do not disappear. His IQ of 81 is of low average ability, but his determination to do the best with his life made him appear more intelligent.

During one of our visits to Bosconia, and before I had met him, I was talking to one of the educadores when Muñoz came to us to ask a question. The educador addressed him as "stump," which I then learned was his nickname. Without waiting for a reply to his question Muñoz left, embarrassed. He went to sit alone in a corner of the patio, his eyes avoiding contact with everyone. After getting to know him better, I realized that he presented contrasting images depending on what he was doing when I saw him. In the midst of a basketball or soccer game he held his own, the master of his disability. Although he was not the star player, his performance did not in any way impede the natural flow of the game and he was accepted as a valued member of the team. Hopping, using his crutch as if it were a normal leg (in spite of the fact that the metal would often slip out from under him, causing him to drop to the floor as if slipping on ice), he always found a way to move the ball forward, keeping it in play.

At one point I saw him fall. He was lying on his back with the stub of his amputated leg twitching. I couldn't see the expression on his face, but after a small crowd inquired about how he was doing, he and the others resumed play, forgetting the incident. On other occasions I would see him on the floor, looking out on the others playing, assuming this physically inferior position with a kind of naturalness. I saw his deeply penetrating dark brown eyes look up as he assessed the surrounding environment and conversation in a saddened repose. Seeing him like this made it difficult to remember the skills he showed while playing sports; instead he appeared more like a helpless, hopeless, physically disabled young man.

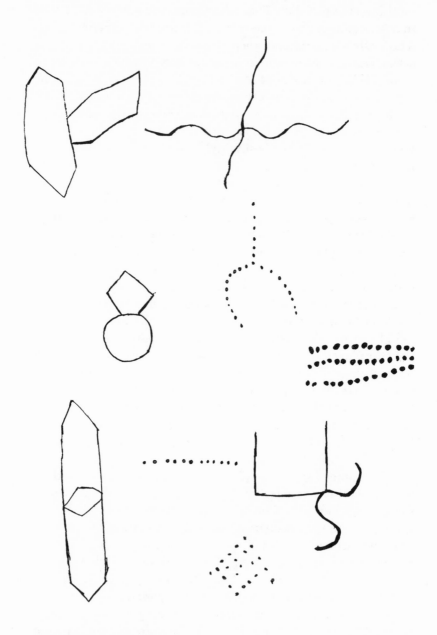

Figure 8 Muñoz's Bender (B = 55)

It wasn't long after we had a few introductory conversations that Muñoz began to ask me about the United States. Eventually he came to the question most on his mind. After almost giving up on the possibility of ever getting a new leg (his way of thinking about getting better, of being normal), he asked me about people with his condition in the United States. All the information he had about North Americans made him feel that if he could get to the United States he certainly would be able to "get better." Could I help him? "No, probably not," I had to answer, after feeling very uncomfortable about the scarcity of resources open to him in his own country and the lack of opportunity for him as a poor foreigner in my own. After that short interchange it was a while before we talked again. When we did I asked him about his daily life, where he went at night, how he ate, what kind of work he was doing, and in general how he was managing. His answer to how was he doing came out immediately, as a pat answer, "sometimes content, sometimes bored."

He was evidently surviving. He had cultivated enough connections to find a place to work and sleep. He was working at being an artisan, having learned, ironically enough, how to fix shoes. When I asked if he could fix my shoes he invited me to his work place. About ten blocks from the center of the business section was a large area equal to about two city blocks that was used by vendors. Here the vendors sold food and clothes, and offered services as varied as sharpening knives and scissors to giving haircuts and fixing shoes. The area was always filled with people and refuse. There were many booths made of cardboard where the people displayed their wares or hawked their services. We walked through mud streets and found, tucked away in a distant corner, the shoe repair shop where Muñoz worked. The owner, Fredrico, was himself an ex–street child. He had met Muñoz when Muñoz was walking around the shopping area looking for something to eat. He offered to teach him how to mend shoes. After proving that he was reliable, Muñoz was allowed to sleep there and protect the booth. When I took off my shoes and asked to have the heels built up, Muñoz went to work and Fredrico and I watched. For the next half hour I saw Muñoz mastering the skills, with an occasional good-hearted directive from Fredrico, who obviously enjoyed having a "partner."

We returned together for lunch at Bosconia, which was about a mile away. I offered to treat him to a bus ride, which would have been beyond his means. As was common, the bus was filled to near overflowing. I paid and he got on behind me. I moved and shoved my way toward the back. As I looked back I saw Muñoz on the floor. The passengers were trying to avoid him, but some stepped on him. The bus driver yelled; Muñoz was obviously embarrassed. I tried to reach him but it seemed to take minutes before I could get him standing. Everyone apologized while Muñoz grew more frustrated. At last we arrived at our stop and got off. Trying not to embarrass him further, we walked the block to Bosconia without talking. As soon as we arrived he left me and went to play with his colleagues.

His friendships at Bosconia and with Fredrico were his new family since, unlike most of the children, he had no connections with his parents. Observing the cycles of his activities at Bosconia over the several months I knew him, I could often see a sadness in his eyes as he sat alone staring into the distance while the others were in conversation. It was as if he was always, at least in part, out of the nexus of activities because of his physical disability. Yet the support he received from his friends at Bosconia, and his gameness in participating successfully on the very turf of his more able-bodied compatriots was a testimony to his strength and his desire to make it, to not give up on his life. His fortunate friendship with Fredrico and the skills he had learned from him served Muñoz as an antidote to his ills. Whether or not he will become a beggar living off his handicap or an artisan living in spite of his disability will depend in part on the way luck, in the form of companionship, supervision and, not least of all, palanca come his way.

Many of those who seemed to be coping best in their status as jóvenes were the ones who were beginning to assume an adult form of the chupagrueso style. This style demonstrated that they no longer wanted to be part of the street culture, but were ready to take on the most accessible role open to them within the larger community, that of being a *trabajador joven*, a young worker.

Giraldo appeared at Bosconia about halfway through our

study. He came from the parent program of Padre Nicolo in Bogotá in order, he said, to help with painting the Cali building. It was obvious from the start, when he immediately introduced himself to me rather than waiting for me to introduce myself to him, that he had a different style than many others. He did not have much interest in meeting any of the Colombian university students; instead he wanted to meet the person apparently in charge. Within minutes of the beginning of our first conversation he told me that he had spent five years in the Nicolo program and that he was in his third year of *bachillerato* (high school).

Giraldo was fourteen. His HFD and Bender are shown in figures 9 and 10. According to the report from La Sucre, he was abandoned at age six and found on the streets. He was transported to a state home and a relative was found who agreed to take him home. He stayed there for a couple of years. During the time he was with his relatives he worked by helping his uncle make bricks for construction. When the relatives left to find work in Bogotá he stayed behind, spending some time on the streets and some time in a state home, where it was noted that he adjusted well. He had some schooling in the institution and learned to read. Because of this he was released to a foster home, but he only stayed there for a short time before returning to the streets. By the time he was nine he had entered Bosconia and committed himself to the program, where he had remained for the last five years.

The figure in his HFD is of a person clearly not of Giraldo's social class. The man he drew is wearing a tie and sports jacket. A square jaw is anchored on what appears to be another square jaw. Both rest on the middle-class figure as if bolted to an image of prosperity. One ear is missing. The other ear is wide open, as if the figure is listening intently to directions from one side, but not at all from the other. Likewise, one arm is missing, as if it were amputated. The body is not whole; important parts are just not there. Good reproductions of the Bender figures gave him a non-pathological score, but the lines were made by drawing them over and over in bold strokes, as if making overstatements to simple questions. His IQ is 92.

Figure 9 Giraldo's Human Figure Drawing
(age = 14, IQ = 92, HFD-EI = 2, HFD-NI= 1)

When I met him he had very short hair that looked like it was cut in an institution. When we talked his eyes stared through me without making contact and he seemed sad. I had the impression from his appearance that he was intellectually slow. As if to counterbalance his appearance, he began to tell me about the Nobel Prize-winning Colombian writer, García Márquez, not in the context of Márquez's political orientation (García Márquez supports the leftist guerrilla groups in Colombia), but more as a kind of name-dropping, as a way of identifying himself to me as an intellectual.

In another conversation he told me about the Nicolo program in Bogotá. Giraldo said that the director, Padre Nicolo, was "the best person in the world. He completely changed my life." He said he had been "three years on the streets robbing" before entering the program. I asked him if he was a gamine. He said no,

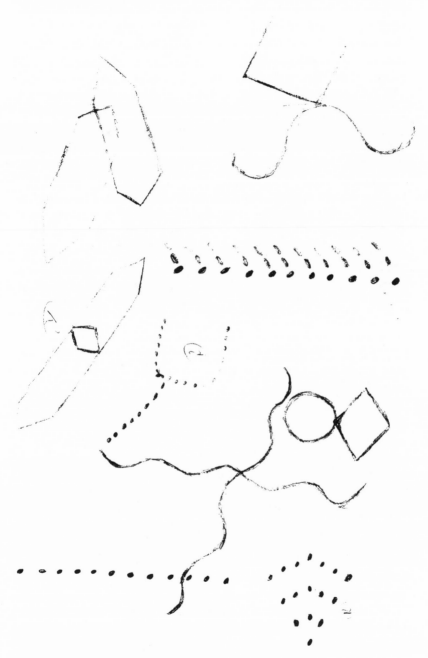

Figure 10 Giraldo's Bender (B = 42)

he wasn't, because gamines rob and kill. He repeated this twice because I questioned him about gamines killing. I had not heard that response from any street child, only from people in the society. As we talked more about gamines, he mentioned in a disgusted tone that their principal vice was smoking marijuana. When I brought up the alleged practice of inhaling gasoline and its possible effects of brain damage, he admitted that this had happened to him. "But," he said, "I am better now."

As we began to talk more about the meaning of gaminismo and of their argot, we agreed to get together another day for lunch. On the day of our lunch date we walked over to a neighborhood restaurant that specialized in preparing chicken. While we waited for our food to arrive we began a conversation that I was to reflect on many times over the course of the study. What exactly is a gamine? I would work hard to untangle the pieces of reality from the answers given by the participants and observers of this public drama of street life. Where in the midst of tragedy, delinquency, repugnancy, and even envy would each person's feelings lie? Within the multitude of attitudes and opinions are reflections of each person's reactions to what otherwise cannot be ignored. While Giraldo talked about the difference between gamines and delinquents, I sat there only partially taking it in because I was thinking about why some people make moral judgments and others grant psychological immunity to the same phenomena. Why is it that some people see one situation worthy of "help," while in another circumstance the same set of facts calls for damnation? "A gamine steals only to eat while a *ladrón* [which translates into "robber," with a connotation of delinquency] robs out of vice, because he doesn't want to make something out of himself in life." While Giraldo wrote the answers to the questions about the differences between gamines, ladrones, and child workers out on a piece of paper, he was at the same time talking to me as if he were giving a lecture to a large audience. "Life," he wrote and said, "is very sad because the *gente* [the people in general] are looking down on us and finding faults. They are always looking for a foul word to give us."

When the food arrived Giraldo continued his descriptions and writing for what seemed a long time, even though I encouraged him to switch gears, hoping that we could enjoy a relaxed luncheon while the food was still warm. He was compelled to tell his story and that of other street children as he saw it, and his views were not very different from the views expressed by the middle class. During this time two beggars—an older man and a woman—came to the table. Giraldo at first looked up at me in embarrassment, giving me the aside reaction that a host gives to a friend when an unwelcome visitor appears, then he dismissed them. As we started to eat, two children came by also asking for food. Giraldo gave them one of his three pieces of chicken. He ate the second, and the last piece he wrapped up neatly in his napkin "to give," he said, "to my girlfriend."

I had another appointment at La Sucre, about a mile away, and he insisted on walking with me to show the way, in spite of my assurance that I knew the route. When we arrived he had to explain the institution to me, even though I had been working there for a couple of months. When I went in to talk to the director he waited outside. Before I could get him to leave, I had to promise to keep in touch and, as proof, we exchanged addresses. As he was beginning to walk away he asked me for some money to get his shoes fixed.

When I finished with my work at La Sucre it was late afternoon and I took my usual walk home past the familiar paths that the children from Bosconia would be traveling on their way to resume their street lives. Seeing their usual haunts, smelling the odors of food and garbage, and hearing the never-ending battle of cars, buses, and pedestrians, I fell into deep thought about the conversation with Giraldo. His answers to my questions had been so rote that it seemed as if he had been converted to a newly found religion. His talk of gaminismo made me feel that I was listening to an upwardly mobile and ambitious, if not nationalistic, Colombian. He told me that the essence of being a gamine was dirtiness in both body and clothes, and vices, by which he meant taking drugs. His eagerness to be an apostle of the Nicolo program and his desire to get ahead in the world by distancing himself from his past were in sharp contrast to most of the other street children. His point of view about street life was not casual. It seemed rather like a duty that he not only was eager to perform, but one he wanted me to share. In a similar fashion he advocated the goals of the Nicolo program to the chiquitos at Bosconia, who either avoided him or made fun of his insensitive advances.

There was no doubt that he had taken one route away from the risky life of being a street child by adopting attitudes and a way of life that would be helpful to his goals. He may have been different as a chiquito, but I could see that in his firm attachment to the upwardly mobile life and to those like myself who might help him get there, he had formed a kind of dependency on people and goals that was similar to that of the chupagruesos. They, too, became servile to the powerful elements in their circles as a way of achieving a self-recognition that they were not able to obtain from a more independent path. His determination and the way he fought for my attention, which was a form of making his own palanca, would help him establish himself in the larger society. His academic skills and his acceptance and desire to become part of the broader culture were to his advantage. His problems, however, were far from few. He looked less intelligent and more like a thug than he was, which was a dangerous proposition for someone with little palanca. And worse, there was not enough substance underneath his ambition to earn the kind of self-acceptance that could only come from something deeper than his obvious sales pitch. I suspected that, like Gatsby, he would not be satisfied even if he should get what he thought he wanted.

I do not wish to imply that the only successful adjustment for a joven is to assume the values associated with the middle class. Far from it. It is probably accurate to say that this is the easiest way, particularly for the chupagruesos. It is the path most often advocated by the many programs for street children. But it is problematic for those gamines who do not want, or are not able, to forget their past.

Palmira is a city near Cali and also the nickname of another postpuberty street child whose home it was before a long list of adventures and talents took him to other places. His nickname was merely a mark of origin for a seasoned traveler. Unlike Giraldo, who used the style of the chupagrueso to establish a new identity, Palmira dealt more directly with his former gamine life.

The first time Palmira and I talked, he asked me about the United States, not to ask for a favor or show his worldliness, but specifically about the eruption of the Mount St. Helens volcano. He was using me as a source of information, a potential resource, but not as a conceivable ally to secure help. When I asked him what a gamine was (once again using the term in the generic sense) he said, "It is something you choose to do and it has to be given up by the time you are eighteen," at which time "you either have to become a delinquent or find work." Although he said he "liked the streets because there was plenty to do and learn," he was happy that he could come to Bosconia because "I can get something to eat and a place to sleep."

Palmira was a handsome boy, with a full, eager smile. On the streets he wore a clean shirt. His overall demeanor was in sharp contrast to that of Enrique. And although Palmira was one of the boys accepted in the Padre Nicolo program, his style was very different from that of Giraldo, who identified the program's success with himself, thus evading the more difficult task of finding his own place in the world. Palmira had already spent enough time in Bosconia to have had the opportunity to weigh its good features against its demands, and he was circling around the decision to move ahead to a more independent existence. He was being swayed to stay at Bosconia by the desire to have "a place," as a traveler who had found a worthy way station for rest, but not a permanent residence. He felt not quite ready to give up on the adventures of his travels, which fueled his interests and intellect; yet, during the time that we knew each other he was finding that the demands of street life were becoming more difficult.

Figures 11 and 12 show Palmira's HFD and Bender. La Sucre reported that Palmira's parents had a common-law marriage that dissolved after three children were born. Palmira was the youngest. His mother remarried and his stepfather was described as being an itinerate traveler and an alcoholic. The two of them had four children. In the stepfather's absence the children of the first marriage worked to support the half brothers and sisters. At age seven Palmira accompanied his oldest brother to work in the streets begging for money. He was reported to have begun staying away from home by age eight, which was the first time he was in La Sucre. He was there several other times. Each time his mother would come for him immediately. The institution described her as attentive. Palmira was known at Bosconia, where he had been for several years. He was also known to the

Figure 11 Palmira's Human Figure Drawing
(age = 15, ɪQ = 94, HFD-EI = 1, HFD-NI = 1)

Bosconia program in Bogotá and to other state diagnostic centers
in different cities.

La Sucre wrote of him that he had "a good self-concept. He
needs to be the dominant one in social situations. He is aggressive." His HFD presents a man reminiscent of a Canadian Mountie.
The drawing is neat, orderly, and straightforward. The man is
wearing a uniform, with a star representing a badge on the left
side, above his heart. There is no violence in the man's appearance. He appears to be comfortable with himself. With his well-
formed eyes looking directly out at the observer, he appears
honest and interested. There are no erasures here or in his Bender,
which is also well within the normal range. The lines on the
Bender are definite, accurate, and large. His ɪQ is 94.

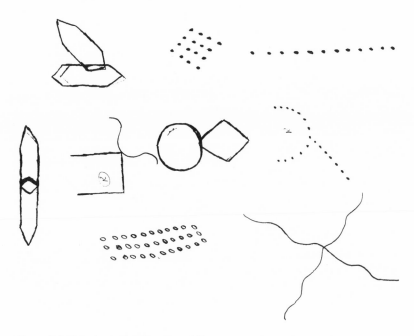

Figure 12 Palmira's Bender (B = 36)

When we met for a Coke one afternoon he told me that he had been on the streets for about five years, until he turned fourteen. He had traveled around Colombia with a friend until his friend had been run over by a car and suffered a permanent back injury that had put him in a state institution. The loss, coupled with the coming of puberty, had forced Palmira to begin to think about himself and his future. He had left home five years earlier because there wasn't much reason to stay and because he had the desire to see the country that his padrastro talked about when he was drinking and feeling reminiscent. When his padrastro left home to resume his travels, Palmira was not far behind. He also was following in the footsteps of his older brother, who had left a year earlier. So with the sad but nevertheless accepting recognition of his mother, who with four younger children was willing to let the older ones go earlier than we would normally condone,

Palmira was off to see the world. Palmira came to this meeting
with a hardcover book under his arm. I thought he was going to
read something to me as he sat down and opened it. Instead,
hidden between the pages was a letter that he had written to his
mother. He wanted me to check and see if it was all right,
meaning—I was to learn—was it legible and grammatically correct. His letter was quite neat because he had copied it over before
I saw it, but it was filled with many grammatical and spelling
errors. Still, the message was clear; he was doing well and was in
good health. It was a traveler's letter written to touch base with
his people back home. It talked about his future plans, which
included "having my own room to rent and to just live like everyone else."

He was one of about twenty boys who were "sleepers." These
children had to go to school, keep their beds made, and participate in the upkeep of the program and building. In exchange they
were given a place to sleep, three meals a day, and were expected,
at least to some degree, to show commitment to "their new life,"
which might well involve some renunciation of the past. Palmira
had done well enough in the Bosconia program that he was receiving some pressure to move past the "sleeper" level and become
part of Marcelina, where he could begin vocational training. He
was in the process of thinking about this, but up to that point he
was avoiding the decision because, as he said, "there are too many
restrictions there."

Palmira was positioning himself to leave one style of life and
begin a new one. He was facing this task in an honest fashion. On
one hand, he was skeptical about too many restrictions and
doubtful about his own skills, but on the other hand, he presented himself with a demeanor and style that was ready to win
the acceptance of those in the larger society. There was a good
chance he could achieve acceptance, particularly if he got enough
of a break to find some work that did not prevent him from using
his curiosity and satisfying his desire for excitement. He probably would not be able to meet these needs if he had to work as a
common laborer, sweating out his days in repetitious servility.
His gamine history on the streets would not allow him to accept
that kind of life.

Moving into Adulthood

To understand what will become of the jóvenes as they pass into adulthood, it is necessary to take several factors into account. The reactions that their images elicited were important. If they were perceived as being "ready" for acceptance into conventional society, as Giraldo and Palmira were in their different ways, then their chances of finding a place in the adult world were greatly improved. If, on the other hand, they were unable to restrain themselves from meeting their immediate needs, from acting eccentrically, or looking like thugs, as was true of Enrique, they were more likely to be forced into a delinquent life in order to sustain themselves. If, like Muñoz, they looked neither threatening nor self-effacing, and were trying to become adaptable, they had a decent chance of making a successful entry, even if it was less than dramatic.

The haughtiness and independence of the gamine attitude were other variables that the jóvenes had to reckon with. They either had to temper these qualities greatly in order to allow for a traditional entrance into society or, if they maintained anti-establishment values, the values had to be curbed enough to avoid abuse by the authorities. The best way that this could be done was for them to work as small-scale entrepreneurs, perhaps as vendors, finding a niche in the urban subculture of poverty that could support them. On the other hand, the chupagrueso attitude could be functional, as we have seen with Giraldo. The ability of the chupagruesos to accept servility, as well as what they learned about going along with the crowd, would help them move into the world of common laborers.

At the heart of the problem of resolving how they might adapt to adult life were their desire and ability to deal with the conflict that their childhood drama portrayed. Living on the streets while still physically small, appearing to be independent of adult authority and not beholden to it, they had lived as if on a stage. The audience was the adult society, which viewed the seemingly independent child as an actor who potentially threatened the sacrosanct power and authority of parenthood. Before the widespread phenomenon of street children began, it was assumed that the family, by its very nature, deserved respect, obedience, and sub-servience. But since the advent of the street children phenome-non, both actors and audience began another act of this drama. Ultimately, the drama will be resolved when the street children convince their audience, by the way they read their lines and dress for the part, that they are ready to step offstage and take on the roles of adults.

It is clear that the commonly accepted notion that all street chil-dren turn into delinquents or criminals is not true. Just as unlikely is the idea that many of them will become psychotic or more emo-tionally unhealthy than their counterparts in the poor neighbor-hoods, or more troubled than the rest of us caught up in the mainstream of society. When compared to their counterparts in the lower social classes who were beginning to assume adult roles, the street children were found to be like them in many respects. That is, some of the street children were going to be steady work-ers, others—those with a sense of independence—would become small-scale entrepreneurs, while others would not be able to func-tion very well, either becoming alcoholic, delinquent, or other-wise emotionally unfit for productive adult life. Our data from the subgroups indicate that this latter group will be a small part, per-haps only a quarter of the total. Another quarter might become rather successful, particularly when compared to the rest of the children in the neighborhood they left behind years ago. The re-mainder seemed on the verge of being fully functional.

One difference that will contribute to their future prospects is the advantage of having lived more independently, having known more adventure, and having had a broader world than more tradi-tional children. This will make them different types of citizens than the many complacent, parochial, and defeated ones who have not left their impoverished circumstances. Possibly they will become more political, in the sense of knowing how to influ-ence society and how their citizenship is influenced by society. These former street children should have a keener insight into the nature of life in their country and may not be so easily swayed by the traditional forces of church and state that have in the past molded the opinions and attitudes of the lower social classes.

That the state is aware of this potential independence is not surprising. The street children are often referred to as "urban guerrillas." This repeated association suggests that they may indeed be a new political force. Although for the most part they will join the traditional work force, their unusual past will certainly make them open to alternative ways of looking at the existing forms of political power. Their education, rather than leading them to adopt and promote the status quo, has taught them to deal with and desire change, perhaps in a manner not dissimilar to the radical changes that the guerrillas are proposing: a more equal distribution of wealth and land, the opportunity to work based on qualifications instead of on palanca, and an elimination of the wide gap between rich and poor.

Most important, I predict that their experience on the streets, particularly for those who made the decision to leave their families, will affect their future relationships with their own children. It is possible to imagine a different scenario than the one often reflected in the literature, which claims they will merely perpetuate the cycle of abandonment.

Walking in the early morning hours around Bogotá I saw several ex–street children, adults who might be referred to as junkmen, their horse-drawn wagons full of a variety of flotsam and jetsam. In the late mornings they parked their horses alongside a grassy place, lighting up cigarettes, talking among themselves, and enjoying each other's friendship.

After weeks of buying my morning milk near the spot where Sergio's horse ate, we got to talking one day. Seated next to him was his son, a boy of twelve or so. Their work, Sergio told me, was to look on the streets for anything of value, making note of another place where they might sell it at a profit. After becoming known in the neighborhoods, they eventually would pick up odd jobs—moving a refrigerator from one house to another or bringing wood from the forest to an apartment. Sergio said he made enough money each day to keep his horse, son, and himself in food and shelter. He was getting by, if not getting rich. In his own way he saw himself as successful. Having long ago left his family, he now had one of his own. He was independent, outside the forces of the state, the bureaucracy, and the demands of a boss. Just as important, he was free from the dependency he had had as a small boy on his "intolerable family."

Thinking about the relationship he had with his son, and comparing it to the one he had wished for as a small boy without "having a father," I could not help but be impressed with the difference. He was not the angry, defeated, unemployed man that he was told his father was. I imagined how he might well be friends with his child. He would understand that fatherhood is not bound irrevocably by blood, but that the bonds could be broken by either father or son. Knowing this, the two of them may have dealt with each other with more equality and more independence than most children and fathers will ever know. Perhaps they came to realize that their relationship was ultimately based less on blood and more on friendship.

The lives of Sergio and his son seemed in many ways to exist in a closet, with the quality and meaning of their reality unknown to the inhabitants of the city who, in spite of walking around them every day, were unable to open the door that would allow them to see the value in the way Sergio and his son lived.

4
Galladas and Camadas: The Street Children at Work and Play

In the two preceding chapters we have examined the lives of the street children as individuals, as if we, too, have gone into the closet without paying much attention to the society that placed the children on the streets. We have done this in order to see the variety of psychological styles the children possess, and the rational and functional qualities of many of their behaviors. Much of a street child's life is spent not alone but with other street children, and their group characteristics and behavior are just as important as individual behavior in determining how they live and the quality of their lives.

When we began our study of the street children they were routinely described to us in the plural, as masses of children with certain characteristics associated with psychopathology of one type or another. The view of the children in the plural sense coincides with the perceptions that North American or European visitors have of Colombia. The children are seen as herds, running uncontrolled and uncontrollable, infesting places where they do not belong, giving the impression that they are trampling on cultivated land. Colombians portray the children with the verb *deambular*.

Coming from the noun *ambulante*, wanderer, *deambular* can be interpreted as an incessant roaming, a constant movement without direction.

This chapter is devoted to the behavior of the children in their groups. Viewing this aspect of the children's lives is helpful for two reasons. First, it gives further information about them and their characteristics, and second, it helps us understand some of the misperceptions that exist about them.

The groups of street children have been labeled *galladas* (*gallo* is rooster), *pandillas* (gangs or bands), *chinos de las calles* (*chino* means children in Quechua, the language of the Incas), and *camadas* (litter or brood). Depending on who is describing them and which historical epoch is being referred to, their groups are said to vary in size from five or six to as many as a hundred. Most of the professional literature written about them comes from the decades of the 1960s and 1970s, when it was claimed that there were large numbers of children and many groups. By the mid-1980s the groups had dwindled considerably in number and in size. This might have been due to the new organizations that had emerged to serve them, or perhaps because the authorities no longer permitted them to be in the streets. Nevertheless, they were still being described in similarly ominous terms. As recently as 1984 a newspaper article appearing in the Bogotá daily, *El Tiempo* (Samper 1984), referred to the groups as a "plague," a word that indicates an infection of otherwise healthy tissue.

These ominous perceptions contributed to several myths about the children's groups. For example, one commonly accepted notion was that the street children slept when and wherever they wanted, as if the world were their bed, their sleep as easy to come by and as deep as that of a small child in the comfort of his parents' bedroom. One author wrote that "they make their bed when they want and they sleep when they are tired" (Téllez 1976, 66). When our research team first went to one of the state institutions we were told the same thing by the director. We came to understand that this particular misperception was based on the fact that the children were seen late at night after most adults had long since put their own children to bed.

One night, near midnight at the football stadium, where a soccer game was in progress, two small boys from Bosconia, whom I knew to be eight year olds, were sitting on the curb across from the stadium. Having contracted with a guard for a place to spend the night in the doorway of the stadium, they had to wait until everyone left the game, including the adult beggars, who would search the grounds immediately after the match for something valuable to wear or eat. Thus, in plain view of the public, they appeared to be staying up as late as they wanted. But in fact, as they told us the next day in Bosconia, they were thoroughly tired and depressed while they waited to gain the safety of a prearranged place to spend the night.

If a group of children had made an arrangement for a place to sleep with a restaurant owner—a fairly common phenomenon— then only after the place was closed and the workers had left would they be able to assume their bed. It was not unusual for them to wait around the restaurant, in full public view, until they could go to sleep unmolested.

A more accurate description of how the children perceived their liberties with regard to sleeping was revealed to me when I asked one of them about it. I used the verb *querer*: When do you *like* or *want* to go to bed? In his answer he corrected my verb, saying that it was better to ask when "am I able" (*poder*) to go to sleep, changing the meaning from desire to necessity.

Another related and commonly accepted misconception about their alleged freedom is that they live only for the moment. Being carefree, we were told repeatedly, they did not need or know how to plan for the future. The way they allegedly spent the nights was an example of this larger principle. However, in following them through their daily and nightly routines, we found that they had many concerns about the future.

One of these concerns had to do with the problems of living on the streets, which necessitated a good deal of advance planning. The way they used the word street, *lleca* in their language, indicated anything but being carefree. As one small boy described it, "*lleca* wants to mean passing the night on the streets, but it is more like the day, with fear placed on top of it. I am uncomfortable with the idea that the police are coming. I wrap myself with papers but it doesn't stop the cold, which is tremendous. We make our beds like the soldiers, pressing against each other in order to keep warm. Almost without breathing, we pass the night

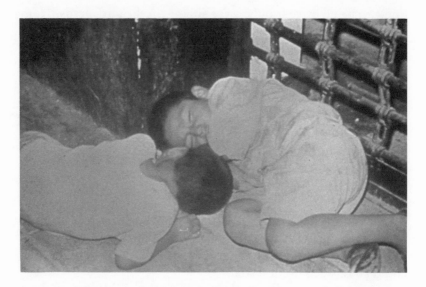

There were many problems with sleeping on the streets. After these two eight year olds had intoxicated themselves by inhaling gasoline, they found a back entrance to a restaurant. They had made the mistake of not planning in advance for a safe place to spend the night, a mistake that could be costly.

this way while we encourage each other to guard against the panic we all have" (Gutiérrez 1972a, 12). The night, rather than being a mere interlude between daytime adventures, was at the heart of their worries and was always present on their minds. Sleeping arrangements, which were often made by small groups of children, were not random or haphazardly arranged; they were well planned in advance.

The elements, particularly in Bogotá, which has a cold and rainy climate, posed such considerable problems that many of the children had traveled to warmer places such as Cali. But even in this semitropical zone getting out of the weather was always on their minds. They often bedded down in the doorways of hotels and dry-cleaning shops, where there was a heating unit and the walls remained warm. These places were often in public view and thus contributed to the general perception of the children being down-and-out, incapable, and irrational. Their clothes, which presented such a picturesque image of vagabondage, being worn in layers one on top of the other, were in reality used for protection against the elements. Because they had to be leery of certain people on the streets, the children sought out well-populated places to sleep, such as restaurants or public transportation facilities. This selection gave them protection in numbers and put them in full public view.

Since they were in danger of being robbed, they rarely kept anything of value on them when they were asleep. To avoid being accosted and losing everything, what material possessions they had were hidden away in separate places and not carried on their persons, making them appear more destitute than they were. The only possession they invariably showed to the public was their cobija. Using it as a shawl during the day and a blanket at night, they were inadvertently aligned with the more traditional peasants, who wore shawls over their shoulders and were also perceived to have inappropriate behaviors for living in the modern world. On more than one occasion I saw the children in the privacy of Bosconia cling to their cobijas as a pampered child clings to a favorite old blanket. In public they portrayed an image of being carefree vagabonds. Such an image could have been interpreted from their frequent appearances in public places, their style of wearing clothes, and their dirtiness; however, such an image was less than accurate. Much of their group behavior, although apparently random play and movement throughout the city, had one real objective: securing a safe place to sleep at night. Although in their groups they may have appeared carefree, they were still small children, reacting remarkably functionally to the demands that street life made upon them.

In short, trying to reach out and touch their "real" presence, to palpitate their group life in order to describe and categorize it, proved more elusive than we had anticipated. Yet we knew that by failing to discuss the nature of their associations among themselves, as well as the information that was used to describe them, we would not only lose much of what they did and who they were, we would also not grasp why society looked upon them with so many misconceptions. Thus we concentrated on investigating the phenomena of what they did when together, how many groups there were, and why they were described in such pejorative terms.

Part of the confusion about their groups resides in the fact that it is very difficult to get firsthand information. Methodologically there were several problems, not the least of which was that it is difficult to see them au naturel. The children are keenly aware of anyone who might be trying to influence their group life, and in groups they have to contend with what their peers will think of them if they allow themselves, even for a moment, to be distracted into paying attention to an outsider. Unfortunately, the majority of information about groups of street children comes from the easier method of giving questionnaires that merely assume that what the children say about themselves is true. We found such an assumption to be invalid.

We were able to distinguish two forms of groups: the *galladas* and the *camadas*. The children's relationships to each other in these two associations are as different as the ways people relate to each other in families and in businesses. The *galladas* were groups of children who associated together principally for economic reasons. Membership in the galladas was controlled by postpuberty children, and prepuberty children were their underlings. They stayed together when working in order to divide the labor that could make them all more successful. As is the case with other business partners, they rarely associated outside of work, but instead broke up their groups to return to their "homes" and sleep.

Camadas were small groups of two or three children who shared the intimacies and camaraderie of being together. The membership was exclusively prepuberty. These groups were more like family and friends than business partners. At the end of each day's work, the children who were in the same camada left the larger business arrangement of the gallada and went to the spots they had arranged for sleeping. In the morning several camadas got together to rejoin a gallada for working.

In spite of the fact that the galladas were perceived by the public as delinquent gangs, they were for the most part groups of children who were learning to work and live in the established subculture of urban poverty. They related to each other under a fairly adequate and consistent set of checks and balances that worked toward preventing abuse between them.

The children in camadas were together for reasons of mutual

support and friendship, which was just what they needed given their family histories, developmental period, and needs. By forming friendships among themselves that worked toward mutual support, they were able to deal with the demands of street life in a rather healthy manner. They related to the galladas for economic reasons and used the help of the older children when it was time for them to integrate into the adult society.

Since all the groups of street children were referred to en masse, the public rarely discriminated between the camadas and the galladas. But there were indeed many differences. The group ethos was different and the several subgroups of children identified earlier related to their groups differently. The gamines and the chupagruesos did not relate to the galladas in the same way.

Essentially there are two theories that account for the existence of groups of street children. One theory is economic and states that children band together to have more of a chance to survive. This is applicable to the galladas but not to the camadas. The second theory is psychological: children have suffered from being abused, neglected, or abandoned by their parents; thus they form groups to establish their own families. This does pertain to the camadas but is not an accurate description of the galladas. While the economic theory allows us to see the galladas as business groups promoting the children's entry into an existing subcultural milieu, it neglects the implications of the psychological theory, which emphasizes the coping skills that the children have developed in the camadas. These skills were not only present, but manifested themselves in many children's remarkable resiliency in adapting to the high-risk situations they faced. As we shall see, this discovery can teach us a great deal about helping not only street children, but other groups of children who do not have adequate family support.

Societies of children have been viewed by adults in dramatically opposite ways. Either they share their accumulated goods between them in a manner that abuses power, with the strongest children taking advantage of the smaller ones, or the economy of children's societies is seen as benign, caring, and socialistic. These two extreme views touch upon deeper questions that are automatically posed by the existence of a society of street children. What is the basic nature of children? Are they innately good or evil? Or do they come into the world with a tabula rasa? What is the role of adults in teaching children to learn to live as responsible citizens?

The existence of children's groups brought these questions to the attention of Colombian society. On one hand were those who claimed that the children took advantage of each other. Homosexual abuse was widely given as an example of this. On the other hand, there was the phenomenon of *pormis*, a socialistic method of sharing goods during times of short supply. Pormis helped to keep everyone alive and functioning. One point of view saw the children as immoral, the other as moral. There are policy implications from this, since programs for the children often stress how they "should" respond to one another. For example, the theory of socialistic distribution was used by the Padre Nicolo program. "If there is food for one boy," a large sign in the doorway of the home in Bogotá read, "then it will be shared by everyone." It should not go without notice that the advocation of socialism in the programs for them could only make the children look more critically at their society's extreme discrepancy in wealth. Socialistic programs, at least indirectly, pointed out to the children that part of the reason for their own street life was based on the inequality of economic life in the larger society. That the groups of children had been labeled "urban guerrillas" was an indication that society was a bit frightened about these prospects.

Whether one saw the groups of children as immoral or moral, as long as there were groups of street children roaming around the cities most of society felt itself in danger. The solution to this "problem" depended on resolving the fundamental question of whether or not the "free" child was by nature good or evil. Consequently, the distribution of their goods and food, and the ways they dealt with each other in their groups was important, because how these children were judged determined the kind of treatment they received.

Pormis: A System of Dividing the Goods

In the abstract, pormis is a method of equal distribution; when something was obtained by one, it was divided equally among all. Pormis was of vital importance to the quality of interactions between children in their groups, and there were significant differences between the galladas and the camadas with regard to pormis.

In the galladas the jefe collected the goods and subdivided them to his sub-jefes. They in turn doled them out to their underlings. This process established power relationships instead of friendships. Each person with the power to distribute did so with options and choices about who got what and how much.

What was being divided in the galladas was usually of little direct use because the items were often stolen materials like clothes or car paraphernalia, which had to be exchanged for the more primary staples of food or money. This was accomplished with differing amounts of ease. The types of goods, and the way they were finally doled out, meant that the items had a subtle, intangible value. In order to be prudent every member of the gallada soon learned what was valuable and how much each item was worth. Disputes arose and ultimately it was the jefe who adjudicated them. He had to know what things were worth, where they might be traded for food or money, and how to keep the sub-jefes (who often had their own self-interests) honest enough that everyone was reasonably happy. To do this the jefe had to be both knowledgeable and respected. If necessary, he exerted his influence by applying sanctions to those who were not participating appropriately. Thus, in the galladas the pormis represented a bureaucratic and businesslike way of getting a job done, which in turn supported a specific kind of interaction among the children. This interaction maintained and controlled the power relationships between group members.

Within the camada, which was composed of fewer and younger children, the level of organization and delinquency was considerably milder and, for a variety of reasons, the jefe less important.

In part this was because the preadolescent children usually were fairly successful in getting food. By relying on their youth—and thereby posing less of a threat to the public—they secured their needs, while the bigger children had to resort to more delinquent acts. The younger children, because they got the essentials, had less need to obtain goods that would have to be fenced. By being in small groups and being able to solicit the essentials directly, they merely divided up what they had on the spot and shortly thereafter consumed it. Their system of pormis demanded less organization, relied more on friendship, and worked against having a powerful jefe.

There was quite a difference between how chupagruesos and gamines responded to the demands of pormis in the galladas. This type of organization was just right for the chupagrueso who learned quickly what was expected of him. He was reliable to those whom he saw as powerful and did what was necessary to stay in their good graces. The chupagrueso style helped to maintain the integrity of the hierarchy and the bureaucratic way of doing business. However, the gamine used the gallada only as long as it helped him. He had little respect for authority per se, and maintained his allegiance to the powerful only as long as it served him better than he might have been able to do on his own, or in another gallada. The gamine therefore was in and out of any one gallada and of galladas generally. Although the gamines did not try to destroy the integrity of the group, they did very little beyond what was absolutely necessary to support the leader and the ladder of power. Gamines often traveled in the smaller groups of camadas, where the quality of the pormis was quite different. This in part explains the difficulty of ascertaining the number of galladas, as well as the numbers of children in them.

Given these facts about the pormis, certain conclusions concerning camadas and galladas become clear. The camada is an association based on friendship and composed of a few preadolescents. The children of the camadas played together and ate together, and they did so without much hierarchy. This type of organization was more akin to the gamine spirit because it was an association that benefited their life-style, and only as long as it did so did the camada continue. The gallada, on the other hand, was a grouping of adolescents, young adults, and some preadolescent children. It was larger and based on a division of labor that was well organized to secure economic ends. Order was maintained by the more powerful controlling the less powerful. The gallada demanded a different type of membership, one that was more akin to the chupagrueso, whose style was conducive to following strict rules and accepting sanctions from authorities.

The gallada cannot be viewed as a separate entity apart from the poor urban subculture; it is integrally related to it. The leadership of the galladas, as well as the majority of the members, had been on the streets for a long time and adopted a somewhat delinquent life-style, along with the associations that such a life-style brought. The membership of galladas was composed mainly of adolescents, but there were also adults who helped integrate the children's economy into the larger culture, and preadolescent children who helped bring in goods.

The survival of this kind of group depended on several factors. These factors included the recruiting of younger children who could be successful at begging, the ability of the jefe to work with adults who could exchange their goods for food, and a strict organization that allowed them all to survive in a scarce economic niche. The organization within the galladas relied on a bureaucratic division of labor. Each member knew his responsibilities and his rights. There was only one jefe, but there was also at least one sub-jefe depending on the size of the group. The existence of sub-jefes made the power in the group bureaucratic. In order to ensure efficiency each member of the group had a place and a "superior" from whom he received directives.

The ultimate authority of the gallada resided with the jefe. He maintained his power and prestige by physical prowess, intelligence, and the ability to "fence" the products of his labor. The jefe not only had to control his sub-jefes and members, he also had to have the appropriate skills to deal with the established criminal element. This allowed him, and thus his gallada, access to more lucrative goods and a place to cash in what they already had. These skills cemented the jefe's power over the group, since they relied on him and his connections to bring them what they needed and wanted. The jefe knew how to cultivate and maintain friendships with adults such as street vendors, restaurant owners, and taxicab drivers, all of whom occasionally fenced his materials, even if they were not fully committed to a criminal existence. The jefe was the bridge between the street children and the subculture of urban poverty.

Because the relationship of poverty to criminality in Colombia (as well as in many other Latin American countries) is more ambiguous and ambivalent than it is in North American culture, the bending of rules and the buying of certain favors is more widespread and tolerated. These forms of quasi-illegal activities are generally not considered criminal, and are viewed as just another way of dealing with urban poverty. Almost everyone in these circumstances is expected to be involved with such activities at least to some degree. The jefes knew how to push or withdraw pressure and when to do so with each person involved, and they did so in a way that allowed them to maintain their contacts over time. In this context it was not just the brawn of the jefe that kept him in power but his intelligence, which had to be ample enough to deal with the ambiguities between these legal and quasi-legal affairs.

The jefe was successful by being able to keep his gallada well fed, clothed, and occasionally (if not consistently) entertained, and when necessary he did so by resorting to physical violence. He managed his sub-jefes in a way that ensured that they controlled their charges, but in doing so he had to be careful that they did not become too powerful and try to take away his leadership. Thus his role was clearly more than that of a thug: he was at once an elder statesman, an experienced businessman, and a politician. What he was not was a friend.

Nevertheless, the leader's role as an intermediary between the members of the group and the larger adult society placed him in the position of having to negotiate constantly between both worlds. If he was not successful at this by bringing into the gallada what its members had joined to receive, the children were more or less free to leave, and often did. This limited the power of the jefe to abuse members. And, contrary to general opinion, younger children were not routinely abused. They were often well cared for because of their ability to be successful beggars. This also meant that the pormis was maintained so that everyone received more or less his fair share.

Chums

The galladas were not groups of friends, but economic units preparing themselves to become, and beginning to be a part of, the urban subculture of poverty. Camadas were different. They were together more for psychological than economic reasons. When looked at in a developmental sequence it is possible to explain why the camadas were composed of preadolescents and the galladas primarily of adolescents. Between the ages of eight and ten these children (not completely unlike other children) were asked by their parents to do a great many things they did not want to do and that forced them to conceal, to lie, and otherwise to learn a variety of deceptive techniques to evade these demands. During this time the children learned to cover up their true feelings in order to satisfy the demands placed upon them by parents or their surrogates. It was during preadolescence that, for the first time, they often gained a close friend with whom they could discuss their reactions to authority. The feelings they sensed to be inappropriate or unusual could now be shared. The pleasure of relieving the guilt and uncertainty about such feelings could well be intoxicating.

In the middle childhood developmental period friendships are composed primarily of two-person, same-sex dyads. But soon these groups of two interact with a third person and with other groups of two. Thus, one friend begins to find a friend who belongs to another dyad, and so the formation of preadolescent groups is derived. Although there were many reasons for street children to be in groups, the value and pleasure of friendships during middle childhood and the ease with which dyads became larger groups focused our understanding away from the notion that they were together only because of economic or pathological reasons. The children were in camadas because such groups were based on the invaluable quality of mutual friendships at the very time in psychological development when such friendships were most needed. Such values are no different for street children than they are for children of more traditional families. These groups, then, were not a pathological response to being without families, but a normative developmental coping mechanism that the street

children had utilized remarkably well, but perhaps more in-
tensely than their more traditional peers.

This type of friendship has been described by Sullivan (1953) as
"chumship," a form of love between two children, generally experienced between the ages of eight and ten and motivated by a
desire, for the first time, to accept another person as an individual of personal worth. Sullivan describes chumship as

> a specific new type of interest in a particular member of the
> same sex who becomes a chum or close friend. This change rep-
> resents the beginning of something very like full-blown, psy-
> chiatrically defined love. In other words, the other fellow takes
> on a perfectly novel relationship with the person concerned: he
> becomes of practically equal importance in all fields of value.
> Nothing remotely like that has ever appeared before. All of you
> who have children are sure that your children love you; when
> you say that, you are presenting a pleasant illusion. But if you
> will look very closely at one of your children when he finally
> finds a chum—somewhere between the ages of eight and a half
> and ten—you will discover something very different in the
> relationship—namely, that your child begins to develop a real
> sensitivity to what matters to another person. And this is not in
> the sense of "what should I do to get what I want," but instead,
> "what should I do to contribute to the happiness or support the
> prestige and feeling of worthwhileness of my chum." (Sullivan
> 1953, 245–46)

The relationship of chumship is a same-sex phenomenon that
ends at puberty and works to validate for each of the two children
a feeling of affection for equals. Sullivan not only praised the
value of chumship, but clearly saw it as a necessary force for
forming future adult love relationships. He also ascribed to
chumship the power to ameliorate prior emotional problems, including delinquency. "I would like to stress, at the risk of using
superlatives which sometimes get tedious, that development of
this chumship is of incredible importance in saving a good many
rather seriously handicapped people from otherwise inevitable
serious mental disorders" (Sullivan 1953, 248). The comparisons

between what was learned about how the preadolescents behaved together and the information that led Sullivan to his understanding of the importance of chumship were striking: mutual daydreams, spending hours carrying out a kind of spontaneous mythology, intimate caring for another person, and intense and joyful play were some obvious ones.

Even if we accepted the worst of scenarios about these children's pasts—that they all had been abused or abandoned—the camada, with its powerful associations of chums, did much to ameliorate this history. These preadolescent chums, while playing amid traffic, or jiving for a place in line where most likely they should not have been anyway, or controlling the exits of buses to raise a few pesos for a planned adventure, or in whatever other demonstration of agility and play, were at the same time also learning the curative qualities of chumship.

Chumship ended at puberty when, as Sullivan says, "lust" for the opposite sex pulled the relationship apart. This natural ending of chumships placed an additional burden on the children. One chum in a pair we studied, for example, began puberty and an interest in expanding friendships with the opposite sex earlier than his companion. This forced the other into a kind of loneliness that was, on occasion, consuming. He sought out another chum in a child who was younger. When that didn't work for him he joined an adolescent group (a gallada), often becoming an isolated and marginal figure, which only added to his loneliness. We observed this phenomenon many times, as it was rare that the breaking of a chum relationship was equal.

The period of transition into adolescence was particularly difficult. Facing the loss of their chums and giving up the advantage of their youthful imagery, the children tried to find some method to begin integrating into their adult roles. The galladas provided the place where this integration often took place. One book, *La Metamorfosis del "Chino de la Calle"* (Beltrán 1969), indicates in the words of the title what happens during this time. The children are changed, metamorphosed from rather benign little children into full-scale street people.

Recocha and Homosexual Exploitation

In the context of the relationships of street children during this phase, a variety of claims were made hypothesizing that younger children were misused by their older colleagues because of their fragility. Perhaps the most frequent conclusion from this point of view was that of widespread and abusive homosexuality. When younger boys went into the streets and sought to become members of the galladas, they were allegedly used as sexual objects. The leader of the gallada was often called by the children, and by those in society who knew this terminology, the *perro* (dog) or the *largo* (best translated as brute), while the young children who permitted themselves to be used either homosexually or, more metaphorically, in any dominant-submissive fashion were referred to as *coico* (limp or lame) or *compinche* (crony, used derogatively). We were led to believe by the public, the people who worked with the children, and those who had written about them that the younger children submitted to whatever demands were made on them by the older ones in order to maintain their security.

In my experience working in a federal penitentiary, the inmates used a term, "going down," when describing the necessity of the underdog to fight this kind of attack, even if the outcome was inevitable. If the newcomer fought the advance he was able to parry the power play, avoiding the "punk" role and the consequences of being perceived as one who can be scared into doing anything. Having thus "gone down," the initiate satisfactorily completed this routine initiation test. If the initiate did not "go down" and fight, then his role in the prison was always that of one who would be submissive, and he would be referred to as a "punk." Of the great majority of newcomers who face this initiation only a few, who generally come to the prison with a history of being submissive, end up as punks. In the terms used by Colombian street children a punk would be a coico of the perro.

The coico-perro relationship was relatively rare, as was the kind of homosexuality that it implied. In part this was because of the value and power that younger children have in getting goods, a power based on their small size and the cognitively dissonant image of being children. It is worthwhile to note here the difference between the street children and North American "run-aways," who are almost exclusively past puberty. Since we simply do not allow small children to be on the streets without adult supervision, the North American runaways do not experience this interdevelopmental phenomenon, which protects the younger street children in Colombia. When the reference to widespread homosexuality was advanced, it allowed the emotive nature of the term to be used by the Colombian public in a way that implied the kind of homosexual rape that occurs in the North American prison systems. These references to abuse of the younger children by the older ones did not imply any developmental form of homosexuality, which might have been considered a normal form of homosexual play or exploration. Such forms are considered a common aspect of the Freudian latency period and of the isophyllic relationship described by Sullivan's chumship.

Our research revealed a unique style of play that street children exhibited when seeking entry from the camadas into the galladas. *Recocha* was a passionate, almost violent mixture of friendship and aggression that combined a seemingly paradoxical form of intimacy and hostility. Its essential nature was total abandonment of emotional restraint, which resulted in friendship and aggression being fully expressed and likely to occur almost simultaneously. It was a type of play that could easily be misunderstood as being abusive, but it represented a fairly adequate method of testing the children from the camadas who were seeking entrance into the galladas during the preadolescent transition into adolescence.

The first time I saw recocha was in the courtyard of La Sucre. Its intensity rocked me with a kind of seasickness while I tried to keep abreast of which emotion was being acted out by the children involved and which emotional reaction I was having while watching them. Initially, I could not tell if they were engaged in a fight or intense play.

The courtyard at La Sucre was a cement square, about twenty yards on each side. The walls around the patio were built high enough to prevent escape, and they also had the effect of preventing the children from seeing over them. The farthest view any child had was across this sixty-foot expanse. On one side of the courtyard was an alcove where a television was mounted high above the reach of the children. On the floor in front of it was a series of metal benches. As I entered on the day I first saw recocha, the children were watching a movie where the hero was a man dressed in a gorilla costume. Behind the children were two guards, observing the boys while they watched the show. As I watched, one of the guards told me about a new boy of twelve. He was small for his age, not weighing more than ninety pounds, and he "had a problem with aggression." Shortly thereafter I noticed that the boys sitting on the first bench were passing this boy down the rows from one lap to the next. While they were doing this they pulled his hair and ears and smacked his stomach, producing loud sounds. They did not touch him in the groin, leaving that most delicate part unmolested. The boy, Jesus, whom we later got to know better in Bosconia, was in return showing his teeth like a dog ready to attack. Neither side ever scored a decisive victory; Jesus never actually bit anyone and the others never hurt him enough to cause real pain. Jesus, who appeared to be on the verge of tears, was on occasion flung off their laps but, surprisingly, he would return to their grabbing hands on his own volition.

The recocha continued for a while but the intensity declined, like an unannounced, yet agreed-upon truce. Jesus, certainly less developed than a full adolescent and obviously chupagruesic, settled down comfortably in their laps on one of these occasions while they, like the parents they didn't have, nestled him softly against their stomachs and held him close to their nipples, as if they were breast-feeding him. The recocha resumed and its intensity became apparent when, in his excitement, Jesus vomited. Even though a few of his companions received a little bit of the spittle on their laps, they just laughed, holding him gently while the boy relaxed to take a moment to compose himself. Then he jumped back at them, baring his teeth while the older ones continued as before, slapping his stomach and pulling at his ears.

I was stunned and did not know what to make of this. Were they playing? I thought at first that he was being abused, yet he never left the scuffle even though he had plenty of opportunity to do so. I then realized that this must be an initiation, that he had to show them that he wanted to be part of their group. In spite of the rough rules in the ceremony, he would have to go back for more until he was finally held as an infant and accepted his role as the newest and smallest member. Was the ritual abusive? It was apparent to me that the older ones were more intent on arousing an emotional reaction than hurting him, as they did not either go for his groin or otherwise cause him obvious pain. Yet the teasing was intense.

After the movie the children left the benches and recongregated in small groups in the courtyard. Two of them played with Jesus. At one point they picked him up, one holding his legs, the other his arms, and carried him over to the faucet, which was mounted over a six- or seven-inch basin full of water. On the way to the faucet they dropped him on the cement, where he lay waiting to be picked up again. He was picked up and carried to the wet basin. As he was being lowered to the standing water, one of his carriers reached with one hand to turn the water on. Jesus began to scream but did not try to break away. The worker on the floor calmly but decisively yelled for them to stop. They did, letting him go immediately, and then all three of them went on to the next encounter at once, completely leaving this episode behind them, as if turning a page.

As demonstrated by his participation in recocha, Jesus might have been the type of child who could have been involved with the form of homosexual rape that we were led to believe existed in the galladas. In this scenario Jesus would at some time be asked to perform some type of masturbatory behavior for one of the larger boys. And because of his emotional need to belong and his physical need to maintain his safety he would have submitted. It did seem likely to us that in the quietness of the dormitories at night Jesus might be asked to share some physical warmth with another boy and might do so, perhaps seeking to diminish the loneliness that was forced upon him by being incarcerated and thus having to leave his chums. But this form of homosexuality is different from forced rape. The social worker at La Sucre said that the extent of homosexuality was not great, and it was more in the form of "youthful friendships of caressing" than in the starker form of coico rape. What she was describing was more like the affection of chums, which, as Sullivan maintained, is a normal, if not necessary, step in learning to be intimate.

Because the preadolescents had the unusual advantage of being more productive than the adolescents, there was a limit to the amount of distress the older children could inflict in their initiation ceremonies. They were not so rough as to turn the preadolescents toward another group. Yet, by demanding something of the preadolescents, they could ensure that the younger children would become good members, not only loyal to the group, but capable of the rough life that the streets would demand of them.

The intricate way in which the adolescents made the initiation ceremony fluctuate between the two extremes of being overly easy and too difficult to bear was quite functional. By being forced to plead his worth before the group, the preadolescent initiate viewed his own entrance as valuable and felt more pride in being a member by having done something to be one. When Jesus relaxed the larger boys cuddled him, demonstrating that they would take care of him when he needed it, sending the important psychological message to him that if he would tolerate the nearly abusive play and participate in it fully, there would be some rewards at the end. Thus, as the preadolescents sought admittance to the gallada, their two concerns—needing protection and wanting to be accepted—were defined. At the same time the adolescents were spending less energy than was commonly believed on the preadolescents, as their attention was more correctly focused on gaining admittance to the existing adult subculture of urban poverty. It was here that the adolescents would eventually take their places as adults, and an excessive amount of involvement with the younger children was unnecessary for those adolescents who were, in a mentally healthy way, looking toward acceptance in the appropriate reference group of their future. The older children enjoyed the company of the younger children only to the extent that the younger children were economic assets to their world of urban poverty. This view of the rite of passage makes more sense in relation to both groups of children than that of inevitable homosexual rape or physical abuse.

There were younger children who violated their side of the initiation by becoming overly submissive or by homosexual gesturing. One incident, which involved the only overweight boy we saw at Bosconia, illustrated the group code with respect to effeminate behavior. On the day of this incident the pudgy eleven year old was wearing a red pullover and sitting in a circle composed of several children and a few members of our research team, learning to play a game that was new to us. In this game a lit cigarette was passed around a circle, and each person took a puff until the ash fell. Then the person holding the cigarette had to run around the circle and find a place to sit. This was always difficult because the others tried to exclude the runner. After securing his place in the circle he was allowed to light the cigarette, and the cycle continued until there was no more cigarette and the one holding the butt was the loser. When the overweight boy had to run around the circle, we noticed that his gait was more like skipping than running. He seemed unable to run with coordination in spite of the fact that this should have been an easy task given his age. The boys sitting around the circle laughed at him and tried to trip him by grabbing at his legs and clothes. As I was observing this, I also noticed one of the physically handicapped boys who, despite using two crutches, was playing and appeared more in control of his physical actions and was more accepted by the group than the overweight boy. By ostracizing one and accepting the other, the group obviously had identified with the ethos of the Latin American majority about inappropriate male behavior. It was more acceptable to be a tough, crippled boy than an unathletic, effeminate, overweight one. The group was simply not ready to be "liberal" about the prescribed traditional roles of gender.

When we asked the boys in Bosconia about homosexuality they did as much as possible to avoid the question. When they did talk about it, they expressed a very low regard for homosexuals. In part this was because they thought that the word was used pejoratively by society to persecute the street children, another example of the abusive attitudes that society showered on them. One boy, keenly aware of this, described how he had to be careful not to show his friendships in public. "Gamines are not able to demonstrate their friendships. This would be dangerous because the rest of the world is against us. Policemen persecute us and wealthy people denounce us, inventing lies that are more miserable than the poverty. They don't understand how we feel when they say vulgarly that we are *maricas* [effeminate, sissy, homosexual]. To be coico or compinche is to be a slave, a maid, or a homosexual of another person. This is the worst thing in the world" (Gutiérrez 1972a, 36). The intimacy of their preadolescent chumships was not tolerated by Colombian society, which prematurely labeled this normal affection as weak and deviant.

Whereas society drew no distinction between the homosexual play of preadolescent chums and the more brutal forms of homosexual rape, this boy and others whom we talked with understood that the use of the word homosexual, when applied to them, was directed against the very way in which they defined themselves: living independent of authority and not submissive or beholden to the more powerful. Since the street children perceived that the term was applied to them in order to discredit their attempts to be independent, they did not encourage their own groups to function in this manner. And they did not look favorably on those who engaged in forceful or submissive homosexuality.

We found that when relations among street children fell into the submissive-dominant homosexual pattern, those who were involved were avoided by other children, often having to leave the gallada and seek another one that would be more tolerant of that kind of behavior. Usually the new gallada tolerated them for only a short time. Moving from gallada to gallada, these submissive boys eventually found a perro who had such tight control over the gallada that the coico was shielded from the insults of the other members. But even in this case the children of the gallada who were neither perros nor coicos did not enjoy seeing this dominant-submissive abuse and often left. This response reduced the ability of those abusive perros to treat their younger members in this fashion because before long their gallada would be sufficiently reduced in size and power to make it ineffectual.

As they grew older, the chupagruesos were still dominated by outside forces. One example of this would be an exploitative homosexual relationship. Another, more likely possibility, the one we imagined for Jesus, was to be a minor member in a delinquent gallada, running errands for the more powerful. Ostracism by his peers might actually prove to be helpful by driving him away from associating with galladas and moving him in the direction of adopting the more routine work that society offered poor children who were comfortable with being subservient and servile. If he was lucky enough to find a benevolent benefactor, it might turn out to be rather comfortable for him. If, instead, he encountered the more delinquent adolescents who were the perros or largos, another future awaited him.

Gamines would not be involved with brutal or obvious homosexual domination. Taking part on either side of this physical or sexual exploitation would entail giving up their gamine identity because it was part of their creed to be haughty and independent. Homosexual rape was a form of brutality, not mischievousness.

Using Drugs

In addition to the misperception by society about the amount of homosexuality exhibited by street children, there was an equally alarming amount of misinformation about the use of drugs. Since the children were perceived to be without the restraints of guardians, and thus prey to immoral influences, it is not surprising that drug abuse was allegedly high among them. The fear of drug use by society was fueled by the misperception that peer pressure applied by the more sophisticated older children would make the smaller children into addicts. This fear was compounded by the fact that a new, extremely dangerous drug, *basuko*, was available.

Basuko is the Colombian name given to the unrefined residue of coca leaves that is left over after the purer cocaine is distilled. It contains a variety of substances beyond the cocaine hydrochloride: kerosene, wood alcohol, sulfuric acid, benzoic acid, and others. It has allegedly been used widely by children. Jeri (1976, 1978, 1982), a Peruvian psychiatrist, has studied the drug for many years in Peru, where it is called *pasta de coca*, or cocaine paste. He describes the effects of smoking the drug to be initially pleasant, but then manifesting within a matter of minutes a variety of negative side effects such as dizziness, headaches, hyperactivity and, eventually, auditory, visual, and tactile hallucinations. According to his reports, the compulsion to keep smoking basuko is so strong and the effects so transient that the user may smoke as many as fifty cigarettes in a day. Inevitably, as Jeri and others state, users became addicted, brain-damaged, and psychotic. Although some people have said that the use of basuko is similar to free-basing cocaine in the United States, the residue substances are different and therefore the side effects are purportedly even more dangerous. Jeri (1982) says that there is no effective treatment short of performing a type of lobotomy (bilateral anterior cyngulectomy) for the worst offenders, which he claims helped 82.3 percent of the patients he treated.

How common was the use of basuko? Data from *El Tiempo* [Bogotá's leading daily] indicate that 60 percent of the youth under fifteen years of age in one town "have followed the path of drug addiction" (Patiño 1983, 11A). The article goes on to say that in many cities the statistics are even more alarming. In one city "of one thousand youths, six hundred are drug addicts in the extreme. . . . Nothing is incredible here since entire families started to consume basuko as easily as if they were trying a piece of fried banana." On June 27, 1983, *El Tiempo* said that "every five minutes another Colombian is a victim of basuko" (Andrade 1983). On September 28, 1983, *El Espectador*, another of Bogotá's leading newspapers, said that "in Colombia 38 percent of the children below fourteen years of age have problems with drugs" (p. 5A). The article continued by saying that "the problem is made worse because each of these children contaminates ten other children." The speculation, presented as evidence in these articles and others, attempted to show that the use of basuko was widespread and debilitating. However, if the street children were using basuko, then we would expect that they would be severely affected by it and the results would have been apparent in their test scores.

Besides the reported physical and psychological damages that resulted from using basuko, there were also political implications for Colombia's cocaine-generated economy that explained the increase of public attention in the Colombian press. We had to contend with this political climate when we tried to discern the amount of drug use in our sample. The export value of cocaine to the United States was $80 million per year, which made it second only to Exxon in business revenues (Samper 1983). In the past the use of cocaine by Colombians had been fairly rare and very private. The publicity that drug abuse was receiving at this time was based in part on the alleged connection between drug traffickers and the leftist guerrillas who, in exchange for arms, were said to guard the illicit laboratories that were refining the coca leaves sent from Peru and Bolivia. The street children, being perceived as both poor and beginning to live outside the law, were believed to be potential allies in this connection, a thought that scared the populace and to which they reacted with great concern.

The motives behind the assault on drugs that went on during our work in Colombia were never clear. The American ambassador connected the leftist groups with the drug traffickers and engaged in a struggle with the Colombian president to reverse the president's decision to refrain from extraditing narcotics suspects. The American position was confusing because it was not clear if the Americans wanted to eradicate the danger of the left or the narcotics traffickers. By connecting the two threats, the Americans tried to gain more popular support. Since the government was already in debt to foreign creditors, and because of the revenue that was put into the economy by narcotics money, this became a sticky issue. In the process of working out the American plan several violent acts occurred. These included the assassination of the attorney general and an assault on the Supreme Court, both of which were said by the American embassy to be the result of this connection of leftists and drug traffickers.

Colombians had mixed opinions about the American plan. I visited one city in a region that was "owned" by narcotics chiefs who had built schools, sewage systems, and public parks, and made other improvements for the local populace that made life for peasants considerably better than in nearby towns where the distribution of wealth was less corrupt. When the government decided to extradite the main chief of this city, who allegedly had offered to pay the national debt out of his pocket, the value of the national currency dropped by 40 percent in a matter of weeks.

The ambiguous relationship between the government's debt and corrupt money took on humorous tones when a leading paper announced in an editorial that there was a problem of what to do with this person's personal zoo, since the animals had to be fed with food that was imported from as far away as East Africa. On one hand, the editorial said the cost of providing for the animals was prohibitive, but on the other hand, the killing of them was inhumane. In the interim, while working on a decision, the government continued to pay the bill.

In any event it was likely, in such a highly charged political atmosphere, that those involved in attempting to eradicate the drug problem would have reason to heighten its alleged menace and otherwise call attention to the severity of the situation, emphasizing the effects of the drug and its leftist connections. Since the street children were seen as possible coconspirators in the drug problem, they were also subjects of the antidrug campaign and there thus would be reason to overestimate the amount of their alleged drug use.

The street children were considered at risk because they had all the characteristics of children who would start using drugs, being poor, disenfranchised, and antisocial. The street children became particularly vulnerable to this attack when they were in groups, since all gangs are allegedly breeding grounds that lead to criminal acts, including the use of drugs. We wanted to ascertain if their alleged use of basuko was a misperception or if in fact it was as high as claimed. In other words, were the children being consumed by their use of drugs or were they unjustly accused by the larger society, which was unwarrantedly pointing a finger at an easy target to defray the larger issue of the society's ambivalence toward income from drug traffickers?

In order to see if time on the streets affected the children's performance, as drug abuse suggested it would, the sample was divided into three age groups. Table 11 illustrates the descriptive statistics for the three age groups on the four variables studied. Twenty-four children aged eleven and under were considered to be prepuberty. They represented 42.9 percent of the sample. The twelve-year-olds, 19.6 percent of the sample, were placed in the transitional category. Thirty-seven percent of the sample were thirteen or older and were labeled postpuberty. Table 11 also shows the results of the Kruskal-Wallis ANOVA test, which was run on all four variables. By assuming that on the average the children left home at approximately the same age, we could assume that the older children had spent more time on the streets than the younger ones. In support of this assumption, several studies already cited suggested that older children had spent more time on the streets and that the ages at which most children started street life were similar. Most children left home before puberty. By comparing the three age groups, using group

Table 11 Age Differences on All Variables

Variables	Prepuberty (N = 24)		Transitional (N = 11)		Postpuberty (N = 21)	
	Mean	Standard deviation	Mean	Standard deviation	Mean	Standard deviation
Age	9.37	1.34	12.0	0	13.95	1.24
IQ	89.56	13.83	93.18	6.27	84.57	13.21
Bender[a]	78.04	39.65	49.18	12.75	46.19	25.84
EI	3.12	2.05	2.54	1.69	2.30	1.38
NI[b]	3.70	1.83	2.72	1.95	2.09	1.61

a. Results of the ANOVA ($N = 56$, df $= 2,53$, F ratio $= 6.78$, F probability $= .002$) and the Tukey HSD procedure indicate that the prepuberty sample differs significantly from the transitional and postpuberty samples on their Bender scores: $p \leq .05$.

b. Results of the Kruskal-Wallis test ($N = 56$, df $= 2$, $H' = 8.28$) indicate that the samples differ significantly on their NI scores: $p \leq .05$.

means, it was possible to determine the psychological effects of time spent on the streets. Thus, the prepuberty children had an average of 3.7 neurological indicators, while the postpuberty group had an average of 2.09 neurological indicators. This difference was significant at the .05 level. This reinforces the conclusion that there is no evidence to support the hypothesis that the children were using an excessive amount of drugs as a result of being on the streets. The same comparisons were made on the Benders, which showed that the scores improved with age. This was significant at the .05 level and indicated that the general emotional health of the children was not deteriorating but improving. The EIs also improved, although not significantly. The IQs remained stable. These comparisons suggest that life on the streets did not necessarily lead to poorer emotional or intellectual health, which in turn suggests that the use of drugs was not as pervasive as we were led to believe.

In our participant observation notes some members of the research team mentioned that the children talked about using drugs, but they rarely actually saw the children using them. Our data on drug abuse come from these occasional direct encounters, a review of the psychological testing, which was in part aimed at detecting the effects of excessive drug use, and the variety of conversations we had with children concerning drugs. When the children themselves talked about drugs, they did so in a way that illustrated that they were indeed aware of drugs and that they used them, but they did not hold any great respect for the drug abusers in their midst. The greatest amount of prestige went to those children who were able to outwit authorities. If this involved drugs, they were just a part in the script but not the essence of the drama. Some of the older chupagruesos, particularly those who were advanced in the Nicolo program, mentioned to us that they had used drugs but had given up the "vice."

Gutiérrez (1972a) talked about the children sniffing gasoline, often at night, in order to reduce their anxiety. He also mentioned marijuana use and explained that much of their labile emotionality was a result of it. He did not allude to actually seeing the children using drugs, nor did he assign drug use a big part in their lives. Felsman (1981a) also did not make drug use a prominent factor in his description of street children. What, then, are we left with? We don't think the children that we observed, or those that Gutiérrez and Felsman observed, are a biased sample. Drug use for the most part simply was not central to the street children's lives. The amount of critical thinking and judgment that the children needed and showed in their daily lives indicated that the children in our sample were not heavily under the influence of drugs. The statistics on the neurological indicators support the lack of significant brain damage, which the use of basuko allegedly produces. The sample's relatively healthy emotional functioning likewise indicated that drug abuse was not as flagrant as the newspapers' reports suggested.

Street children were almost never seen on the streets intoxicated. They almost never publicly drank or consumed drugs. The public's conception of their drug-taking behavior was based on what the public thought the children did in the privacy of the times they spent together in groups. We cannot say that we know what they did in their private times, for they were for the most part private to us, too. Yet, we can say that if they were "addicted," their addiction did not spill over to the public domain, nor was it revealed in their test scores. This testifies to a certain amount of control over drug use that the articles in the newspapers claimed was unavailable to those who use basuko.

The galladas would not tolerate those children who were too drugged to perform their part of the work bargain. There was drug use in the camadas, but that was most often curtailed by lack of access to drugs. The drinking, the smoking when it was available, even the use of inhalants was done mostly as a way to celebrate friendships and to avoid the fears of the nights. But the widespread use of drugs was not necessary to the children in the camadas because they had friendships, because they were more economically solvent than their older counterparts, and because the value and necessity of having friends meant that drug abuse, which encouraged passivity and submission, destroyed the value of the child for being a chum.

Because the connection between drug use and criminality is stronger in Colombia than it is in the United States (due to the stricter laws against their use), it was difficult for children to get drugs. And if they were caught the consequences were graver. This made regular drug use more common in the older children, who had begun to integrate into the criminal subculture. The younger children most commonly used alcohol or inhalants in their groups, and tried marijuana or basuko less frequently, when interacting with older children. The shift from legal but inappropriate drugs (alcohol and cigarettes) to illegal and more potent drugs usually occurred when the young children were interacting with older children in galladas. The older children were more likely to use marijuana or basuko. If the children were still using alcohol or inhalants by the time they were past puberty they probably had a drug problem that would continue into their adult lives. The children most commonly started drug use through certain rituals that were connected to friendship and working activities, while those who continued drug use into adolescence were slowly weaning themselves out of the street culture and into the delinquent subculture.

The alcohol used in the camadas was usually a mixture of aguardiente, or cane liquor, and a variety of other alcoholic beverages. As chums waited for sleeping places they would on occasion steal the leftovers from patrons at an outdoor cafe. Sometimes they did not have to steal the leftovers but were able to entice the patrons to give them alcohol. In one camada we observed that the children carried a clay pot about fourteen inches tall for the specific purpose of carrying the alcohol into their sleeping spot. For the younger children, another way of securing alcohol was to put on a public performance where they would pretend they were drunk. On San Nicolas square we saw two young children pretending to be tipsy, staggering, acting foolish, and making inappropriate lewd jokes. A third child carried an empty bottle for the observers, who laughed at the children's theater and applauded it by pouring some of their liquor into the bottle. One reason why alcohol was the most common drug used by the small children was that it was easily available, since it was used widely by almost everyone in the society.

The children's insistence on independence also contributed to the fact that illegal drugs were not used widely, since it was difficult for the children to get illegal drugs without compromising themselves to those who had some to sell. This kind of attachment often involved several compromises that the children as a rule were not willing to make. Children in the camadas often lived outside the cash economy. The person giving a small child a drug wanted something in return. The child would have to opt for a promise to sell drugs or to perform a compromising act, which the majority of children did not want to do. The children were very careful about relationships with adults, and the more an adult appeared as if he might take control over them the less likely the children were to engage in the relationship. In one of our conversations with Adolfo, a thirteen-year-old boy in our sample, he told us that "drugs are pleasurable but not needed. What we need is a place to stay and food. We get our kicks from laughing at the drunks, not from being drunk ourselves because that's a sure way to be taken advantage of." Another reason why children avoided illicit drugs was that the children who were successful at street life took a good deal of pleasure from their success. They found great satisfaction in being so independent at such an early age. When they saw other children forced to follow the directives of parents and teachers, they often went out of their way to laugh at them. Their pranks in public places were one way that children took advantage of the adults' fear of them. This increased the children's satisfaction and self-esteem. As long as

they had these sources of triumph, drug abuse, often tied to losing independence, was considered not worth the price. This is not
to say that they wouldn't or didn't use drugs, but to be involved in
a drug life was not necessary or desirable for the majority of
them.

The young children who were less successful at street life
were the ones most often involved with drugs. For them the drug
of choice, beyond alcohol, was inhalants. Since inhalants were
cheap and not illegal, they were easy to come by. However, the
majority of street children would routinely tell us that inhalants
caused brain damage and many children would shun those who
used inhalants. Some of the children who were involved with
programs actively incorporated this point of view and patrolled
their peers. Those using inhalants had to avoid being caught by
these colleagues. Only on one occasion did I see children using
inhalants. One evening, near the bull ring in Cali, I saw two
small boys with a group of five postpuberty children. The older
ones were offering the contents of a brown paper bag that contained some type of inhalant. I did not see the larger boys sniffing the bag, but each smaller child inhaled its contents for about
twenty seconds while the larger ones laughed and encouraged
them to continue. The younger children were barely able to
walk straight. I did not see the end of the drama because my
presence forced the older boys to scatter. I approached the two
children and found them barely able to talk. As they regained
their composure they too ran away. The next day I mentioned
this event to the children at Bosconia and tried to ascertain their
reactions. They told me that this was a typical way to test certain
younger children who were suspected of not being tough
enough to join a gallada. However, there was no winning because the inhalants were considered a drug for *sapos*, or sissies;
thus, if the children did follow the orders of the older boys, they
would gain admittance to the gallada with the role of a coico, or
slave. These comments on the practice reinforced our idea that
the children looked down on inhalants.

The greatest prestige in the galladas and the camadas went to
those children who were indifferent to drug use, accepting mild
doses for themselves, avoiding heavy use and users, and seeing
drugs as a minor part of street life. There were some exceptions to

this rule in the older children. Occasionally a gallada would be run by a more delinquent leader who was associated with those who could supply him with drugs. *El Tiempo* reported in early 1984 that there were forty galladas in Bogotá, and "seven *galladas* could be considered dangerous" (Cortes 1984, 7A). This is 17 percent of the total and a fair estimate of the link between the street culture and the delinquent subculture, which was more likely to be involved with drug use. As the children got older some of them opted to join or were forced into a criminal element.

The galladas were usually the place where younger children would first encounter marijuana and basuko. Peer pressure often resulted in many children trying these drugs. After taking the initial forbidden fruit the majority of children found that it was not as delicious or important as claimed. Those younger children who had started on alcohol or inhalants were the ones most likely to use the illegal drugs and then to follow the older children into the delinquent subculture.

The chupagruesos were often led into drugs by peer pressure, but the power of the drugs, as well as what the children had to do to use them, often was the primary reason why many of them joined programs for street children. This was fairly typical in Bosconia. Giraldo, the child advocate for the Nicolo program, readily admitted to using drugs, to having had a vice. He was now devoted to stopping drug use by other children, which was part of the reason why he was successful in the more protected environment of the Nicolo program. The gamines, who were devoted to their independence and successful in their street lives, often avoided illegal drugs because their use entailed giving up too much freedom. Thus, it was the early style of prepuberty life, that is, whether it was gamine or chupagrueso, that often determined future drug use in the galladas.

Before sunset one evening I was walking through the older part of El Centro and came upon five boys from Bosconia in a gallada. Two of them were under twelve, three were past puberty. They were in a darkened alley laughing and talking loudly, and smoking what smelled like marijuana. As I approached, the oldest boy, Eduardo, held the handmade cigarette next to his body, meekly covering it up from my view, while one of the two younger boys, Esteban, greeted me. For a moment we all froze, none of us knowing what to do next. Then, in a brazen move, Eduardo offered me a smoke, which I refused, but I made a point of showing that I was not unnerved. Nor did I offer a reprisal or make any statements about their smoking. Instead I merely started up a conversation about the afternoon activities in Bosconia. After a few moments of conversation the two younger boys left, saying they had to meet friends to see a movie. I stayed with the three older boys, who continued nervously with their illegal cigarette. Eduardo, the leader, kept the cigarette, taking three drags on it before passing it on to the next boy, who inhaled hurriedly and ended up coughing. The third boy took a deep puff and let it out as quickly as it reached his mouth. Then he rolled his eyes and remarked about how good it was and didn't I want some. I said no once again, feeling more than a little nervous about the possibility of an unexpected person coming along and thus finding myself in a very difficult position. About halfway through the cigarette Eduardo began to act very "stoned," laughing loudly, making jokes that were designed to make me feel uncomfortable, and organizing the remaining two boys to go and get something to eat. The two boys acted as if they were too intoxicated to fetch his food, which was hard to imagine since they had hardly inhaled any of the cigarette. This was the only encounter I had with children using illegal drugs. The event ended with the two smaller boys leaving early, being uncomfortable in my presence and quite possibly feeling unpleasant about the whole scene.

Eduardo, the leader of the group, was growing out of street life. At sixteen he had been on the streets a long time. By now he had chosen a more delinquent life-style. He consumed drugs frequently. When confronted about drug abuse he first denied it, then admitted that he used drugs, liked them, and was not being hurt by using them. His two adolescent partners were not expert drug users, but under peer pressure they partook. This example reinforced what we considered to be fairly typical for these children. The majority tried drugs, including alcohol. Some got caught up in their use, usually later in their street careers. Some of the children inadvertently got into drugs to mask their depression. Some used drugs only in social situations when they felt that they would suffer more if they refused them. These children were unlikely to become habitual drug abusers.

The group code of the majority of street children was not directly involved with drug use and certainly not with drug abuse. The heart of the group code was freedom from adult authority and the ability to make a living without being beholden to anyone. This was difficult to achieve under the best conditions, and drug use was no help. Consequently they avoided drugs.

As some of the children got older, their use of drugs escalated toward more potent substances. However, there were other choices for children who did not pursue this path. Since the galladas were open groups, children were able to leave and find another group, which they often did. Many children chose to leave galladas that were involved with drugs and return to a program for street children, enter the work force, or go to another gallada that was less involved with delinquent elements. Those children who were moving toward the delinquent style of life often became involved with drugs. Yet even this involvement did not always entail abuse. For many of these adolescents drugs were more of an economic reality than a question of addiction. The worst prognosis was for those children who were using several drugs. This was most often the case with children who had a history of alcohol abuse beginning in the camadas.

The street children's use of drugs was viewed by society as a political and moral problem of great dimensions and importance. To the children it was more limited and practical. At younger ages it often involved a special way of easing fear or celebrating friendships. At times it had economic motivation; for the young children, in their theatrical displays of feigning drunkenness, it served to help them gain money and to display their aggression against a society that devalued them. Adults' own use of alcohol demonstrated to the children a morally indefensible position that in anger many children sought to confront. For the older children drug use often had the economic advantage that many illegal activities bring.

It was the unusual choice of the Spanish word *vicio*, which was routinely used to indicate drug use of any kind, that helped us to understand the confusion around, and often the misinformation about, the children's use of drugs. In spite of all the allegations about the children—their delinquent behavior, their abusive families, and their homosexuality—nothing about them was perceived to be as dreadful as the vice of taking drugs. Drugs emphasized the intergenerational gap, which was becoming wider as the country moved toward a more complete participation in the modern world. From the confusion, the fear, and the unfortunate political opportunity that exploited the misery of drug abuse, the problem was elevated to a moral issue.

Control of drugs became the ultimate weapon in a struggle between the generations and between the modern and archaic ways of life. Through the fog of these overlapping issues we tried to focus on the children: why they took drugs, how much they used, and how drugs affected their lives. We discovered that drug taking occurred, but nowhere near the amount or for the reasons commonly believed.

In order to understand this discrepancy, as well as the other misinformation about the children presented in the case studies and in the details of how the children lived in groups, it is necessary to see the children beyond the context of their personal and social lives. The perceptions of the children's drug activity emanates from historical, political, and cultural realities. To understand the dimensions of this more completely, the next chapter explains why the misperceptions of the children exist. Examining the hypotheses concerning the causes of street children helps explain why society is so offended by their existence.

5
Solving
the Riddle of
Abandon-
ment and
Abuse

Three major hypotheses attempt to explain the causes of street children. The first alleges that the families of street children are headed by mothers who are victims of abusive male partners. In this scenario the mother has no alternative but to endure the abuse because she needs the man for economic survival. Her children either leave because of the abuse or are forced out of the home. The second hypothesis states that the families of street children are recently arrived rural migrants to urban areas who are culturally unprepared to deal with the modern world they find. The cultural disorientation of these families produces street children. The third hypothesis holds that street children are the natural products of the impoverished neighborhoods they live in.

Although these hypotheses are useful in explaining some of the causes of street children, they are often inaccurate because they ignore important differences between family structures. These hypotheses also have served to discredit the street children, who have become symbols in a larger struggle, a struggle that has to do with who will participate in civic life.

The Newly Emerging Civic Identity

Contrary to reports, street children were not "everywhere." They lived in certain parts of the country and came from areas that represented different cultural traditions. Two studies (Pineda et al. 1978; de Galán 1981), for example, compared the predominantly patrifocal and more Spanish-descended areas of Bogotá and other cities in the central highlands with the matrifocal and more African-descended regions of the north coast. The latter had few street children while the former was known to have many. This information was valuable because it led us to see that the different cultural and familial conditions were related to the origin and number of street children, the way they were described, and ultimately the way they were treated.

Although it is common to use the term "Latin American family," Gutiérrez discussed some of the difficulties of naming a monolithic concept of family in Colombia. "Social science in Latin America has taken as a model the European puritan family" (1972a, 328). This type of family is patrifocal, of Spanish descent, and it has functioned to protect and support its members from whatever external tribulations they faced in society. The less dominant, matrifocal African and indigenous family structures have less power and fewer opportunities to help their own members, and thus have been less able to take advantage of family connections.

Until the mid-twentieth century the traditional Spanish family was so tightly closed in on itself that it prevented modernization, because to become modern was to have more of a civic than a familial outlook. The modern society is characterized by its ability to form groups of citizenry for a variety of causes that are more related to the state than to the family. In Colombia, "for this modern identification to exist, it is required that there be less maternal or paternal tyranny, less dependence on them [parents], and a warming up to the simple notion of citizenry" (Gutiérrez 1972a, 329). Connecting the participation of cultures and family structures with the struggle to come into a modern civic world, it becomes clear that street children are a part of this battle. They have, even if unwittingly, protested the reign of the feudal family and have thus participated in the protest against access into modern society based solely on family name. This helps to explain why they were treated poorly by a large segment of society.

The children were thus engaged in or found themselves in the middle of a very old conflict. Plato was the first to discuss the advantages of abolishing the family as a social institution. The family, he said, established an obstacle between the well-being of the community and the citizenry (Blustein 1982). Citizenship was squelched by family loyalty, which siphoned off the energy to act for the larger good. Plato objected to the notion that children's obedience to the family worked for the broader welfare of the larger community because, he argued, the ideal state had to have a sense of public versus private responsibility. The demise of the Roman Empire, he said, was the result of the family working toward improving their own members while rejecting the concerns of those outside the immediate family.

Kant maintained that the most important moral training was one that allowed for a knowledge of universal laws. Family life would not adhere to universality, but would dwell on its own concerns for the welfare of its particular offspring. Thus, children in families could not learn the important truth of the Golden Rule. What they learned from their parents' wish to give them the best was that only their families would "really" provide for them. Children must learn, said Kant, to differentiate between the role of family member and that of member of the citizenry, which entails a commitment to a more universal sense of right and wrong and fairness (Blustein 1982).

Historically, Colombia has been controlled by families who were given their wealth by the king of Spain. The tradition of family life in Spain was strongly influenced by the Roman conquest. The Spanish families in the New World, guided by the Roman tradition, maintained their privileged status through the privacy of family. As they did everything to favor their kin, they reduced the possibility of non–family members getting a share of the goods. This also reduced the financial resources of the state to care for the general well-being of citizens who needed help. In Colombia, with a rigid division between those who were wealthy and those without any resources, it became apparent that the family, acting as an institution of identity, deprived those outside its boundaries from getting some share of the goods. It also caused the poor to be alienated from what they perceived to be their just benefits from society. This deteriorated the belief in the moral values of equality and justice that were necessary for a sense of community. Without these values hostility and disorder prevailed.

It was therefore not the poor families who were jeopardized by the presence of street children, but the wealthier families. They had gained wealth by maintaining "the family," merging it with state control and access to material well-being. Accusations by the dominant society of the poor families' irresponsibility, lack of education, disrespect for their spouses, and cruelty toward their children were in part politically defensive maneuvers to protect their rights to control their children and to provide special favors for them. The issue was not one of poverty, but of the nature of the family and the power of the family unit.

The church, which has helped many poor children by establishing programs for them, has unfortunately missed the most important point. The church has maintained that families need to control and provide discipline so that children will grow up to be respectful, less egocentric, capable of postponing gratification, and able to curtail the evil that is within all of us. These beliefs rest on the notion that the ultimate purpose of the family is to help children develop the capacity to distinguish good from evil. This could come about only through the authority of parents to maintain the rights that the children of the streets had allegedly usurped. The church, even though it has helped many in poverty, has also aligned itself with the notion of family shared by wealthier groups.

On April 9, 1948, Colombians experienced what they refer to as *La Violencia*. On that day the dictatorial government of Ospina Perez was overthrown and the populist leader Gaitan assassinated. According to Alape (1983), one set of customs was totally lost, while others began that would dictate the country's future. La Violencia spread a level of tension throughout the country that had never been felt before. Gaitan was the first man of the masses to have won the hearts of the people as well as the support of the political system, instilling a renaissance of possibility in the populace. On his death, people felt robbed of their idol and their hopes. Hordes of people flocked to the streets and stormed what they perceived to be symbols of corruption that had taken their leader and their hope away. In the aftermath Bogotá was burned to the ground and 200,000 people were eventually killed.

Before Gaitan, access to political life, as well as to prominent society, depended on one's family name. Civic life was dictated by family connections. Different families not only belonged to the different political parties, but the very identity of those parties was inextricably associated with various family names. Thus, political parties were not civic responses to national or regional life, but feudal, patrifocal family empires. Different families participated in different social groups and referred to each other by the single monicker that made their claim to identity: their father's name.

After Gaitan and La Violencia, the country began to come into the modern world. Life became more egalitarian and meritocratic, which increased the individual's opportunity to participate in civic, social, and political life. After Gaitan's death and La Violencia it was possible to be someone without having to rely on family name or family history. La Violencia broke down the tradition of family as the sole determinant of citizenship and started a process of modernizing the country and the family.

There were regional differences of involvement in La Violencia. The greatest contributors to both sides of the struggle came from the regions where the Spanish patrifocal families still had feudal control over participation in civic life. These were the same areas in the heart of the country, surrounding Bogotá, that produced the great majority of street children. The north coast, with its principally African, matrifocal family system had little involvement in La Violencia. These areas have also produced fewer street children.

Many scholars traced the origins of street children to the epoch of La Violencia (de Mantilla 1980; Muñoz and Palacios 1980; Néron 1953; Pineda et al. 1978). Unfortunately, they saw this essentially as a result of the economic turmoil and the rural-to-urban migration that followed La Violencia, rather than as the result of the civic changes that it produced. For the first time there was an opportunity for the non-Spanish racial groups, with their own cultural patterns, to become participants in the civic politic. Rather than dealing directly with the social problems caused by opening up the society to all of its members, certain indirect, insidious, but powerful tensions emerged.

It was at this time that the label "abandoned" was popularly applied to street children. The emotional nature of this term implied that their families were remiss, irresponsible, and in need of restructuring. Verjan and de Lujo (1982) and Ricaurte (1972) trace the linguistic history of the word gamine to 1874, when children began to protest inhumane working conditions in the mine at Zipaquirá. At that time there were so many children in the streets that the viceroy, Manuel de Guirar, ordered the state to round the children up and put them in custody. But according to Meunier (1977), there was no mention of improper child rearing or remiss families. It was not until the aftermath of La Violencia that they were called abandoned. With this change the children and their families were being judged and moral values were being applied to support the claims of those making the accusations. In great part this was connected to the turmoil of opening up the society to different social and racial groups, as well as to a different set of rules that would change the nature of participation in civic life from one based on family identity to one associated more with personal merit. Vying over the degree that this change would eventually encompass, those who had the power and those who sought it found in the presence of street children a symbol over which claims for each side's positions could be made.

A new expression emerged, "losing the children to the streets," which became a metaphoric flag that identified the nature of this deeper struggle. The term was a paradoxical one. "The streets" were a nearly archetypal place of anonymity, where family name had no meaning, where family connections were worthless, but where one's personal abilities to get the job done were paramount to survival. "Children," on the other hand, belonged in families, where family name was essential to identity and participation in society.

With the presence of children on the streets, the families in jeopardy of losing power felt even more at risk. The street children questioned the tenets of the accepted forms of child rearing.

Within Colombia the two forms of child rearing created a dynamic tension not only between family structures but also between social classes. As Villar (1978) illustrated, the socially acceptable, class-dominant, Spanish patrifocal form of child rearing demanded that children stay close and loyal to their families. These families were patriarchally controlled. The lower social classes, with matriarchal family structures, allowed children to drift away from home and parental authority (Fromm and Maccoby 1970). Because of this dualism the street children were viewed as evidence that the need to be under the control of parents (in a form of compulsory dependence) was imperative.

After La Violencia both an abundance of children on the streets and a newly emerging civic politic existed. If the children had been seen as healthy, the irreplaceable necessity of the dominant family structure would have been jeopardized. Street children, if seen as functional, might well have debunked "family" as it was perceived from the patriarchal point of view. This was ample motivation to secure the common view that the children were unable to manage their lives and were in need of moral supervision. Thus the street children found themselves inheriting a particular social class and cultural struggle that put them and their families at center stage.

Matrifocal Africans and Patrifocal Spaniards

In a recent study funded by the government's national welfare agency (Pineda et al. 1978), the structure of poor families and women's place in them were described in terms that reinforced the commonly held beliefs about the origins of street children and the characteristics of their families. The authors claim that

the mother is the stable progenitor figure, placed in front of the family group as the result of the fruit of successive unions with men. The biological father almost always abandons his descendant and many times another man replaces him as father. In her status of covering the roles rejected by the man, the woman's job is very difficult and rarely successfully accomplished. The ambiance of the home is one of conflict between the stepfather and his stepchildren. This conflict also involves the mother. The pressing economic needs of the family, only semi-protected by the stepfather, threaten the family with dissension. When the domestic tranquility is threatened, the mother has to choose between working to protect and provide for her children or accepting the stepfather who can help her out of this economic difficulty. Very often she chooses the stepfather. The female status is very precarious in a labor force with very few options and the mother is confronted with the fact that if she is going to be economically active, she must also face the consequences of her children becoming gamines [the term is used here to indicate all street children]. The alternative, which is also very difficult, is that she chooses to live with her *compañero* [male friend] who works, but then her children, because of the tension that his presence creates, will still go to the streets. (Pineda et al. 1978, 12)

If this point of view was as salient as claimed, we would have been faced with much more psychopathology in the children than we found. Since our data showed many of the children to be functioning adequately, we carefully examined two points about the family expressed in the above view. The first was that the stepfathers were uniformly portrayed as negative. The second was that the women were portrayed as victims. Accepting these two points would have forced us into the same nondiscriminatory stance that, as we have seen, lumped all street children together. These points also needed further clarification. They did not explain why, when faced with identical sociological circumstances, only some children left home while the majority of them stayed.

Since the two family types—Spanish patrifocal and African matrifocal—represent not only different cultural traditions but also different sources of power in the society, there have always been tensions between them. Not the least of these is that the dominant patrifocal family was threatened by the dynamics of the mother-child bonds in the matrifocal family. This is why such bonds were considered to be not just different, but pathological or pitiful. This has resulted in a good deal of misconception about the matrifocal family and its children.

Peatrie's study (1968) of a poor and middle-class settlement outside of Caracas, Venezuela, described some important differences between these two types of families. The typical patriarchal family began with marriage in the Catholic church. It was composed of middle- and upper-class *Venezolanos*, whose families had the following characteristics:

> The husband is clearly the jefe of the family. The house and property are generally his, and the husband's economic and social role is highly status-defining for his wife and children. . . . The marriage is formal and consummated in the Church where relatives from both partners exchange kinship ties. The man is the head of the household and not only assumes economic responsibility for the home but also has the authority to determine the direction of child rearing. The kinship network surrounds and supports him for doing this. His wife and family are considered assets. He and his kinship ties have the power, authority, and responsibility to define and carry out the course of events that define the direction of "his family." (Peatrie 1968, 45)

This was nearly the opposite of what Peatrie found in the poor neighborhood. Here "the primary axis of kinship structure is the relationship between a mother and her children" (Peatrie 1968, 43). In the matrifocal family the relationships that were made beyond the woman's bond to her children were more like alliances than mergers of family or kin groups. Unions were consummated without legal, church, or even kinship sanctions. "Marriages" were bilateral, nonbinding agreements between two consenting adults. Even when the men in the matrifocal family had fathered a child, they were not always considered a part of the family. The nucleus of the family was the mother and her children. The father was given the status of family member only if the mother decided to give it to him. She gave and took away this status depending on his behavior and how she perceived that her needs and those of her children were being affected by him. "Marriages, especially common-law ones of the matrifocal type, may be and are, terminated by either party" (Peatrie 1968, 46). In this matrifocal barrio, marriages were most often broken when the woman left her husband, which she did if he was abusive, or if he sought other women. She was not only able to leave him, but more often he was told to leave her for whatever emotional reasons she found intolerable. Rather than making the family unhappy, the common-law, matrifocal family, because it allowed for an easier exclusion of abusive men, was often psychologically more healthy than the formal, patrifocal church marriage, where there was almost no option for divorce.

In Colombia the commonly accepted and erroneous notion was that a woman would not leave her husband because she was unable to live without a man's income. However, Peatrie discounts this: "The point must be made that for many women in La Laja, having a man in the house is no firm solution to the economic problem, either because the man is likely to be unskilled, to be employed intermittently, or to be expensive to keep in food and beer when out of work" (Peatrie 1968, 46). De Jesus's (1962) account of a Brazilian *favela* (a word used to describe a type of poor neighborhood in Brazil) near São Paulo also testified to a different set of options for women. She described the hardworking women of this favela as supporting, rather than being supported by their husbands. While women worked, husbands, she said, "remained at home under the blankets. Some because they can't find jobs, others because they are sick, others because they are drunk" (de Jesus 1962, 39). A World Bank report (Mohan 1980) stated that in Colombia the work force for unskilled men has become more competitive and restrictive, while unskilled female employment, because of the growing middle class and its need for service workers, has been enlarged. There are more opportunities in petty trade and domestic service for poorer women than there were a decade ago. This has often created more economic security for them than they have had in the past.

Even though the role of the poor woman in Latin America was generally perceived to be that of the victim, historical and contemporary studies of women in poor families have not always borne this out. In a historical review of the nature of family life in Peru, Ecuador, and Colombia from the sixteenth to the twentieth centuries, Jaquette (1976) questioned the presumed role of submissive women. She argued that there has been a long history of matrifocal families, headed not by stereotypical, submissive women, but by women in full command of their families and of civil affairs. Equally as noteworthy was the misconception of the man's role. Students of Latin America had been led to believe that the Andean man of Inca ancestry had been dominant in the family and in charge of civil affairs, but:

> In recent years, anthropologists and sociologists have discussed the character of the *chola* [Mestiza woman] in Andean towns and cities. She is depicted as a strong, willful woman, either Indian or Mestiza, aggressive economically and socially. She stands in sharp contrast to her *cholo* [Mestizo man] brother who is seen as drunk, bumbling, meek and not very bright. The sources of such differences, for they do not seem to exist only in the minds of scholars, have provoked little analysis. Most scholars avoid the question too easily, pointing their fingers to the latest and easiest explanation for everything: modernization. But reading through the records of the sixteenth century, researchers are struck with similarity in the picture of that era to modern times. The Indian man appears infrequently, and when he does, it is as criminal, field hand, drunkard, or lackey. Yet the Indigenous female emerges in an aggressive stance. Not only does she appear very often as servant, wife, or concubine, but also as author of a detailed will, prosecutor in a civil court case, and defender of her rights. The difference between the sexes is striking. (Burkett 1978, 117)

This difference is exactly the opposite of what we had been led to believe. The more commonly accepted view describes the contemporary Latin American woman as the male is depicted above.

More compensations are made by both men and women in these matrifocal families than were commonly assumed. And the relationship between spouses is not always the stereotypical woman as victim–man as abuser. One ethnographic study showed how the men and women of the eastern slope of the Colombian Andes have made family life different from the stereotype. "The picture of family life acquired from observation of the facts of family affairs and from the life stories told by people of Ita differs strikingly from the ideal picture of family relationships. Rather than the dominant male controlling and fully supporting his family, a woman is just as often the central figure of the household. Few men in Ita are as aggressive, even at the moment of discovered adultery on the part of their wives, as the picture of the dominant jealous Latin male has it" (Wagley 1976, 165).

Even the stereotype of the evil stepfather is belied by the evidence. One long-standing compensation for illegitimate children that Colombian peasant families have had, and in direct contradiction to the evil padrastro versus women-as-victim point of view, is the custom of *entenados*, adopting stepchildren. The following information on rural Colombian life explained how the phenomenon of entenados has traditionally helped to maintain, rather than break up family unity.

> No stigma is placed on a woman because of having had a child prior to marriage. Even if she does not marry the father of her child, she and her family continue to live a normal existence. When a new suitor comes, he is completely informed of the situation, and if he loves the woman, he is expected to take her children along. These semi-adopted children are called entenados, of which there are quite a few in Saucio. Neither ill feelings nor tensions are apparent in families having entenados. On the contrary, there is much solidarity and love among half brothers and half sisters, and the usual considerations and respect for both parents. (Fals-Borda 1955, 206)

Part of the confusion caused by using a single concept of family is that it brings about misconceptions because it ignores the cultural origins of the people involved. In Colombia there are descendants from Africans, indigenous Incas and Amazonians, Spaniards, and other Europeans. All these groups intermarried, forming all possible mixtures. However, because of the importance of social class and racial identity, two cultural family traditions emerged. One tradition was the Spanish, or European, and the other was the African and indigenous. The latter, of course, was the poorer of the two.

The Colombian families of the lower socioeconomic status —of more indigenous or African descent—showed "male kin marginality" (Siegal 1969), which meant that men were marginal to these homes. When present and appropriate they were valued, and the economic products of their labor were used. When either of these two factors was not present the men were asked to leave. Children, both boys and girls, were raised with a subjective, if not intellectual understanding of this. The mother was the source of wisdom, and her children turned to her when there were issues or dangers that had to be clarified. The girl child remained with her mother, perhaps until her mother, usually late in life (in her forties, as one study of Caribbean culture suggested [Mintz 1984]), was ready for a more permanent union with a man. Even if the girl became pregnant at puberty she often remained close to her mother, usually in the same home. Sometimes three generations of women lived in the same home.

The boy child in the matrifocal family faced an opposite scenario. He was socialized to leave home before puberty and to be independent of his mother. This ensured that by the time he reached puberty he would have had many experiences on his own away from home, and often with other children, on the streets. As he reached puberty his welcome at home depended on bringing in money and thus contributing as an adult. The mother was the source of wisdom during prepuberty and up until puberty, when she remained the person he could ask for clarification of experience.

In the middle and upper social classes the dominant family tradition was Spanish and patrifocal. Both boys and girls were encouraged to stay at home far longer, and neither left without the blessings of both parents. Boys learned from their fathers, usually in sanctioned social groups or clubs, how to be "men." The streets were out of bounds. Girls were socialized to be women by the mother, and they were only disciplined by the father when the mother sought his help. The father was considered to be the principal source of family wisdom, although the mother, in spite of her "inferior position," was on many occasions consulted in private about relationships between the sexes.

Thus, in the matrifocal family the woman's role as mother instead of wife was of primary if not sole importance. On the other hand, in the patrifocal family the woman was both mother and wife. This changed the role of the mother-son dyad, which was extremely important because this dyad often mirrored the roles the children would have as adult men and women, both separately and in relationships with each other. In the families that purportedly were producing street children (and which we are postulating are matrifocal), men were only serial companions to women until a woman reached middle age. Then they would join in a union that resembled marriage in terms of durability and effect (Mintz 1984).

A woman's relationship with her son had some similarities to her relationships with her serial companions. Her son, after his immediate dependency needs were met, was encouraged to leave home and be independent. When the son reached puberty the emotional ties of mother to son were lessened, and he was valued and held responsible in the home as an adult. Thus, only later in life, as an adult, after a son had made secure his own economic situation and was able to contribute to his mother's home, would the affective care he received before puberty be resumed. This prepared him for an adult male-female relationship in which the two parties would be independent. His expectations, at least during his early adult years, were not such that he assumed, ipso facto, that he would have an enduring relationship with one woman.

In the patrifocal family the mother cared for her son, often excessively demanding his attention and obedience. This often created a dependence on her that mirrored her dependence on her husband. Contributing to this was the role of the father, who controlled the extent to which the son was dependent on his mother. The father saw to it that his son was not made overly dependent and a "sissy" by the indulgent, emotional mother. This, too, mirrored the adult relationships between men and women that the boy was likely to inherit. He treated women as if they would be overly emotional and potentially controlling, which he wanted but knew was inappropriate. He was taught that men should be in rational control of their emotions. He had learned that women tended to pamper men, who were allowed to bathe in their emotions only in private. In public men, and even pubescent boys, were expected to shun such extravagances.

Studying these two forms of family life helped us to understand why men and women have been described so differently in the Latin American literature. The dominant class in Colombian society had the ability to influence public attitudes and policy.

Underneath the lack of recognition given to the matrifocal family in Colombia was the belief that it was dangerous to the welfare of the male's role in the patrifocal society. The matrifocal family gave the conjugal unit less value, thus rearing girls and boys to expect that the relationship between husband and wife had less importance and was less necessary. "What we find is a priority of emphasis placed upon the mother, child and sibling relationships, while the conjugal relationship is expected to be less important and less affectively intense. It is this aspect of familial relations which is crucial in producing matrifocal family structure" (Tanner 1974, 156).

Under the matrifocal system girls were socialized to become independent of men, since girls were taught to look for their identity without being dependent on intimate relationships with men. This posed quite a threat to the integrity of the patrifocal family, which saw the conjugal relationship as the basis of their family's ties and the backbone that instilled and maintained authority and obedience within the family. The conjugal relationship was also important for the patrifocal family in defining the family publicly and placing it within a hopefully higher stratum of the civic order, hence the overweighted value Colombians placed on the *apellido*, the father's family name.

Matrifocality was viewed as pathological rather than as a different and equally valuable way of child rearing. These views came from a defensive posture and were expressed as an ethnocentric notion that a family structure other than one's own was not just different but must be flawed. As the children of matrifocal families sought entry into society, they created tension in the civic politic, which contributed to the pejorative view of them and their families.

Street children did not arise because their mothers were victims of poverty or dependent on men. The padrastros did not have total power to disrupt the lives of their mates or abuse their children or those of another union. Street children were developing normally in matrifocal homes in a tradition of urban poverty. It is not accurate to say that they were a result of pathological families. Given this information, we are ready to examine the apparent fact that street children were exclusively boys.

Girls in the Streets

Although there were some programs for street children in Colombia that offered assistance to girls, it was considerably more difficult to find programs or literature about them than it was for boys (International Catholic Child Bureau 1984). There were street girls in Colombia, but they were not recognized as such because in the eyes of those making this classification they occupied another psychological niche.

The popular notion in Colombia was that girls without homes were prostitutes. Even though the girls who were in the streets were defined as sex objects or as vendors of sexual favors, the reason for the prostitute hypothesis had more to do with the fear they elicited in the larger society than it did with the facts of their lives. The definition of street children has always included some pejorative qualities. The boys are defined as delinquent or psychopathological and the girls as prostitutes. This pattern is neither random nor accurate.

Such misconceptions illustrate certain fears that were associated with the larger issues concerning street children. Since street girls may have altered the interpersonal relationships between men and women in the existing patrifocal family system, they were portrayed as sexual deviants, while fear of errant boys was related to their possible menace to the perceived safety of property, person, and the civic order.

The niche that defined all street children was dependent on specific gender roles as defined in a patrifocal-dominant society. Certain actions committed by boys classified them as delinquent, while the same actions by girls classified them as prostitutes. The adjective "irresponsible" was often used to define the psyches of street children. In Colombia boys were irresponsible if they didn't go to school, while girls were not expected to go. Boys were irresponsible if they engaged in premarital sex, but only *really* irresponsible if the girls got pregnant, while girls were irresponsible right from the start. Playing aggressively on the streets, being dirty, wearing ragged clothes, experimenting with drugs, or sneaking into the movie theaters were all socially irresponsible actions for boys, ruining them for future roles as reliable workers. The same actions for girls were signs that they were spoiling their purity, making them undesirable as women and mothers.

This patrifocal view of appropriate adult gender roles was reflected in the institutions that served the street children. The most common programs for girls were private "homes." These were often run under the direction of nuns, applying the rubric of Christianity in an effort to change wayward girls into women less frivolous about their bodies. They concentrated on changing the girl's character. In contrast, homes for boys centered on vocational training. Institutions for boys made themselves visible to the public, and they sought media attention to compete for funds. Institutions set up to serve girls operated more like convents. They remained difficult to find, rarely seeking and usually trying to avoid public attention.

Girls did occasionally appear in Bosconia. On one occasion during lunchtime a girl of about twelve was sitting on the ledge with a small boy in her lap, picking lice out of his hair. He, in turn, was lying on her stomach with his hands limply over her legs. On his face was a smile of extreme contentment. There was nothing overtly sexual about the two of them, yet his body, which was limp with satisfaction, reminded me of a postclimactic relaxation. Physically, she had a developed bosom that was covered by a long shirt reaching almost to her knees. She had no other clothes or shoes on and her body was covered with dirt. Her dark, Negroid hair was dirty and matted. After a while an older boy, more her size, sat next to her and began to demand her attention. The small boy was forced off her lap and, although the larger one wanted the same attention, she ignored his demands and stared off into the distance until he finally left her alone. Since I had not, up to that point, seen a girl in any kind of interaction with the boys at Bosconia, I did not immediately realize that she was female. It was as if she was not really present because she was a girl. More from the posture of the boy on her lap than from her own appearance, it slowly began to dawn upon me that she was not a boy. If it were not for this I would have been unaware of the presence of a girl who was clearly part of the street culture.

One person who worked with street girls said that "since girls have something to market they choose to sell their bodies rather than live as poor street children." Behind this were several possible assumptions: either street life was so unbearably difficult that a girl would rather sell herself than live on the streets; or, since girls were not capable of defending themselves, they would be sold into sexual slavery, or literally raped, and then from necessity assume a life of prostitution. Neither our evidence nor common sense allowed us to believe that these generally held assumptions were accurate. For one thing upon examining the numbers of street children, we would have expected many more prostitutes than there were. If there are forty million street children in Latin America (Tacon 1981a, 1981b; Betancur 1983), then nearly half of the forty million would be girls, and if only half went the way that was presented to us as inevitable, there would have been ten million prostitutes in Latin America. Taking the more conservative estimate of the numbers of street children in Colombia used by de Galán (1981), approximately 4 percent of the Colombian population, then almost 500,000 children would have been street children. Conservatively then, that would mean that there would have been a quarter of a million girl "prostitutes" in Colombia. These figures are, of course, way out of bounds.

There were similar assumptions about homosexuality. Homosexuality, according to those who proclaimed it to be widespread, was the result of the inability of small boys to protect themselves. Defenseless, they sold their bodies for physical and economic security. It was far more likely that boys would avoid this at all costs, as it represented a step over a line that had considerable negative consequences.

If the definition of "prostitution" refers to prostitution that was organized, situated in a fixed place, and involved older people who for a price solicited for the girls, then prostitution was in fact a very minor part of the lives of street children. Another possible view of the phenomenon was less pathological. In this case the girl asked for some type of remuneration in exchange for sexual favors, either food, a place to stay, or money, which was then used for her necessities. This last possibility, particularly if it was not done regularly as a life-style, but out of periodic necessity or as part of a serial partner arrangement, carried few of the emotive qualities associated with the first definition. This was more common.

The problem of ascertaining the number of prostitutes below

age seventeen was as difficult as ascertaining the number of boys below the age of seventeen who were homosexuals, even if a definition could have been agreed upon. Obviously, very few people put such titles down for an occupation on a census or a social science research report. Thus, who and what the public was referring to was very complex. The way the term prostitute was used, to whom it was intended to apply and for what reasons, ended up giving us just as much information about those who were using the term as it did about the people for whom it was intended. We knew there were girls on the streets, but they were labeled as prostitutes, not street children. This gave us very little information about the girls beyond the fact that they, like the boys, were viewed pejoratively. Several possible reasons were given for not including girls in the definition of street children.

One was that they were socialized differently than boys. The matrifocal homes that we have described did not have boys over the age of puberty living at home. By the time they reached puberty boys had secured enough *contratas* (benefactors) to become independent. On the other hand, girls well past puberty were still encouraged to see their mother's home as their own. Since they had been socialized to stay at home, girls in the streets from matrifocal families might well have been more pathological. But this did not mean that their only choice was prostitution. There were in fact several work options open to girls that were not available to boys, such as domestic service. This indicates that prostitution was more of a choice than a necessity due to family disintegration or economic need.

Although girls were socialized to remain at home, as indeed most did, it is also valid to say that some girls were socialized into street life in the sense that their mothers were often street vendors or street marketers. The young girls not only routinely accompanied their mothers, thus gaining access to life on the streets, but they were also instructed by their mothers to wander off and scavenge things that could be marketed, or simply to beg for alms. Our most frequent view of girls on the streets was of them begging, but upon closer examination we usually discovered that the girl was within a few hundred yards of her mother, and was acting on her instructions. Felsman (1981a), in his ethnographic study of Colombian street children, often saw girls who

The twelve-year-old girl in this photograph is not the mother of the girl in her lap. She is her older sister. The mother was three blocks away and had taught her daughter how to ask for alms under the guise of a child mother.

were apparently alone on the streets but he noted that they were close to their mothers.

As already suggested, it was very difficult to discern by appearance the difference between many street children and child workers who were involved in similar activities but had happy family lives. Although it is partially true to say that there were fewer street girls because they were socialized to stay at home, "home" in the matrifocal family structure was often away from the house. When the mothers went to the streets to become vendors they brought their girls with them, giving them plenty of opportunity to be socialized to street life. Thus, girls were indeed socialized to work on the street, not as prostitutes but as child workers. There were many girls on the streets who looked like orphaned street children. In fact, many were purposely taught to dress and act like street children. They begged, they committed petty thievery, and they were often quite dirty. In short, many girls who did not leave their matrifocal families were doing the same things as the boy street children.

Another reason that girls were not defined as street children, in addition to the notion that the girls were socialized to stay at home, has to do with gender differences in cognitive styles. The dimensions of field dependence and field independence refer to the cognitive styles of people who are either capable of working independent of background information or who are consumed by, or dependent on, the irrelevant background. There is some evidence that girls are more field dependent than boys (Witkin and Berry 1975). Since girls are considered more field dependent, it was thought that their cognitive style helped them adapt to their homes and made them less able to cope with the demands of street life, which entail a good deal of field-independent skills. Felsman's (1981a) adaptation of the embedded figures tests made it clear that the boys on the street were very field independent. But it is less clear if there is a difference in field independence due to differences in gender, and if there is, how important this might be in accounting for fewer street girls.

Minturn and Lambert (1964) indicate that there is a great deal of diversity in child-rearing practices, and different cognitive styles, not only between but within cultures. Their data, as well as that of Berry (1976), suggest that subcultural factors related to child rearing in any one culture are quite important in determining cognitive style. Berland pointed out that gender differences with regard to cognitive style are not uniform across cultures, or within cultures, and are not biologically based. Such differences depend on the particular experiences of child rearing. In fact, he noted that "while biological mechanisms undoubtedly contribute to perceptual and cognitive functioning, their effect appears to be mediated through social and cultural experiences" (Berland 1982, 177). The cross-cultural evidence does not suggest that there is a gender difference, with boys being more field independent than girls. Since it was quite typical for girls to be seen in the streets doing the same things as the boys, they should have been operating, as Felsman has shown for the boys, quite field independently. The girls assumed child care for their younger siblings. They were frequently left alone to fend for themselves while their mothers were working, during which time they were expected to function in a manner that was often developmentally well ahead of their female counterparts in patrifocal families. There is no evidence to suggest that the girls were less field independent than the boys. What differences there might have been are not large enough to have impeded girls from entering street life, or to account for the presumed gender difference.

Another hypothesis suggested to explain why there were no girl street children is that girls develop more contextually, or within personal relationships, than boys, who develop more in direct relation to objects or to the outside world, which they will inherit as workers (Gilligan 1977, 1979). This might have been partly applicable; however, our evidence suggested that the boys did develop within contextual relationships. They were with other boys in the streets, on whom they relied for survival and enjoyment.

One reason that was given to support the idea that there were no girl street children was that the padrastros forced the boys out of their homes in order to have the girls in the home without other males. The tensions that resulted from this should have caused girls to leave home also, since their fear of sexual abuse from stepfathers would have been higher. It probably did cause some of them to leave. However, since the majority did not leave, our contention—that in the matrifocal home it was generally the stepfather, and not the girl child who was forced out by the mother—was supported. His place in the matrifocal home was only temporary and lasted only as long as his behavior pleased the woman who had agreed to let him in her home in the first place.

By the time the street boys were young men they had had many experiences with contratas, informal arrangements with benefactors that were easily dissolved by either party. As young men assuming the role of stepfather, the arrangement made with a woman to live in her home was only another in a series of contratas. Given their developmental histories these men (or even late adolescent street boys) were aware that they were making a temporary arrangement that would continue only as long as it was beneficial to their woman benefactor. This knowledge would temper their supposedly irresponsible attitudes toward their stepchildren.

Inasmuch as the stepfather was not really a stepfather, that is, he did not assume the same role of father seen in a patriarchal family, he may have played a much smaller role as a causative agent for either boys or girls to leave their families than was normally assumed. The psychoanalytic perspective of oedipal tensions could have explained some of the problems between stepfathers and non–blood sons, but this explanation also assumed the cultural context of patrifocal families. Viewing padrastros within the matrifocal cultural context, they could be seen merely as older street children who had found another benefactor, not on the street or the premises of another person's property, but from a woman in a matrifocal household. From this perspective, only those women who were willing to rupture the integrity of their families would allow the stepfather to win in this hypothetical struggle for her favor. Although this happened, it was the exception to the rule.

In matrifocal families the padrastros would have affected the girls more adversely than the boys. Since the boys would have been socialized to leave the family early, it would have been easier for them to adjust to being forced out on the streets. The girls, who belonged in the matrifocal home, would have to be driven out. It may well have been that girls, rather than being the victims of padrastros, were coping rather well in homes where their mothers were not allowing them to be abused by stepfathers. Thus, padrastos and oedipal tensions, although occasionally significant, were not overwhelmingly responsible for either girls or boys going to the streets. This theory thus does not adequately explain the gender difference in street children.

Chodorow's psychoanalytic perspective gives some important reasons why girls did not flaunt their sense of independence from their families as the boy gamines did. "It seems likely that from their children's earliest childhood, mothers and women tend to identify more with daughters and to help them differentiate less [find earlier independence less easily], and that processes of separation and individualization are made more difficult for girls. Women in patrilineal societies, if they are oppressed, often express this resentment against their sons while their daughters become allies against male oppression" (Chodorow 1974, 48). From this point of view, the girls who were on the streets would have resembled the chupagruesos more than the gamines, in that they would have been less likely to define themselves as being opposed to authority. The chupagruesos, like the girl street children, posed little threat to authority and thus appeared more like child workers instead of "street children." Girl child workers could be devalued by labeling them prostitutes just as the boy child workers were devalued by labeling them delinquents.

Gutiérrez (1972a), in discussing the issue of the prevalence of boys on the streets, emphasized the phenomena of rebellion and submission that characterized the two forms of street life, the gamine and chupagrueso. For the boys on the streets the motivation became how to establish an identity different from what was expected of them. They fought between two extremes: either they accepted the role of servant to the authorities or to the wealthier class, which is what the chupagruesos did, or they struck out against authority, as the gamines did by opposing this exploitation. By acting submissively, the chupagruesos were not much different from the stereotypical girl house servant, who either accepted a demeaning attitude from her employer or possibly lost her opportunity to become independent. If the girls were to rebel, thus becoming gamines (which we think some did), they might rebel in another way than by taking to the streets.

Boys on the streets made a public display of opposition to the traditional adult roles open to them. Their conspicuously dirty appearance, their flirtation with the dangerous, and their cunning thievery all took place in full public view. These acts were, at least in part, a symbolic defiance against the predictable routines of conventionally accepted, mature, male adult life. It was not hunger or family disintegration that impelled them to be so public in their displays, but defiance and rebellion against the inevitability of inheriting the lowest places in an economy that forced them into servitude. The boys "form a type of miniature guerrilla band at large on the urban areas of Colombia" (Gutiérrez 1972b, 45). They were perceived by the public as potential disruptions to the stratified society and many sniping remarks were aimed at defeating their attempts to live as independently as they did. The boys' existence was a fragile one and, like all guerrillas, they lived between the battles imposed upon them by their biggest enemy, the state.

Matrifocal families in Colombia, without political power or

public status, were less of a threat to the state, but they were an enemy to the traditional male-dominated family structure. The girls' struggle was not with the nature of the work force or with the body politic, but with men who might oppress them. They thus had less reason to go into the streets. That they were perceived as prostitutes indicated that their potential threat was viewed as more personal than civic, as a disruption of the sanctioned relations between men and women. The boys, who were perceived as delinquents or guerrillas, were viewed appropriately more as political liabilities, as possible disruptions to the economic disparities. In this context there was little sense in calling girls *street* children. Given all the reasons usually associated with girls not being on the street, none was more germane than the fact that their battles were more interpersonal than civic.

Those few girls who became prostitutes may have demonstrated, in a self-defeating way, a form of self-effacing rebellion similar to that of the chupagrueso. It is more likely that the majority of girls who sought independence from the domination of patrifocality were not prostitutes. But as they struggled to identify their relationships to their future husbands, less as victims and more as the independent women they saw in their mothers, they were motivated and behaving in much the same way as gamines. These girls were taking on the role played by street children when they assumed an independence from their preordained future roles as wife and mother in a patrifocal society. The lack of girls on the streets was because they did not have to seek their adult identities outside of the home. Coming from matrifocal families in a patrilineal society, the girls were learning from their mothers, while they stayed at home or accompanied them in the streets, to be self-sufficient, and not to be submissive to, or victims of, men.

Living Marginally in Barrios and Suburbios

Following La Violencia of 1948, the process of modernization radically increased the flow of people to the cities, where for the first time many of them encountered life in a cash economy. This migration, which was both a physical and cultural journey, dramatically changed the lives of rural peasants by making them a part of the modern industrial world. In the generally accepted scenario, these migrants found themselves caught between their traditions and the demands of their new urban life. They were without skills to compete in a modern urban economy. Families lost their capacity to maintain themselves and broke apart. In their demise they produced street children.

Unfortunately, this faulty train of thought also led to inaccurate and pejorative statements about the kinds of families and neighborhoods that produced street children. Both the children and the neighborhoods where they lived were labeled *marginada* (marginal), a word that implied that they were unnecessary, if not unwanted.

> In Latin America, the growing number of unskilled, semi-skilled and abysmally poor urbanites are often called the "marginadas." The term is apt. The people to whom it is applied are economically marginal, in that they contribute little to and benefit little from production and economic growth. Their social status is low, and they are excluded from the formal organizations and associations and the informal and private webs of contacts which constitute the urban social structure. To the extent that they are rural in origin, they may be culturally marginal, clinging to customs, manners, dress, speech, and values which contrast with accepted urban patterns. They lack ties to or influence on the established political institutions. Many are marginal in a geographical sense, living in squatter settlements on the fringes of the cities. (Nelson 1969, 101)

The above quote makes several claims about the people who are referred to as marginadas. Among these is that rural-to-urban migration causes such severe problems of adjustment that it precipitates family disintegration and produces street children who are the products of this turmoil. Representing this point of view, Muñoz and Pachón say that "the majority of the children interviewed are children of rural migrants who have had difficulty adapting to urban life" (1980, 102). Yet our data, as well as that of other authors, showed that most street children were not rural children recently arrived in the city. "A gamine, boy or girl, has an origin in a neighborhood or a large city. There is a small percentage of gamines who come from small cities or from the country, but in general they are urban children from the large populous cities" (Villota 1979, 473).

Téllez's study of the origins of Colombian street children reported that "53.7 percent of the gamines were born in Bogotá and Cundinamarca [another large city], while 46.3 percent are migrants from the rest of the country. They have come alone or with their families, but always from their capital cities or from other cities of more than 50,000" (1976, 37). In another study that examined the origins of the people who occupied the poor areas of the city, further evidence is given that street children were not recently arrived rural migrants. "Some migrants to El Carmen [a poor barrio near Bogotá] are peasants but a significant number also come from towns, while others are native-born residents to the city. Most of the migrants moved a short distance to Bogotá but only 22 percent of the immigrants were born in population centers of less than 20,000 and moved directly to the shantytown fringe" (Flinn 1968, 88). Rather than wandering the streets in àn aimless manner as a result of being confused and defeated by the process of rapid cultural change and modernization, the children were discovering their own niche, finding and creating their own employment, in an existing cultural milieu of urban poverty.

Part of the modernization hypothesis concerns the economic skills of the recent migrants. A World Bank report on immigration to Bogotá made it clear that it was ill advised to accept the popular notion about who the migrants were.

> Migrants are not essentially poor; they do not concentrate in specific areas of the city, the center or the periphery; they are not concentrated in particular occupations or activities, they are not less educated, nor perhaps less skilled than the natives [in Bogotá]. Such are the indications from the data counter to the popular ideas of poor migrants streaming into the city. That more of them are poor is merely a reflection of more of the whole country as well as the city being poor. Furthermore, there is little evidence that they are disadvantaged in the job market. One might even say that they are basically "normal"

people and consequently the less urban poverty problems are associated with migrants the better will be the chance of alleviating it, or at least analyzing it. (Mohan 1980, 7–8)

What, then, is the economic condition and the style of life in the marginal areas of the city? First of all, there is more than one type of poor settlement and more variety in the poor urban areas than was commonly believed. Leeds (1974) mentioned eight different types of poor neighborhoods in Latin America, including *favelas, turgios, barrios, suburbios,* and *invasiones.* Although these terms were popularly used interchangeably in Latin America, according to Leeds all of them were different with respect to rural-urban migration, economic well-being, and in their interrelationships with the larger society. The economies of these poor areas were more complex than generally perceived. Our study distinguished between two types of poor neighborhoods, *barrios* and *suburbios.* The poorest neighborhoods were in the central part of the city (barrios), while the newer slums (suburbios) were on the outskirts of the city. Even though they were referred to as marginada, both were well integrated into the national economy. "Immigrants who possess financial assets and skills tend to settle in the shantytown fringes [suburbios]. Thus the clandestine area in this study [on the outskirts of Bogotá] appears to be a 'shantytown suburb.' Though definitely not a 'middle class suburb,' the area represents a higher socioeconomic level than the transition zone and the working man's barrios of the central city" (Flinn 1968, 88).

On a windy day I went with a Colombian architect to the top of a large hill about seven hundred feet above Cali. Below, nestled in the protection of a valley, we could see a small settlement of about five hundred people, who were occupying what could be referred to as a suburbio. My friend described how, two years earlier, several families who knew each other moved here, onto what was then a deserted piece of land. These migrants, as was often the case, came from another area of the same city, where they had settled after moving farther from the center of town. They had seen this latest move as a form of homesteading, a way to better their condition. Having no money but plenty of time to build a home, they were not much different from other homesteaders or immigrants who also had dreams of improving their condition in life. Soon they had constructed the minimum of housing, which consisted of no more than cardboard frames. Shortly afterward they began to tap the nearest electrical lines for power. During this time they carried water from the closest public pipes.

After some additional time passed other people moved in and the settled area got larger. A sense of community began. A make-shift church started to give communion, offer them minimal health care, and provide them with some education for their children. As we looked down, we could see that some children were carrying water while their parents walked down what was now a well-traveled path to the center of town, where they sought and often located work. Men found work as vendors or helped with construction projects in the downtown area, while the women worked as domestics for established families. Community groups were formed, and by developing some political skills they began to lobby for roads, schools, and other services. As they prospered, the government pressed them for land titles that they did not have. But they refused to leave the land and gained support in numbers and in organization. The government was placed in the position of having to either remove them or grant them some form of title to the land. Granting titles in these circumstances was often the response of other Latin American governments, who did so rather than face the political fallout of ejecting such groups. Eventually, in this and other suburbios, roads were built, sewers put in, electricity installed, and bus routes moved closer. All such changes contributed toward making these residents a part of the national economy.

The strength of the purchasing power of a similar, but larger suburbio outside of Caracas was estimated to be on the order of $200 million per year (Peatrie 1968). Another study in Bogotá "calculates the formation of capital only in dwellings in squatter settlements and 'private urbanization settlements' [another descriptor for suburbios] as equal to $146 million" (Departamento Nacional de Planeacion 1978, 80).

An accurate description of a barrio, as opposed to a suburbio, would place it in a central part of the city in an old and established neighborhood. Bogotá runs north and south and is divided by the central downtown area, which is still the major place for commerce, banking, and government. The northern edge of the downtown area has expanded to include the older, middle-class areas. Farther north are newly emerging areas where the more prosperous middle class was building. To the south of downtown were the barrios, areas that long ago had been without adequate housing and facilities. Decades earlier they had started as suburbios in a fashion similar to the one described above; now they were definite communities—poor, but with churches, hospitals, and schools, and within easy reach of employment. They were overcrowded in part because relatives had moved from the rural areas in greater numbers than those who had chosen to leave, and in part because many people had chosen to remain where they were, either too old or too content to move.

Neither barrios nor suburbios were single-class communities. The level of economic self-sufficiency was quite varied; some people were very poor, others were upwardly mobile, and some had established a comfortable level of working-class stability. Although there was a great deal of unemployment in the suburbios when compared with unemployment in the larger society or in the central parts of the city, it was not excessive. "My little barrio [suburbio in our nomenclature] for example, at the time I censused it in 1963, had a third of the adult males out of work. But, the situation locally was not strikingly different from that in the city as a whole, and indeed nationally" (Peatrie 1977, 102).

As important as the differing economic levels in these areas was the existence of an informal way of redistributing the wealth within the communities. "In squatter settlements, as among other groups of people with low and intermittent monetary incomes, networks of mutual help develop, often of kin, within which goods and services may be exchanged outside of the framework of the market" (Peatrie 1977, 104).

It was generally assumed that the people who lived in barrios and suburbios had different cultural values than those of the larger society. People in the barrios and suburbios where we did our study were hardly marginal with respect to the national culture. Their clothing and hairstyles were imitations of the latest in Bogotá's fanciest areas. Jeans were equally as visible in the poor settlements of our study as they were in the wealthiest of social clubs. The parents of our street children shopped in some of the same stores, occasionally attended the same movies, often went to the same hospitals, and used the same buses as the great majority of people in the city. Peatrie (1977) noted that the people in her study outside of Caracas were quite similar in this respect. Mangin's study in Peru likewise noted that "not only do squatters do much of the service work of the city, but they also patronize the movies, bars, soccer games, musical tent shows, tv broadcasts and other amusements. They attend Catholic and Protestant services. Without exception education ranks near the top on the list of desiderata for children in every area referred to in this survey. Newspapers and magazines sell in large numbers in squatter settlements and transistor radios and plug-in radios are in practically every house" (1967, 78).

Although the prevailing view of the people in these neighborhoods was that they were helpless and hopeless, they had developed a much better way of life than they were given credit for. They also showed great coping skills, such as in the creation of informal economic networks that were in many cases perfect examples of small-scale businesses (Lomnitz 1977; Peatrie 1977). Their coping skills were also expressed in their adaptations to child-rearing practices, which they altered by fully utilizing their children as child caretakers. They coped with cramped space by making changes in housing arrangements that gave them more room (Mintz 1984).

However, many times these coping skills were not well understood by outsiders and therefore were judged inaccurately. For example, in the description of the Mexican kinship system of *cuatismo* (close friends of the same sex), Lomnitz (1974) demonstrated that drinking, rather than being solely a vice or a reaction to a frustrating life, also involved a process of mutual aid.

> Drinking relationships amongst *cuates* [close friends] are exceedingly important. . . . From a psychological point of view, drinking together is a token of absolute mutual trust which involves a baring of souls to each other. From an economic point of view, cuatismo implies a mechanism of redistribution through drink which ensures that all cuates remain economically equal. And from a social point of view, it reinforces existing social networks and extends the influence of networks in

many directions, since a drinking circle may contain members of several networks. (Lomnitz 1974, 151)

This is not to say that drunkenness was not a problem, surely it was, but drinking also served as a mechanism to redistribute what little wealth there was, as well as a way to develop important relationships between friends that fostered what Lomnitz referred to as a "duty of assistance" to one another. The street children, particularly in their camadas, where they developed their informal and friendly manner of dividing their goods through the system of pormis, were following the cultural pattern of the urban poor. Their coping skills had developed to serve particular needs, a fact the larger society did not always understand.

The groups of street children and the poor urban areas where they lived were not composed of alienated and isolated people. Even those without good incomes, or much chance of getting one, had either blood relatives, extended families, or cuates to assist them. In the case of the few street children who did not have access to their families, extended families, or friends of their extended families, the camadas constituted a supportive network of friends that helped them to cope with their poverty and gave them a personal space to call home.

Although the poverty of the suburbios and the barrios was no doubt a partial cause of children being abandoned or abandoning their families, it cannot explain the phenomenon in full. Only a small number of children from families living in these conditions were not living at home. By one estimate about 5 percent of the children in Colombia were street children, whereas almost one-third of the population lived in conditions of poverty. Using the statistics from de Galán (1981), which she took from the ICBSF national study, we have made the following calculations. Of the twenty-six million Colombians, almost twelve million, nearly 50 percent, are below the age of eighteen. One-third of twenty-six million calculates to eight and one-half million people living in poverty. The arithmetic also shows that there are over four million children living in poverty. Only 5 percent of these four million poor children, or 200,000, are street children. These figures are greater than those found in Felsman's study (1981a) of Colombian street children. About 20 percent, or one in five of the children in his sample, who were from the same homes, with identical economic and cultural conditions, lived on the streets.

The hypotheses that pointed to urban poverty, rural-to-urban migration, and different cultural values of poor urban dwellers as being the sources of street children must be viewed with caution. Not only did the assumptions about poverty, urban migration, and cultural values fail to explain the source of street children, they also failed to take into account individual differences. Why was it that only some children (anywhere from 5 to 20 percent, depending on the source of the data) in the same family became street children, and why did only some families in these circumstances produce street children? The prevailing hypotheses emanated from and expressed some essential differences between the two different cultural groups in Colombian society. We have concluded that most street children were not abandoned. What was being referred to as abandonment and neglect was a method of child rearing that was deliberate and helpful in training children to be independent and self-assured in the existing subculture of urban poverty.

The poor urban families that allegedly produced street children had a functional approach to child rearing that helped their children in the most productive and likely ways to find a place in the adult world. If the child-rearing practices of these families were not such a threat to the patrifocal family structure, then they might have received appropriate support so that the children would have been considered part of the labor force. An ombudsman was suggested by Cobos (1979) in his government-authorized study of ways to help Colombian street children, but his plan was never implemented. Instead of having an ombudsman to offer economic opportunities and to protect them, the government attitude suggested that something had to be done to get them back in line, to curtail their early independence. At the heart of society's attitude was the question of authority and conformity to the patriarchal family in precarious control of a newly emerging and more meritocratic society.

Since the use of the word abandonment implied a morally repugnant act on the part of the caretakers who were abandoning their children, its use by a large part of society could be seen to have a political focus. To be accused of abandoning a child had a clearly reproachable moral connotation: the accused received a devalued status, a place in society close to the bottom. Likewise, a child who was considered to be abandoned would automatically have had a history of being with an immoral or otherwise pitiful parent(s). Therefore, "abandoned children" were in need of assistance, which must include moral training, or more appropriately, a moral reeducation.

Abandonment without Malice

A more detailed phenomenology of abandonment can now be described. Three different parent-child interactions that increased the likelihood of children assuming a street life were defined in this study. In the first of these interactions abandonment was passive; the child was merely allowed to roam the neighborhood and to find his company as he saw fit. No emotional pressures from their families to stay at home or to stay away were put on these children. The children were neither neglected nor actively pushed away. In some cases parents accepted that being on the streets, and away from home, had its value and place in the education of their children. As has been pointed out in the Caribbean, with its matrifocal, African traditions, the areas away from the house, far enough away to be out of sight from parents, are not considered outside of the protected area called home (Mintz 1984).

This is similar to what Fromm and Maccoby (1970) found in their study of a poor indigenous Mexican barrio. Children were not considered extremely vulnerable and therefore they did not need to be protected by their mothers from harsh experiences. The authors found that large numbers of children were allowed to roam away from home at an early age. They were either left to care for themselves or left in the care of older siblings who were often no more than seven or eight years old. This was almost the opposite of the attitudes toward child rearing found in the dominant class. The authors noted that this difference between child-rearing practices made for tension between the two social classes.

The same kind of child rearing existed in Colombia and Brazil,

which, along with Mexico, are the three Latin American countries that have the highest incidence of street children. In Oscar
Lewis's *La Vida* (1965), Fernanda, a Mexican mother, demonstrated an apparent lack of concern for her children, an apparent
neglect of them at all times except when they were hurt or hungry. She allowed them to roam about, coming and going seemingly as they wanted. De Jesus (1962) wrote quite lovingly about
her children in a poor São Paulo favela (suburbio in our nomencla-
ture). She allowed them to leave the homesite much earlier than
would be acceptable generally in the United States and Brazil.
Nevertheless, de Jesus accepted this as a functional way of child
rearing. During the times her children were roaming the neighborhood, learning what would be necessary for them to survive in
their cultural circumstances, de Jesus, with exemplary motherly
care, was working to support them as an urban gatherer who collected scraps to resell at a profit. In fact, rather than neglecting
her children, it was her extreme care for them that made her auto-
biographical account so poignant.

The assumed connection between parental rejection and abandonment is culturally specific, and it is difficult to assume willy-
nilly that the connection existed in the poor urban areas of
Colombia. When parental rejection is connected to abandonment, we agree with the findings of the cross-cultural work of
Rohner (1975) that the experience is never benign. But there
often is a difference between being away from the family at a
rather young age and being abandoned, that is, rejected. One reason why street children were allowed to wander away from their
parents was that their siblings often assumed a good deal of the
child-rearing responsibilities. Although cross-cultural research
in Third World countries indicates that nonparental caretaking is
either the norm or represents a significant amount of caretaking
in most of these societies, this phenomenon was rarely taken into
account in Colombia, where the information was presented
through the point of view of the patriarchal family structure.
This is particularly unfortunate because Ainsworth (1967) has
shown that separation from one's mother and from one's home
was less stressful for young children exposed to a multiple-
caretaking environment than to children who were raised only by
adults. In Whiting and Whiting's cross-cultural child study

(1975), the authors concluded that children taking care of younger children (as opposed to solely adult care of children) promoted the development of prosocial, responsible, and nurturant behavior. As shown in the photo on page 169, it was not uncommon for us to see a young boy or girl of ten or so begging while simultaneously taking care of one of their younger siblings. As this child caretaker grew older and left home at twelve or thirteen, it might well have been something different from being "abandoned." She would have been more like an adolescent beginning to leave her family and starting to assume adulthood in a quest for her identity than a twelve- or thirteen-year-old rejected child.

When siblings take care of siblings instead of children being attended by their parents, developmental stages are altered. Street children did not leave home, as a rule, before the age of eleven or twelve, at which time they were no longer in early or even middle childhood, but closer to early adolescence. By this time the children in our study had slowly learned what life was like away from the home, being allowed to come back to it when they needed the affection or attention that it gave them, and being neither rejected by their parent(s) nor forced to leave the home before they were ready. This gradual testing of the waters, which is what is implied by the passive form of abandonment, was really an early search for an appropriate subcultural identity.

Given this gradual move into the streets, we saw the camadas as a form of support. Mead (1968) observed that in societies where caretaking relied less on parents and more on children there was often a "fostering group" of peers. This peer group forms a "barrier between parents and the child and creates greater similarity in personality across children and less similarity between parents and their offspring" (Weisner and Gallimore 1977, 178). Thus, through the normative child-rearing practices of matriarchal Colombian families, which involved an acceptance of children leaving home early and of older children taking care of their younger siblings, the street children had, by age twelve or thirteen, several years of experience on the streets and caretaking responsibility. This contributed to their maturation and they were, in comparison to those children who did not have these experiences, well advanced in terms of their psychosocial development. On the other hand, in the wealthier social classes a maid, who often was a teen-aged girl from a matrifocal family experienced in child care, took on the role as caretaker for younger children and thus deprived these children of an early independence.

The street children, helped by their fostering groups (the camadas), were ready to leave home at an earlier age than that assumed to be legitimate by the middle-class culture. They often chose to associate with peers and lived with them on the streets without being abandoned or receiving the parental abuse or rejection that was commonly associated with them. Sibling caretaking, "passive" child rearing, and the presence of already existing associations among children all contributed to helping them change into street children in a less abrupt way than "abandonment" implied. In fact, their presence on the streets was part of an orderly process of socialization.

Most people responded to the emotional impact of small children seeming to be on their own by using that image to warn society about being permissive with their own children. In any given group of street children, almost all of whom were over ten, only occasionally would there be a child under seven or eight. In our sample 18 percent were under ten. Nevertheless, the presence of each little child was always portrayed dramatically.

The few younger children who were on the streets became advertisements for the public institutions whose jobs would be made more secure by the existence of such little children in an obvious state of abandonment. On the several occasions that our research team was asked to visit institutions for street children, we noted that the smaller children were invariably given as examples by our guides to illustrate the severity of the problem we were investigating. On one occasion we were only allowed to see the living quarters of the youngest children. On another occasion, when the institution was readying itself for a visit from a dignitary of a potential funding source, we observed that the three smallest children were "asked" to meet him at the door and explain the benefits of the program. The use of the smallest children also appealed to the press, whose articles about the littlest ones sold newspapers. Whenever articles or books were written about the street children, no matter what the content, the front cover was of a very small child, usually in the most dire of circumstances. Each of these groups, in the pursuit of their own goals, knew that "little" could become large, so the image of the smallest children was incorporated into the slogans for helping abandoned children. Putting a fedora on a small child is a compelling, if not marketable image.

Even the children were aware that their smallest colleagues had great advertising potential. That is why they were put on public display to ask for alms, purposefully prepared to look pitiful, and announcing after serious rehearsals that they were indeed "abandoned." They had learned to dwell on the emotive quality of the word's association with rejection. Thus, both the street children and the culture that served them had reason to distort the real nature of the alleged abandonment, making it appear more like rejection than the subculturally normal part of development it was.

The Real Rejection

The second form of abandonment was that of rejection: the case in which, for any one of a variety of reasons, the child was not wanted. Either there was no money in the home, or no one in the home really cared, or the child's behavior was so obnoxious or out of line that the child was rejected. We were led to believe that a major reason for the existence of street children was that the child fled from home after being beaten or threatened with attack.

Rejection was more complex, however, than we had assumed initially. When we asked children why they left their homes, it was hard to get a response that could be relied upon as truthful. This made it difficult to ascertain whether the child was rejected by being beaten, or was rejected more passively through not receiving an adequate share of attention and care, or, finally, whether the child was doing the rejecting. More often than we had thought, rejection was a two-way phenomenon. Some children had left home because they had weighed the value of being at home against their options of being on the streets. Others left home out of a sense of pride or as a demonstration of reprisal about how they felt the home situation was being handled. The children were doing their part of the rejecting, which was made easier since there were so many children already on the streets who were beckoning—if only in their public display of attractive play—their potential colleagues to join them.

Deciphering the true nature of the rejection was a difficult methodological problem. Yet it was important to understand the nature and extent of rejection to see its relation to the causes of street life. The type of answer we received to why children left home often depended on how the child predicted his answer would be received. This was why direct solicitation of information, either through a nonstandardized questionnaire administered anonymously to an incarcerated population (Téllez 1976), or through informal interviews (Muñoz and Pachón 1980), was highly suspect. It also made the information the average pedestrian received from the child soliciting alms in a public place equally suspect. If the child wanted pity because he perceived this would get him something, he would tell his inquirer that he was forced out of the home because of being beaten by his padrastro or because there wasn't enough money to go around and he was the unfortunate one to be forced to leave so the others could survive. If the children suspected that it would be to their advantage to show how well they were taking care of themselves, they gave answers that illustrated that they were faring well. The street children were well aware of which part to play and what rewards were likely from their performance. Their livelihood depended on it.

At the outset of our work in Bosconia we asked children why they were on the streets, and they often said it was because they had been driven out of their homes. After we got to know them they gave us other answers. Some of them reported they left home as a form of respect to their parents. One boy told us he left after committing a robbery because he couldn't face telling his parents about it. Other children said they left after hearing their parents' stories about their own adventures on the road, or their parents' stories of finding more opportunity in another place.

Some children told us they left home because they could no longer tolerate what appeared to us to be fairly legitimate adult demands. They merely opted for something other than being raised in the home. As one twelve-year-old boy said, rather nonplussed, "at the time [when he left] my mother told me not to go downtown because I would start running with the other kids on the streets. Well, I wasn't going to stay locked up, so I left home knowing that I was going to earn my own living and lead my own life."

Some children who said they were rejected noted that their homes had changed. At first they said they were quite content at home, either being taken care of by older siblings or by their mothers. Then something fairly normal changed the home situation. As one boy said, "After my older sister got married, I was bored, so I left." Another possibility was that the relationships between the children and their parents changed over time. As Felsman (1981a) noted, many of the behaviors of young boys, such as their activity levels, their curiosity, and their overall liveliness, at one age period drew their parents toward them, but at a later age the same behaviors became problematic and brought on a series of reprimands that escalated into discipline problems. The result was mutual rejection. In this case the child's home changed, and the time of the rejection was important. The child would have had the advantage of having formed a sense of self-esteem that an earlier rejection would not have allowed him.

The 50 percent of the children who said they were abused by their stepfathers in response to the Téllez questionnaire (1976) was not surprising. This was what produced profitable sympathies. The difficulty of knowing how much of a factor parental rejection was in causing children to be on the streets was evident in the data from the responses to that questionnaire. We noted that 10 percent did not respond and 10 percent said they lived with their families. The remaining 80 percent of the respondents answered in a way that could elicit pity. The most frequent response was that of being physically abused by padrastros. The next was being starved out of the home due to a lack of money. If we had accepted this information, we would have seen more overt signs of psychopathology or of nutritional deficits.

Comparisons with their siblings and neighbors who remained at home showed that the children's physical and emotional health were superior (Pardo and Vergara 1964). In a review of this literature, Beltrán (1969) noted that "the street children have developed a level of life that very adequately compensates for the deprivations in their homes. The authors who have studied this phenomenon note a significant difference in the average weight

that favors the street children when comparing them to their siblings at home, which the authors contribute to better nutrition"
(Beltrán 1969, 43). Felsman (1981a) made similar observations
about their physical and psychological health, noting that the
children who left home were in better physical condition than
their siblings who remained. The physical evidence of weight is
harder to dispute than the claims of the children, when we knew
that it was precisely these "pitiful" words that were used to manipulate others into helping them. Thus, we learned to take with
some doubt the answers to "Why are you on the streets?" when
they came too quickly, when they were in rote response, when the
possibility of gain was associated with the answer, or when the
answer went against our observations.

Rejection must also be seen in relative terms, that is, by comparing what the children were leaving to what they were gaining.
On a visit to a school for poor children one day, I began to walk
around the neighborhood in order to see what the children who
lived there were like. The adults I saw were either at work doing
hard physical chores, repairing their houses, or digging sewage
lines, or they were sitting idly, talking among themselves, seeming to wait for work. Down an alley I saw a gallada loudly and en-
joyably playing. These children were exercising their freedom,
having no adult authorities to alter their play by making demands
on them.

> Before abandoning the home, the child has had different con-
> tacts with street life. When he goes outside, he has observed
> other children who are roaming all day, playing, and getting
> money and food by begging. In the newspapers he has seen pho-
> tographs of street children, children of the same age as himself
> who are treated as heroes. In his mind he begins to conjure up
> ideas; the street children live every day as adventurers, they
> don't have to obey anyone, they eat and have money only by
> asking for it, and besides, they appear to be big shots because
> only important people are in the newspapers. The child begins
> to think of life on the streets as a better way to live and begins to
> think about leaving his home. (Téllez 1976, 13)

In contrast to the lives of their parents, the lives of the street
children were often better. "Life in the streets comes to be seen by

them as a step up in satisfying their necessities for food, a place to sleep, things to do, all of which are better than what they can find in their homes" (Téllez 1976, 36). With their parents and themselves firmly rooted in the lower socioeconomic classes, many of the street children saw moving out of the home less as a result of being rejected or a form of rejecting their families, and more as a move toward improving their socioeconomic conditions.

Given the relative value of choosing to stay at home versus leaving and joining a group of friends, particularly when this choice followed several years of being accepted in the home, we concluded that rejection must be viewed under very particular circumstances. When we dealt with these particulars we were faced with a much different phenomenon than that reported either by the children themselves, who claimed they had been abused or rejected, in order to elicit charity; or by the professionals, who were prescribing solutions in part to change the problem and in part to ensure their own economic condition; or by the dominant class in the populace, who felt their style of child rearing was challenged by having too many street children around who might tempt their children to leave for a "freer" life. We looked at rejection from the experience of the children, which gave us a perspective that helped to explain their physical and psychological resilience and their lack of overt psychopathology. We found considerably less rejection by the parents than was commonly believed, and more rejection on the part of the children, who left home out of a mixture of adventure, good sense, opportunity, because it was expected of them, or because they were angry at being ignored or mistreated.

Rejection through Overprotection

There was another form of abandonment: rejection veiled in overprotection. Some children left home in spite of what seemed to be plenty of love. They learned that one way to find themselves was to seek out relationships with friends that allowed them a more honest assessment of who they were. This is a factor in why many North American children leave their homes. Brennan and

Huizinga noted that "indulgence, which is another kind of over-protection, is significantly associated with runaways" (1978, 188). Although this was generally overlooked in the Latin American context, and indeed we found this not to be particularly common in the street children we studied, we did note that the prevailing patrifocal family, with its restricted role for women as *ama de la casa* (woman of the home), often resulted in many women clinging to their children. Some children experienced this as smothering. This feeling was exacerbated when these children were unable to assume the kind of independence their colleagues had. The presence of street children aggravated this further by making it difficult for many parents to know how much attention was appropriate. Overprotection is the flip side of abandonment, both of which are illustrating a concern over the proper amount of attention.

In an interview for a national magazine about child rearing in Colombia, two Bogotá pediatricians described some of the problems with overprotection.

> I want to emphasize that overprotection is an attitude, not only is it prejudicial but it is one of the most fatal burdens to the child. It entangles him with a false sense of love. Everyone supposes that overprotection is educational for the child and for society. It has as a final goal the betterment and well-being of all. But besides this it also prepares the child for unhappiness and dependency. How else would a child understand, for example, the following from his mother, "I am irreplaceable, there is no one that is better than I am. Without me you would not be able to live. There are always things that I do for you that no one else would." These words would not have such importance if they were just said. But they are also acted out. They are translated into an exaggerated care with a disproportionate amount of attention, with services to the child that are not necessary, in a sacrifice that only appears interested, and in praise that is given not as help, but as seduction. The child understands this. This manifestation prepares the child for sadness and also permits him another option, that of countering with abandonment. (Gaviria and Guerrero 1980, 23)

Thus, a fairly common Colombian form of indulgence has been

associated with children abandoning their homes. I present it here not because it was seen as an important reason for the existence of street children, but to illustrate the dynamic tension in the larger culture over the proper way to raise children. The appropriate amount of love, liberty, and freedom that ought to be given to children was a matter of urgent concern. This was in great part due to the existence of so many street children. Failing to judge properly the amount of liberty or indulgence to give a child could result in losing one's children by having them abandon their family. Colombia was a society that felt its basic and fundamental sense of family to be in jeopardy. Society was unsure about how to raise its children. The presence of the street children made the uncertainty poignant because the limited power of the traditional family to demand the attention of its children, like the unlimited power of the family to control civic life before La Violencia, was eroding.

Leaving the Family and the Quest for Identity

Many of the children in our study left behind bereft parents, who felt they had lost their children in an unfair competition with a street life that had more to offer than they did. On several occasions we saw mothers in Bosconia, looking and hoping they would find the children who had abandoned them. One mother with two small children in her arms appeared at Bosconia with tears falling down her face. She was looking for her boy, who had disappeared several days previously. As I talked with her, she told me that she had already been to the police and had walked around several neighborhoods looking for her missing child. Now she was making the rounds of all the possible institutions where he might be. In her concern she looked to see if her missing boy was there, not believing me when I told her he wasn't. She left in tears, saying that she had surely "lost her boy to the streets."

This woman's words were echoed by newspapers, authors, and other parents. An article in a national paper, *El País*, entitled "Los hijos de la calle" (Children of the streets), made a distinction be-

tween families of street children and families whose parents were
not watching over and spending time with their children. Children from the latter were referred to as children *in* the streets instead of street children. The article implied that there were two
types of families: in the responsible family "being a father and
mother is more than giving children '*comida y regalos para
Navidad'* [food and presents for Christmas]; it means spending
time and caring for them." Children need schedules and discipline. If the parents did not heed this advice, they headed a different and less responsible type of family. Their children, the article
stated, would be lost to the streets (Gloria 1983).

The streets represented a place outside of family control. The
public nature of the streets made people anonymous citizens, as
opposed to being known members of a family group. The streets
were beyond the definite private boundaries of protection associated with the family and were perceived as dangerous. Yet, for
many children who left home the streets offered the possibility of
hope. It was, from their point of view, a type of quest that necessitated leaving the known family in order to seek an identity in the
larger family of humankind. Although abandoned children were
described by the public and by the institutions that served them
as pitiful and delinquent, it is also appropriate to see them in this
other connotation.

In many cultures the orphan is frequently associated with a
number of mythical and legendary figures in a way that suggests
an intimate connection between being abandoned and being heroic. Children dream of being orphans because the orphan "is free
to devote himself to discovering life's mysteries, partaking in
whatever romantic adventures he may fancy, and accomplishing
numerous feats along the way" (Rothenberg 1983, 183–84). From
this point of view, the street children left their parents to pursue a
heroic quest, to fulfill their destiny, and to join in what Jung
(1971) referred to as the myth of the divine child. He wrote that
in many cultures there was a legend about a child born of humble
origins (e.g., Buddha and Moses) who was abandoned in order to
start an important quest. This child was then tested for an important calling. Pursuing this calling meant leaving behind their origins, even if they might later resume contact with them.

Unraveling the concept of abandonment in relation to street

children proved very complex. To the onlooker, who lived in one type of family, the children were aimless wanderers, even possibly enemies of their waning power and life-style. While examining what the children were leaving, we found that they were often making a healthy, even a measured choice. Rather than a desperate escape from abuse or abandonment on the streets, they were often merely accepting the independence that their type of family expected of them. While they abandoned or were abandoned, they might also have been beginning a heroic adventure, often in a community of peers and friends—an adventure that has been portrayed in the literature of many cultures as a requisite to finding one's own identity, which is, after all, the function of adolescence.

6
Policy
and
Programs:
Using
the
Ambivalence
of Envy
and
Disdain

In the first week of the study, when Marta, one of the university students, made arrangements with her mother to drive me home from Bosconia, an important clue to helping the children unfolded. Marta's mother was waiting at the door. As I rode with them Marta's mother said how "cute and adorable" the kids were, but at the same time she told us to "roll up the windows and lock the doors." These duplicitous reactions mirrored many adults' reactions to street children. They described the children with smiles and pleasure, but also with fear, protecting themselves. The uncontrolled energy of childhood and the perceived need of adults to bring it under control were at the heart of the ambivalence society felt toward the children, and it affected the quality of the children's lives.

Meunier, a French journalist who went to Colombia to study the lives of the street children, protested to a French interviewer that misery was not his motive. "Their misery? It is not significant [to his motivation for writing about them]. Misery is here in France, and everywhere. It is not worth the effort to go to Colombia, two thousand miles away from home, to see misery, poverty and families in crisis. These exist at home; in contrast what characterizes the gamines is the spirit of rebellion" (1977, 7). It was the children's liberty, their flaunted sense of independence, and their haughtiness that made his long journey away from home worth the trip. It was these same qualities that allowed me to experience a sense of wonder, admiration, and even envy that contributed to my own ambivalence. They rekindled in my mind fantasies about living without authorities, and the simple pleasures of my childhood unedited by demands from parents, teachers, or even passersby on the streets. Like chocolate candy on my hands, the children gave me evidence of past pleasure while at the same time making me feel uncomfortable.

When asked why there appeared to be little hope of reducing the numbers of street children, Alvaro Lopez Pardo, former director of Colombia's national social welfare agency (ICBSF) said: "There are more than financial difficulties. Life on the streets has a certain attractiveness for the children: such as the liberty, the freedom, and the pleasure of being a Tom Sawyer, which is common to every ten-year-old child" (Gutiérrez 1972a, 276). Every time I encountered someone who could only dwell on the children's misery I felt isolated and irresponsible. Was the interest of Meunier and myself unwarranted because it was motivated by our adult fantasies of wanting to regain some of the memories of being "free" children? As the street children displayed their independence, they caused me (and many other people) to conjure up childhood fantasies of what life might have been like given the possibility of doing what we had dreamt of, but had not done. When I think about Giraldo, the graduate of the Nicolo program, I realize why he depressed me. He had given up on this fantasy and had become, prematurely, an evangelist for adult responsibility.

Childhood eventually leads to growing up and thus being obliged to deal with the necessary trade-offs between assuming responsibility and giving up the freedom of not having responsibilities that is associated with childhood. How these inevitable trade-offs were made by individual adult Colombians, as they reexperienced childhood through the presence of street children, determined in great part how they as adults looked upon and formed attitudes toward street children. Although there were many people with negative attitudes, and a good many others, like Marta's mother, with ambivalent feelings, there were still others whose personal histories made the apparent freedom and independence of the street children appear attractive, even enviable. Adults who perceived that they had earned their livelihood from their own wits, or who had come from the lower social classes and had worked their way up without palanca were often quite empathetic to the street children. Others, who felt they would have liked to have left their parents for the unknown, also vicariously enjoyed the street children. Adults who were not happy with their station in life, who felt trapped and unable to make a change, often looked upon these children with a mixture of envy and disdain.

When asked why we admire certain figures as heroes, Mark Twain said, "We envy them for the great qualities which we ourselves lack. Hero worship consists in just that. Our heroes are the men who do things which we recognize, with regret, and sometimes with secret shame, that we cannot do" (Regan 1966,66). Twain's child hero Huck Finn, while wanting to be individualistic and independent, finally dealt with these desires in relation to the social costs. Huck was what Regan called the "success story hero." This type of hero eventually gave up his nonconformity and accepted what conventional society had to offer: wealth, status, and the security they could bring. In contrast, Regan depicted the "uncompromising hero" as one who refused to make these trade-offs, keeping his individuality and abjuring the goods of civilization. The "uncompromising hero" usually "got the goat" of those who represented conventional authority, often at the price of being rejected by those who represented that authority, either in the family or in the state. Those in power who knew they had given up a great deal of freedom to get where they were felt justified in using their power against those whom they perceived were making light of that compromise.

These two heroic forms are diametrically related. Stories about the "uncompromising hero" often reveal a nearly mythological wish to win worldly recognition without sacrificing freedom or self-respect. The "success story hero" is in fact much less heroic because his tactics are common to so many of us who have bartered away what haughtiness and independence we had in exchange for the security of conventional social acceptance. The drama, played through these two heroic forms, is not unlike the human drama that is the essence of the Freudian view of human nature in a civilized society. In this view children as infants are without complexes, have no neuroses precisely because they receive pleasure without having to postpone enjoying it, as they must do later due to the necessary demands that are placed on all people who live in a civilized world. Freud's pessimistic view of human nature, that we are by definition neurotic, came from his interpretation of this necessary fact of life.

The gamine presented himself as the "uncompromising hero," while the chupagrueso tried to become the "success story hero." Thus, the street children existed as resonating images (even more than they did as individual children) because to the average citizen who saw them daily, the tension between these two heroic forms emerged as an unavoidable reflection on the way in which each observer resolved this human drama. It was precisely this dramatic tension that fueled the animosity between the gamine and the dominant Colombian society. The pariah status given to the "uncompromising hero" by Colombian society was in part envy expressed as disdain. The seemingly self-assured, assertive gamines, with no worldly possessions, must have appeared as personifications of the "uncompromising hero." This was particularly so for the non–street children (who later became the adults who perpetuated the same attitudes), since they were obedient and submissive to authority in exchange for what security their parents had, and what they might look forward to getting. The gamines could easily be used as reference points, as anchors on which to hang the anger derived from their parents' compromise of their independence.

As Gutiérrez wrote, "It is not the gamine per se that provokes fear and disgust, but that which is projected onto him. The disgust is projected out of a fear that every member in the society has toward those who avoid responsibility" (1972a, 337). And as Twain, who spent his life working on both sides of the heroic paradox added, we also admire and make heroes out of those people who have qualities that we ourselves wish we had. It was not just that street children provoked strong reactions; more important were the particular forms those reactions took. The children were responded to with disdain and envy, they were pitied and admired, and they were pushed out and held in. And all these emotions were laid out as if in a set for a play that contained a moral message. The children elicited these reactions because they produced the image of being uncompromising heroes in a society where there were few opportunities to get ahead, where the average citizen held more than one job, had more than one boss, and continually was beholden to many people.

Membership in Colombian society was often marked by which social clubs one belonged to, which schools one went to, or which church was attended. In Colombia, as well as in most of Latin America, social class membership and belonging to appropriate institutions were inexorably combined. Very few people in Colombian society were able to advance in social class status without paying attention to these details. Street children, who obviously rejected these institutions, were seen as a thorn in the side of those who were uncomfortably indebted to these practices. Street children, like all "uncompromising heroes," were antithetical to social climbers. Thus, a questionnaire about attitudes toward street children disclosed "that those who held the most authoritarian concept of family structure and those with the greatest aspirations toward upward mobility were the strongest in their rejection of the gamines" (Gutiérrez 1972a, 55).

To those people whose families formed the reference point for their own identities, and who had pursued success through the established institutions of schools, clubs, and churches, the street children were seen as possible threats to their personal security, to their identity as family members, and to the institutions themselves. From these groups the street children received scorn and, far less often, help. The help, however, assumed that the children were emotionally sick or criminals in need of reform.

In contrast, those Colombians who had left their families and had brought themselves to their current status outside of their family's palanca were likely to view the street children as replicas of their own struggles. These adults were often the small entrepreneurs who were the benefactors of the street children. They were the restaurant owners who gave them food, the street vendors who shared their space to peddle, or the laundry owners who allowed them to sleep in a warm place.

What influenced each of these reactions to street children was the individual's relationship to personal freedom and authority. This explained why so many people saw them as pitiful, dwelled upon them as victims, perceived them as threats, and yet smiled affectionately when making these judgments. It was because of the relationship between the freedom associated with childhood and the responsibility demanded from adulthood, and ultimately the battle between self-expression at whatever social costs or social conformity at whatever personal costs, that resulted in the ambiguous moral attitudes toward the street children. Yet, these very attitudes can supply answers to the question of how the street children can be helped.

Changing Social Attitudes:
The Macroprograms

In reviewing the existing programs for street children and planning for possible future ones, it is best to divide the programs into two categories: macroprograms and microprograms. The macroprograms are on a larger scale and are concerned with changing attitudes of society toward the children. Microprograms are much smaller and attempt to diagnose and treat children on an individual basis. Both types of programs need to be carried out simultaneously.

Since the variety of personalities and experiences of street children must be considered in the programs that are designed to help them, no single plan will work. The best approaches will consider the differences between the children, the variety of personal histories of the adults who are often predisposed to help, and the complexity of the society's attitudes toward the children. Consequently, the most effective programs will make appropriate matches between certain children and certain adults. Society's attitudes toward the role and image of street children must change to allow for eventual success in helping them.

Street children took on several rights that had been excluded from the definition of childhood. The street children chose the right to work for money and use it as they saw fit; they traveled by their own means and on their own schedules; and they had taken the opportunity to live away from home without the permission of their parents. In doing so they had assumed the right to control their time, their education, and the people with whom they associated. It was because of those choices that the street children came into conflict with the majority of adults, who assumed as part of their adult status the right to control and demand obedience from children. These same choices also put the children in conflict with the state, which had assumed the role of civic manager over the rights and responsibilities allowed to children.

Having renounced childhood by choice or circumstance, they had begun to live as adults without being given the opportunity to work productively. Given jobs, or given incentives by the government for business to provide them with jobs, the children would do much better than if they continued to be dealt with only as children. Therefore, macroprograms for street children should start with the assumption that the children can and should be included as part of the labor force.

Macroprograms must also offer the children possibilities of being adult members of the labor force. This means that macroprograms should work to replace attitudes toward street children that are based on emotional responses with more measured, contemplative, empathetic attitudes. The goal of the macroprograms is to allow children an earlier entrance into adult status. Achieving this will involve disseminating information about the diversity of the children, their origins, and the skills they have developed as a result of their street experiences.

UNICEF (Tacon 1981c) has described a macroprogram in Nicaragua worthy of notice. The courts, which in the past had adjudicated delinquent children to jail terms, have been replaced with local social agencies. At the same time a broad educational program that stresses the economic loss to the country caused by having children in emotional crisis and the economic advantages of healthy children has been established. When children are seen as national and local resources they become worthy of more investment. UNICEF estimates that "within a generation, child abandonment will cease to be a large-scale problem in Nicaragua, simply because the community, in support of the family as its primary nucleus, will not permit it to happen" (Tacon 1981c, 75). One advantage of the Nicaraguan model is that all the government programs have coordinated their efforts, using a well-thought-out advance plan. Each local government, often divided down to the level of individual city blocks, is expected to care for its young people. In Colombia and other Latin American countries that do not have such concentrated governments this would be much more difficult to achieve. This points out the difficulty of establishing transnational programs.

Another good example of a macro approach is UNICEF's advocacy of "identity partners" (Tacon 1981c). This system of help allows older street children to have the status of an adult by giving them responsibilities for younger children. Any older child who can supply affection, stability, and support can become "family." Through the adoption of "identity partners," camadas could be utilized to build "families" in this broad context. In the acceptance and promotion of families that do not have to be composed of parents but can be formed by peers, UNICEF is thus making a valuable contribution to changing public attitudes toward accepting diverse forms of adulthood and family. This works toward increasing the acceptance of street children as adults.

Macroprograms can also give direct opportunities to the children by offering them easier access into government employment programs, by giving a certain percentage of government licenses to street children. Another approach is to offer incentives to the contratas of street children, thus strengthening the benefactor relationships. By directly supporting those people who are already involved in informal contrata relationships, a valuable message is sent to the community about the value of street children to the whole of society.

Two national educational programs have supplied information to many people. In Mexico a daily newspaper, *Uno Mas Uno*, provides advocacy information to families who need to learn what different solutions are available. Part of the value of a program of this type in Colombia would depend on the way it could educate the larger society about the individuality of street children and the skills some of them have as potential productive workers and citizens. In Costa Rica the government operates a radio program that responds to write-in questions. The program concentrates on providing diverse information to poor families in language appropriate for those who use its services. Using these mechanisms in Colombia could work toward providing information about available benefactors and existing programs in order to match these with the individual needs of those who write or call in for information. In return to those in the community who offer help, these media programs could offer incentives such as free advertisement and public recognition. These two informational programs could benefit the children by working directly to replace existing sympathetic or antagonistic attitudes toward street children with an empathetic orientation based on information about their abilities and resiliency. Even so, having the information is only the first step toward having the adult status that must follow.

Some macroprograms have offered incentives to hire or train street children by deemphasizing the idea that they are errant and in need of moral training. In Honduras the government operates a program for child street vendors that does not try to take them out of the labor force, but instead offers them a free lunch in the neighborhoods where they work, during which time the children are given psychological support and informal education about health and maternal care for children. The education the children receive about maternal care is designed to make the children the teachers of their parents. Beyond meeting short-term needs, the advantage of this is that it offers a way to elevate the children's status in their own eyes as well as in the eyes of the public, thus changing the view of their value to the larger community. Approaches that enlist the adult qualities of the children not only provide employment opportunities for them but also demonstrate to the public the children's value as citizens.

When the town of Ipameri, Brazil, was faced with the closing of its largest employer, the town council established a new ceramics factory that hired over two hundred adolescent street children for work that was supervised by adults to avoid exploiting the children's labor. Thus, by creating work opportunities, and without creating unfair child labor conditions, "the street children problem has virtually disappeared, in spite of the general economic situation in the city not having improved significantly. Ipameri therefore confirms that the community can do a great job even when confronting serious economic restrictions" (Tacon 1983, 11). The success of the program testifies to the fact that a community that allows itself the freedom of responding to street children as adults can rid itself of many problems associated with street children, and can do so without having to rely on a great deal of financial outlay. More important, the ability of the new work force has helped to correct the inaccurate notion that children must be excluded from being citizens.

Adapting to Individual Differences: The Micro Approach

The essence of any good microprogram is that it deals with street children individually. Microprograms start with a careful diagnosis of the children. Thus the plan, or ethos, of these programs does not override the importance of individual diagnosis and planning from that assessment. The gamines and the chupagruesos, two different types of preadolescents, as well as the three groups of postpuberty children—the desamparados, the sobrevivientes, and the afortunados—all need different kinds of help.

Antonio and Roberto, the two eleven-year-old gamines who roamed the streets in a combination of play and work, used their imaginations to create opportunities. They showed a creative and resilient system of responses that would make them poor candidates for programs that use highly organized, step-by-step procedures and end in artisan training. They were open to different opportunities and would have benefited from using their street skills in work necessitating something other than routine skills. Luiz, the chupagrueso who told his story through a mist of self-doubt and reproach, benefited from a highly structured program. Jesus, the boy who went through the rough experience of recocha in order to seek entry into the community of street children, needed the support of an environment that paid close attention to his ineffectual manner of coping—a program that would dwell on building his self-confidence.

In the postpuberty groups, the desamparados (like Enrique) were usually children in need of psychotropic medication, preferably with supportive treatment. Medication with supportive treatment is probably the most effective method (both in terms of cost and in terms of psychological health) for treating the desamparados, but before it can be utilized Colombian society must learn the value of psychotropic medication and the close relationship between a variety of mental health problems and biochemical disturbances. A single psychiatrist, with several "nurse practitioners" who might be older street children, could serve a large number of children. Most of society inappropriately viewed the street children as "drug addicts," but we found that most children who used drugs did so as a means of self-medication for their psychological problems. Since they had only alcohol or illegal drugs, they did a fairly poor job at it.

One quick and inexpensive change that could benefit many existing programs could be routine visits by a medical doctor who would assess children's needs and medicate them in a more appropriate manner. There are a wide variety of Third World programs that supplement medical personnel with practically trained, nonmedical staff. These impoverished countries have been able to deal effectively with large groups of people in need of medical attention. In Costa Rica mobile rescue units have been used to patrol the streets in search of children in crises. These mobile units could also be involved in beginning a medical treatment plan for those children who need it. By including employment opportunities for older street children who already have experience in quick, effective resolutions of difficult circumstances, and who could be trained in assessing crises and utilizing crisis-intervention techniques, the program would gain low-cost mental health workers. This type of work would not only send a clear message to the children and to society about the children's skills, but it would be quite helpful to desamparados.

The majority of the sobrevivientes needed some supportive therapy. Giraldo's success as a graduate of the Bosconia program was *vocationally* a perfect match between his personal style and the goals of this structured program. His identification with the upwardly mobile, nationalistic segment of Colombia was the result of the continual moral training that was incorporated into the Bosconia program and was helpful to him, given his chupagrueso style. One of the problems that Giraldo faced was learning how to manage personal, noninstitutionalized relationships. In part this was because there was no active approach to integrate girls or relationship building into the Bosconia program. This was often a problem with segregated institutions (particularly those that served only girls), which usually had an attitude toward heterosexual contacts that was based on beliefs about the hypersexuality of uncontrolled children. There certainly was no hypersexuality with Giraldo, who needed to be pushed into heterosexual relationships, and his case is a good illustration of how more individualized treatment would help many of these children.

Palmira, the traveler whose studious, creative manner cautioned him about moving further into the Bosconia program, was seeking his own identity. He realized that in the Bosconia structure, with its program of vocational training for artisans, finding his own identity would have been difficult. His dream of living in his own apartment could have been fulfilled by a program like Chinchachoma in Mexico, which has rented a small, simple house in a poor neighborhood, and offers its services without a great many rules and regulations. The program operates as a halfway house and provides models (through the use of university students as house parents) for advancement beyond artisan employment. The problem with this approach is that it serves only a few children and relies too heavily on voluntary staff. Money is always a problem in poor countries, and there is no easy solution to this. But by using what money there is wisely, more children could be helped. By giving attention to the individual needs of children, some could be culled from government programs that demand more expensive care, and the money could be diverted into less expensive programs such as halfway houses that use volunteers. A voluntary work force can be increased by offering incentives. In this case, in exchange for their work the university students could receive reductions in the costs of attending school.

In order to serve more children, the halfway houses are often extended in a system of cooperatives in which the children are required to work to support themselves and their community. These communities, often called *Republics*, are usually large, and often quite bureaucratic and institutional, which creates some problems. Such circumstances make it difficult to deal with children individually and cause the staff of these programs to separate the children into segregated communities, denying them access into the mainstream.

Most Republics have "creeds" and "programs" with moral overtones. Sometimes these "philosophies" get in the way of individual growth, but at other times they can be subservient to caring between individuals. I found, in fact, that the philosophies were less important to the children than they were in securing funds from outside sources. I visited an international program near Bogotá, with headquarters and philosophy in Europe. Before each meal a hundred children entered the dining room, took their food from a cafeteria line, and waited without being able to talk until every child was seated. Then, as their food got colder, they recited in unison a memorized prayer. Each step of the program was preplanned, each contained a moral message, and the intended outcome was identical for each child, no matter what his history or desires. Yet, in this particular situation the staff was able to put all these procedures in their proper place, since the affection and care of the adults for the children went beyond any preset rules and regulations.

Tied closely to nearly all private programs for street children, and particularly those that operate as halfway houses or Republics with philosophies, is a charismatic leader. The advantage of this is that these leaders, with the help of their philosophies, are able to bring in funds and often have a great deal to offer the children. I visited an sos program in Ecuador. The sos programs, and there are many throughout Latin America, began in Austria after World War II. sos operates by building small homes with the financial assistance of the headquarters in Austria, but with the understanding that the local groups will gradually assume financial control. In the program in Ecuador about a dozen children, segregated by gender, lived in each home, headed by caring volunteer women. These women had other responsibilities that forced them to be away more than the director or the children wanted. The home was considerably separated from the main part of town, making it difficult for the children to live in the community they knew. The leader of this program, the only man around the children, was a Swiss doctor. Not only did he look after the health of the children, he was able to get funds to keep the program going because of his charisma, which was based in part on his stature as a doctor in the larger community, and in part on his considerable personal charm and resources. What would happen to the program should he leave would depend a good deal on who would replace him. In any case, such a scenario puts the children in jeopardy. For the time being, the children are indeed fortunate to have him. Padre Nicolo, the founder and director of the several Bosconia programs that serve thousands of Colombian children, is an international figure in the area of providing services to street children. Yet he has a definite philosophy which, though quite valuable to some children, clearly is less so for others.

Tacon (1981c) mentioned Mi Casa, a program in Guatemala that is typical of Republics because "while the rescuing of all these boys from the streets by one man is laudable, the possession of them and prevention of their joining the community seriously hampers the success of the programme, and, of course, handicaps future youngsters" (Tacon 1981c, 54). Unfortunately, in order to maintain funding, programs that rely on a leader's personal charisma or philosophy often play up to just those sympathetic attitudes of the public that have contributed to the perpetuation of society's misunderstanding of street children. It is easier to get money to segregate children than it is to get money to integrate them into the community in an adultlike status.

The most common forms of work in Republics are agriculture and the making of useful, inexpensive goods such as household items. These work styles often deny the qualities of work that children have learned in the streets, namely, their ability to find something cheap in one place and sell it or trade it more dearly in another. One notable exception to this is in Brazil, where the Republic of Small Salesmen (Tacon 1983, 6) is utilizing an important variant to raising money in a children's community. They have an annual collection of used but still useful objects, which the children collect, refurbish, and sell. This serves as their main source of income. The value in this is that it utilizes some of the skills that street children have already developed. The break with the more traditional forms of agriculture or artisan training is important because it represents a different attitude. This approach advocates, and thus gives respect to, trading skills that are associated with lower-class itinerant work rather than with the

steady, salaried employment of middle- or higher-class working
life. Furthermore, it recognizes the urban rather than rural background of most street children. It is the first sustained effort at
utilizing the children's skills as small-scale entrepreneurs, and it
is certainly relevant to many gamines.

The use of this or other forms of appropriate technology can
also help to keep the children's communities smaller and less bureaucratic. These goals could be accomplished by diversifying the
economy within each program, by seeking out projects that need
little capital investment, by relying heavily on the children's
street skills, and by utilizing cheap but necessary items that can
be refurbished without additional money.

The afortunados, the third group of postpuberty street children, in spite of their histories have made good adjustments and
demonstrated some remarkable skills at being resilient. We think
that one of the major shortcomings in supplying services to street
children is that these children have not been studied to see how
they have managed so well. Their strength, like that of other resilient children, probably comes from a combination of biological
temperament and an active manner of manipulating their environment. Both are worthy of acknowledgment, not only for information that could be immediately helpful but also for a better
understanding of their resiliency, which could be used in preven-
tative programs to pinpoint where and on whom money should
be spent.

Just as important as matching programs with children of particular needs is the assessment of existing programs based on who
is in them. For example, a high success rate might be because the
program is serving only resilient children, or a certain program
might be useful only to gamines or to chupagruesos. Certainly,
information like this, which might come from a study of the
afortunados, would serve everyone who is trying to help street
children prosper.

In the short run little can be done about the great lack of resources and opportunity, and probably little will be achieved by
asking for money from the state or from those who have a good
deal of it to give to the less fortunate. Only some success will
come from trying to change the attitudes of those in society who
feel in jeopardy from the early independence of street children.

So, in addition to the several programs that have been mentioned, a careful study of those children who have left home and have, against great odds, maintained themselves economically and emotionally is well worth the effort. Our observations tell us that these children have learned to control and utilize the ambivalence of envy and disdain that they found in their society, a skill that needs little capital investment to obtain and is invaluable to have.

The further study of Colombian street children also has significance beyond the immediate goal of helping them or the several million similar children in crisis in Latin America. Many societies, for a variety of reasons, have children leaving home at an early age and living without support from families or parents. The study of such children helps us to understand better the interrelationships between families, societies, and children.

The Relativity of Childhood:
Comparisons with North American Runaways

This study has sought to explore the boundaries of childhood and the precepts that society uses to create and define those boundaries. Throughout the study it was necessary to consider the dilemma that faces every cross-cultural psychologist: Are these children merely the poor and outcast examples at the impoverished end of childhood? Or are they, perhaps, illustrative of expanded possibilities of childhood?

The interplay between child development and societal structure in countries with divergent circumstances such as the United States, Latin America, the poorest of sub-saharan African countries, and countries like Cambodia, which have experienced the inhumanity of war, teaches us about the fragility and resiliency of children. I hope the reader will be forced to take into account a new perspective, to reconsider the nature of children and how adult society is responsible for the well-being of those they choose to call children.

After I returned to the United States many people asked me if North American runaways were like the gamines. I told them no,

that they are more like the chupagruesos. In flight from abusive
or neglectful parents, the North American runaways congregate
in certain sections of some North American urban areas, seeking
programs for shelter, finding sustenance without cunning. They
appear not to be happy about their freedom and barely able to
cope without relying on someone who can give them some kind
of help. Gamines in our society are very rare. There is no mixing
of humor and delinquency, no active argument over the boundaries between childhood and adulthood. We have only a violent
group of thugs, or a wounded group of runaways, who present
themselves more as invalids than as haughty provocateurs. We
don't face the kind of dichotomy between cunning and thuggery
that Colombians do.

There are many other differences between North American
runaways and Colombian street children, not the least of which is
the absence of the ambivalent response in the United States. Still,
there are some comparisons. The children on the streets in both
cultures represent a similar problem: what to do with children
who leave childhood before society deems it appropriate.

In each country reactions to the children involve family and of-
ficials representing the state, either in the justice system or from
human services agencies. In the United States most children
leave home after having myriad problems in school, while in Colombia the children have rarely even gone to school. In the United
States being out of school is a delinquent act, but in Colombia
truancy goes unnoticed.

The result of the role that school plays in the definition of
childhood in the United States is apparent in the ages of children
on the streets. In the United States there are virtually no children
under puberty on the streets. In Colombia there are many. People
in Colombia give money to small children, they allow small children who are on the streets many liberties with respect to behavior, and the image of a small child on the streets is commonplace.
Although this image is not easily acceptable, it is also not likely to
produce much public outcry. In the United States the image of a
small child on the streets is almost impossible to envision. Para-
doxically, this may be unfortunate since the Colombian street
children in their camadas know and experience the pleasure and
importance of chums, which helps them cope with being alone

and without families. But preadolescent North American children do not have the opportunity to enjoy chums because their time is fully programmed with school and other activities. The lack of access to chums works against coping with unhappy circumstances and contributes to some children's running away.

North American adolescent runaways also do not have groups with which they can associate freely. Their relationships are similar to the kinds that fugitives have, and those relationships change frequently as circumstances change. Coupled with the fact that they have not experienced chumships, many North American runaways are more lonely and less likely to know intimate friendships than their Colombian counterparts. The insistence of the authorities on close and judicious supervision of North American runaways makes their peer relationships precarious. A friend is likely to fall at any moment to the judicial system. There is no place for independent adolescents in the United States. In Colombia they are commonplace. In the United States the only place for an adolescent is in school, but unfortunately schools usually increase the demands placed on children, and offer even stiffer rules and penalties for breaking them. In North America the possibility of early access into adult status is very rarely realized. The time period for growing up is much longer.

These points illustrate the fact that the study of the Colombian street children also has the benefit of showing that the nature of childhood depends on historical and societal contexts. Childhood is neither a given nor a consistent phenomenon. After returning to the United States and trying to reorient myself to my own culture, I saw a cartoon in the *New Yorker* entitled "Singin' in the Rain." In this cartoon a child is dancing in a rainy scene. His umbrella is folded in his hand and he is skipping merrily along while the reader sees only his back side and the notes of music coming from his mouth. Without parental authority he is enjoying, as an unsupervised child might, the pleasures of singing in the rain. Staring at this libertine child's bravado are the parents of a child who is safely in tow under his mother's umbrella, totally bundled against the rain. This child, who is battened down from heavy galoshes to well-buttoned raincoat, can only contemplate a childhood with such liberty. The parents clutch their umbrellas and child as they look with distraught faces at the happy boy singing in the rain. They are telling their child that this boy is setting a "terrible example" and will "catch a cold." If they were in Colombia they would be seeing not just one "terrible example," but thousands of children like this. The relationship between unchallenged parental authority and childhood submission to that authority would become more precarious. If the child in the cartoon were black and from a poor neighborhood, and if he were multiplied by thousands, the precariousness might lead toward accusations about appropriate child rearing, adequate parental responsibility, and other explanations for "cultural differences." What we in the United States cannot imagine, but as the parents in the cartoon make clear we can fear, is that our children could gain a foothold on freedom and become serious contenders in this age-old battle between parents and their children. This battle is precisely what the street children have brought to Colombia, and the ramifications have reverberated throughout that society.

Glossary:
The
Children's
Argot

The following glossary consists of words and phrases the children used, or that were applied to the children by the society. Also included are the words we used to describe the children. Many terms in the glossary were mentioned in the text, but I have included additional commonly used words and phrases. We were able to ascertain that much of the children's argot came from extending the meaning and sounds of existing Spanish and Quechua words. Mexican words were incorporated from the Mexican movies that the children loved seeing. Modern North American slang was introduced through popular music and other media, and there was a Portuguese influence from Brazil.

Achantado triste. To be depressed.

Afortunados. The fortunate ones. This is the name we gave to the postpuberty children who were functioning well. They made up 42.9 percent of the postpuberty sample.

Aguacate. A police agent, although it literally means avocado.

Aguardiente. Hard liquor or brandy made from sugar cane. Because it is made locally, and is therefore cheap, it is the drink of choice of the masses. The wealthier people prefer imported liquors such as scotch, whiskey, and so on.

Altivez. This means haughtiness or arrogance. Padre Nicolo, the founder of the Bosconia program, used this word to describe the essence of a street child's personality. We have used the word to describe an essential characteristic of the gamines.

Ama de la casa. Literally, the mistress or owner of the house, but the term was widely used to refer to the role of women in the house where they had a position of power but were subservient to men. It also referred to women who put their total energy into managing their house. As a rule it was used pejoratively.

Amanao. When a child was amanao he was satisfied with a particular place or circumstance. It probably came from the verb *amañarse,* to be accustomed or to acclimate.

Amando. This was the word that the street children used to refer to those children who "sold out," or became conformists. When a child was called "amando" he was being warned about inappropriate behavior.

Ambulante. This noun means itinerant or wanderer. *Deambular,* the verb from which the noun derives, was used colloquially to refer to the children's constant movement, which appeared ominous to those who used the word.

Apellido. The father's name, and an important mark of status, either good or bad. The street children often came from matrifocal homes where the apellido was less important than in the patrifocal society, and this often worked against them.

Bacano. For the children, anything that was good or agreeable was bacano. It was used to refer to someone who had money and knew how to live the "good life." It comes from the Portuguese Brazilian *bacana.*

Bachillerato. The degree from a secondary school. A *bachiller* is a person who has graduated from secondary school, which is very rare for street children.

Balurdo. A person with money, but who did not know how to enjoy it.

Bareta. One name street children used for a marijuana cigarette.

Barrio. In Latin American countries barrio refers to any neighborhood. We use it here to refer to centrally located, established neighborhoods that were essentially poor, but which also contained working-class and some middle-class people.

Barro. To be a loyal *compadre* or friend (literally, it means mud or clay).

Basuko. The residue, full of dangerous impurities, left from the refining of cocaine. It is smoked. Allegedly the street children were addicted to it.

Bijaco. One name for the cobija, or blanket, particularly one that was of low-quality material such as newspaper.

Bola. A police car. Literally it means a ball, but it can be used to mean a lie.

Boludo. An automobile with a large back bumper that would be good for hanging onto and riding when *linchando.*

Bote. The literal meaning is little jar; the children used it to refer to any place where they were incarcerated.

Cacharro. A word the children used to describe someone who was furious or someone who easily expressed anger in fights.

Caleta. A secret place where the children hid their valuables.

Camada. A group of two to four preadolescent children who associated together as friends, in what we have called chumships. The children in camadas slept and played together and joined galladas to work. Usually each camada had a *caleta*, or place to keep valuables, that was known only to members of the camada.

Cama de soldados. A soldier's bed, literally, but it referred to how the children slept, which was head to toe, with one person's head over the chest of the next person. This system was the best way to stay warm at night and share what cobijas they had.

Cana. The children's word for jail or being imprisoned. In Argentina and some other Latin American countries it means policeman.

Cayetano. Someone who was trustworthy and could be told things because he was not a *sapo*, or squealer.

Chapa. Literally, a lock, but chapas or *apodos* were also nicknames.

Chévere. A word frequently used to indicate that someone had done something "cool" or good.

Chicanero. A person in a gallada who unfairly dominated others. It was also used as a put down because it indicated that the person was a charlatan.

Chichigua. Used endearingly by the street children to indicate a little friend or a small member in the camada or gallada.

Chichones. Literally, lumps or bumps, but it was used by the children to refer to hematomas from fighting. To have chichones was usually a sign of status.

Chinos de las calles. A term used to describe street children. The word chino comes from the Quechua (the Inca language) for child. Calle, as it was used when this phrase was popular, meant public street. Thus the phrase means a child in the public domain and therefore out of place.

Chiquitos. Literally means little ones. It was also used endearingly when referring to small children. We have used the word to indicate all the prepuberty street children.

Chiri. A word used for smoking marijuana.

Chola(o). A person in the Andes who is of a racial mixture of indigenous and Spanish. However, it was also used pejoratively to mean someone who was crude or dark-skinned.

Chorro. A pejorative word used by the police to define street children who were robbers or thieves.

Chupagrueso. Chupar means to suck or to absorb. *Grueso* means fat or
thick. The street children used the word to indicate a person or child
who talked too much, was too dependent, and often sallied up to others for support. We have used the word to indicate preadolescent
street children who had these characteristics.

Cobija. A shawl or blanket worn by peasants. As the country became
wealthier only the poorest people or those people who identified with
their rural background wore them. The quality of the material was an
indicator of a person's status. The word also means shelter or cover.
The street children always had cobijas. They used them as covers at
night, tables for eating, and tarps for playing. Their cobijas consisted
of a wide variety of materials, from wool to newspapers.

Coico. The street children used this word to refer to someone who was
subservient. This could include subservience in homosexual relationships where the coico sold himself to a perro or largo for sexual factors. For a street child to be called coico by another necessitated
defending one's reputation.

Colorado. Literally, red, but used to indicate blood.

Comadre. A kinship tie between a woman and her goddaughter. It is also
used to indicate good friendships between women.

Compadrazgo. This refers to the compadre and comadre relationships.
These relationships are important, widely used, and sanctioned by the
Catholic church throughout Latin America with appropriate services.
This helps reinforce the importance of the extended family and the
sense of community.

Compadre. The same as comadre, but the relationships are between males.
The street children referred to their good friends as compadres.

Compañero. A companion or partner. The children often referred to
their friends with this word. It was also used of someone who acted as
a watchman for the rest of the children while they were in danger.

Compinche. A friend, but used by the street children derogatorily to
mean a person who was subservient, or a coico, to a stronger person.
The latter was referred to as the perro or largo.

Conseguir pinta. When children went to get clothes they said they were
going to get *pinta*. Pinta could also mean any outward sign.

Contratas. The word means a contract or bargain. The children used the
word for the people who gave them something to eat or a place to stay.
Usually, but not necessarily, the children did something in return for
this. A contrata was also a child who had a place to stay or food because
of having a benefactor.

Cuates (cuatismo). A cuate is a twin, or a buddy with the status of a twin
or a brother.

Curruca. The name street children gave to an ordeal that was forced
upon them when they were incarcerated. To be curruca often meant to
have to squat on their haunches and walk this way for a long time. The

expression probably comes from the verb *acurrucarse*, to nestle or to huddle.

Dengue. A communicable disease resulting from being bitten by a certain kind of mosquito that lives on the Pacific coast. The symptoms are similar to a flu and the fever is also called "breakbone fever."

Desalojarse. Literally to be evicted or expelled from a lodging. The children used it to describe being kicked out of their house.

Desamparados. Literally, desertion or abandonment. We have used the word for the 23.8 percent of the postpuberty sample who were in need of emotional help.

Echar el pato. Literally, to throw out the duck. The street children used the phrase to indicate getting out of an accusation or getting out of the repercussions of being found guilty.

Educadores. The educators in Bosconia were ex–street children who had graduated from the program and were hired to work as leaders for the new recruits.

El Centro. The center, usually the business center of town. Because of the large number of people and the activity in El Centro, the street children could often be seen there.

Entenado. The word literally means a stepson or stepdaughter. It is also a system of social adoption in Colombia. When a male suitor courts a woman who already has a child, he is informed of the child and if he loves the woman he is expected to adopt the child, who is then called an entenado(a).

Favela. The word is Portuguese and refers to a poor neighborhood in Brazil.

Fefe. Another word for jefe, or boss.

Fifi. A boy who was well dressed or from a wealthy family.

Gallada. A group of street children who associate together for economic reasons. There is a boss (jefe) and often one or more subbosses (subjefes). The gallada is composed of many children, the majority of whom are postpuberty, but there are also some prepuberty children. Galladas made connections with the larger society, often with criminal and semi-criminal elements, to fence their goods.

Gallo. Rooster or cock, also a word used to refer to large or strutting street children, or the jefe of a gallada. It was also used to indicate a person who was valiant.

Gamine. In Colombian society all the street children were referred to as gamines. It is interesting that this is the word that has gained the highest currency, because it is not a Spanish word, but comes from the French *gamin*, which means urchin. *Gaminoso*, or to be gaminelike, indicated a child who was dirty, poorly dressed, or in rags. We have used the word gamine to indicate only those preadolescent street children who were functioning well and who were characterized by their sense of altivez, or haughtiness, toward the authority and society who looked down on them.

Garrotero. Literally, someone who fights with a club or a stick. Among the children it meant someone who was cruel.

Gente. The people. When used by the street children it meant people who were common, not much different in origin from them.

Gil. A person who was innocent, stupid, or a clown. It generally meant someone who was a *campesino*, or peasant. At times it was applied to some street children.

Guachimán. Another word for night watchman. The word comes from extending the sound of the English word watchman.

Guerrillas. A small band of fighters. This has traditionally meant a force from the left or right fighting to overthrow the government. There was a new force of guerrillas who were allegedly involved with illicit drug activity. The street children had been referred to as "urban guerrillas" because they were seen as potential threats to the state, independent of authority, and possibly worthy enemies against the status quo.

Hacer la paja. Paja means straw or rough but the phrase when used by the children referred to masturbating. In the third-person singular, *hace la paja* meant "he is masturbating."

Hamaca. Literally, a hammock, but also the children's word for bed.

Iguana. A reptile that looks ferocious but is rather tame, even if bothersome. The children called the police *iguanas*.

Imán. A word used among the street children to refer to a friend. The word literally means magnet or attraction.

Invasione. A poor neighborhood that originated when people moved onto the land without having the title to it. Then they made improvements, and eventually established some sort of de facto recognition of ownership.

Jefes. The bosses.

Ladrón. A petty thief or robber.

Largo. The large one, literally, but it was used by the children to mean a bully who abused them.

La Violencia. In 1948 Colombia went through a severe civil strife in which about 200,000 people were killed. Because of this and because of the economic and social changes of the post–World War II period there was a large rural-to-urban migration, a good deal of poverty in the cities, and according to many, the beginning of street children. When La Violencia ended, a period of political compromise began in which the society became more meritocratic.

Linchar (linchando). Literally, to lynch, but it is also a type of game widely practiced by street children. It consisted of grabbing on to the back bumper of a vehicle and hanging on for the ride.

Lleca. Street, but when used by the street children the word meant the heaviness and loneliness of being on the streets without friendship or an adequate place to spent the night.

Madre de crianza. A woman, usually a friend of the mother, who would take over the parenting of the mother's child. Crianza means nursing, but these women were not wet nurses. Nor were they professional child caretakers, but rather women who for a variety of reasons raised children not their own.

Mano. The word the children used for someone who had accepted life in an institution instead of taking the attitude of being *ser firme,* or against the authorities. It was used derogatorily.

Marginada(o). A term used derogatorily to indicate poor people, or marginal people. It was also used to refer to poor neighborhoods.

Marica. Used by the children to indicate a sissy, effeminate, or homosexual person.

Mica. The word the children used for a prostitute. It literally means a long-tailed monkey.

Motilar. This verb indicated the process of having one's hair shorn at an institution. This was usually done to avoid lice, but it also had the function of marking the child as having been institutionalized.

Niños vagos. Vagabond children. A term applied to the street children.

Obrero. A common worker or laborer.

Padrastro. Stepfather or hangnail; the latter indicates the status given to stepfathers. It was widely believed that street children resulted from living with stepfathers who abused them.

Palanca. Personal connections that helped someone gain access to employment, social status, etc. Much of what got done or who one was in the social world was the result of palanca. The word literally means crowbar, or influence, as in a pipeline of influence.

Pálida. Literally, pale or ghostly, but for the children it indicated the feeling of being faint and light-headed due to lack of food, or from drinking without eating.

Pandilla. A gang or a band, referring to street children.

Papayaso. The word the children used to indicate a very easy scam or a possibility of getting some money easily.

Pasta de coca. Cocaine paste or the residue left from the processing of cocaine. Pasta de coca is a Peruvian drug that is comparable to basuko in Colombia. Its use, which was widely believed to be rampant in street children, was physically and emotionally dangerous.

Pelado. The word the children used to indicate being broke or having no money. It literally means being barren.

Perro. Literally, dog, but it also was used by the children to indicate a bully or a leader who abused his underlings.

Perrón. To be drunken or to be a drunk.

Pilluelo. A word used to describe street children. It means little rascal or scamp.

Pipero. The name used by the children to indicate that someone was a habitual user of inhalants.

Pira. To escape from a place of incarceration or from a home where the child was being abused. Literally it means a funeral pyre.

Pormis. From *por mitad* (in half), the expression was used to describe the way in which the children equally divided among themselves the material things and food they had.

Propina. A tip that was sometimes necessary to get what should have been gotten without one. In large part this was because the prices of services were too low and a tip was the only way to make them worth the effort. But it also led to an intricately defined economy where the true value is the cost plus the tip.

Quechua. One of the two major languages of the Incas and the one used by the Inca descendants in Colombia.

Quedarse gringo. The children's expression for staying babylike or being dependent.

Ranchera. A type of popular Mexican song that is sentimental and speaks to problems of love and the loss of it. It was often the kind of tune that street children sang for alms.

Raponero. An *ave de rapina* is a bird of prey. The word had been changed by society to indicate the kind of stealing that some children did when they grabbed something from an unsuspecting person and then ran away.

Recocha. A passionate play among the children that touched upon love and violence. It was often part of establishing group status among the children. Literally it means to boil over.

Recolectones de cosechas. The children were described as collectors of garbage (*cosechas*).

Regalos (regalitos). The children who were given away by their mothers to be raised by friends or relatives of their parents were referred to as regalitos, or presents.

Ronda. A formal Spanish dance that the children performed on the streets for alms. The contrast between the children's poverty and the elegance of the dance was sure to get attention and money.

Sapo. Literally, toad, but used by the children to describe someone who was a tattletale. It was always used very pejoratively.

Sardina. A sardine, but used to indicate a beautiful woman or girl.

Ser firme. Used by the children to indicate a child who was strong, stoic, and who did not give in to inappropriate demands made by authority. It also meant to be loyal to the street child's way of life.

Sobres. Leftovers that the children would look for and receive from restaurants. They were often their primary source of food.

Sobrevivientes. The term we gave to the 33 percent of the children in the postpuberty group who were the "survivors." They had problems but they were coping.

Suburbio. A poor neighborhood on the perimeter of a city. To live in a suburbio usually meant living in poverty, but as the area became older the economic conditions of some of the inhabitants improved. Suburbios usually started as invasiones.

Taco. Literally a short, fat person, but between the children it was used to mean someone who was putting the "screws" to someone else.

Tombo. The children's word for police.

Trabajadores jóvenes. Child workers or young workers. They looked much like the street children but they lived at home with their families.

Turgio. A poor neighborhood.

Tuso. Literally, cornsilk or a corncob. The children referred to as tusos by society were the ones who had had their hair shorn at an institution.

Vacilar. The children used this word to mean making jokes or jesting. Literally, it means to hesitate or waver.

Vale. To the children a vale was a friend. It comes either from the verb *valer*, to have worth or to be trustworthy, or from the slang word that means voucher.

Vicio. A vice, but the word could also mean a habit or a craving, and was thus used by society to describe an addiction to illicit drugs.

Vigilante. A person who kept watch over someone's property for a price. At night it was common to have houses patrolled by vigilantes. The street children often made friends with them in order to find a place to sleep in exchange for bringing the vigilantes something to eat or drink.

Volarse. Literally, to fly away, or to fly off the handle. The children used it to indicate escaping.

Voltear. For the children this meant to walk about the streets looking for fun, or to see what was going on, or quite possibly to scout out a possible situation that might bring in money. Literally, it means to whirl or to revolve.

Yoly. Slang for a pretty girl.

Zona. A zone or a band, but the word was yelled by the children when there was danger in the vicinity.

Bibliography

Ainsworth, M. S. (1967). *Infancy in Uganda: Infant Care and the Growth of Love.* Baltimore: Johns Hopkins University Press.

Alape, A. (1983). *El Bogotazo: Memorias del Olvido* [The Bogotano: forgotten memories]. Bogotá: Editorial Pluma.

Anastasi, A. (1982). *Psychological Testing.* 5th ed. New York: Macmillan.

Andrade, S. G. (1983). Basuko—Un vicio que carcome . . . y esta moda [Basuko—a vice that is decaying . . . and it is the style]. *El Tiempo,* (Bogotá), June 27, 12C.

Beltrán, C. L. (1969). *Temas Colombianas: La Metamorfosis del "Chino de la Calle"* [Colombian themes: The metamorphosis of the street children]. Bogotá: Editextos.

Berland, J. C. (1982). *No Five Fingers Are Alike.* Cambridge: Harvard University Press.

Berry, J. W. (1976). *Human Ecology and Cognitive Style.* New York: John Wiley and Sons.

Betancur, O. (1983). 40 millones de gamines [40 million gamines]. *El País,* October 30, A6.

Bettelheim, B. (1976). *The Uses of Enchantment: The Meaning and Importance of Fairy Tales.* New York: Knopf.

Blustein, J. (1982). *Parents and Children: The Ethics of the Family.* New York: Oxford University Press.

Brennan, T., and Huizinga, D. (1978). *The Social Psychology of Runaways*. Lexington: Lexington Books.

Brislin, R. W. (1980). Translation and Content Analysis of Oral and Written Material. In Triandis, H. C., and Berry, J., eds., *Handbook of Cross-cultural Psychology: Methodology*, vol. 2. Boston: Allyn and Bacon.

Broman, S. H., Nichols, P. L., and Kennedy, A. (1975). *Preschool IQ: Prenatal and Early Development Correlates*. Hillsdale, N.J.: Erlbaum.

Budoff, M., and Corman, L. (1974). Demographic and Psychometric Factors Related to Improved Performance on the Kohs Learning-Potential Procedure. *American Journal of Mental Deficiency*, 78 (5):578–85.

Burkett, E. C. (1978). Indian Women and White Society: The Case for Sixteenth-century Peru. In Lavrin, A., ed., *Latin American Women: Historical Perspectives*. Westport, Conn.: Greenwood Press.

Campbell, D. T. (1961). The Mutual Methodological Relevance of Anthropology and Psychology. In Hsu, F., ed., *Psychological Anthropology*. Homewood, Ill.: Dorsey.

Chodorow, N. (1974). Family Structure and Feminine Personality. In Rosaldo, M., and Lamphere, L., eds., *Women, Culture and Society*, pp. 43–66. Stanford: Stanford University Press.

Cobos, F. (1979). *Estrategia para una luncha contra el abandono* [Strategy for the fight against abandonment]. Bogotá: Instituto Colombiano de Bienestar Familiar.

Cortes, F. (1984). "Caregato" no perdona. . . . [Caregato doesn't forgive]. *El Tiempo*, January 15, 1, 7A.

de Galán, G. P. (1981). *Se Acaba la Familia* [The end of the family]. Bogotá: Editorial Pluma.

de Jesus, M. (1962). *Child of the Dark: The Diary of Carolina Maria de Jesus*, trans. David St. Clair. New York: Dutton.

de Mantilla, N. (1980). El Gamin: Problema Social de la Cultura Urbana [The gamine: A social problem of the urban culture]. *Revista Javeriana*, 94:457–64.

Dennis, W. (1966). *Group Values through Children's Drawings*. New York: Wiley.

Departamento Nacional de Planeacion (1978). *Diagnostical general sobre la situacion del menor en Colombia* [A general diagnosis concerning the situation of minors in Colombia]. Bogotá: Instituto Colombiano de Bienestar Familiar.

Deregowski, J. B. (1972). Reproduction of Orientation of Kohs-Type Figures: A Cross-cultural Study. *British Journal of Psychology*, 63:283–96.

Díaz, B. G. (1973). Un Ensayo de Autoeducacion de Niños Marginadas Gamines [An essay of the self-education of the marginal children: The gamines]. *Educacion Hoy*, (November–December): 33–58.

El Espectador, September 28, 1983, 5A. Mas de 25 millones consumen drogas en los Estados Unidos [More than 25 million consume drugs in the United States].

El Tiempo, September 1976, 22. El Censo de Gamines [The census of gamines].

Fals-Borda, O. (1955). *Peasant Society in the Colombian Andes.* Gainesville: University of Florida Press.

Felsman, K. J. (1981a). *Street Urchins of Cali: On Risk, Resiliency, and Adaptation in Childhood.* Unpublished Ph.D. dissertation, Harvard University, Cambridge.

————. (1981b). Street Urchins of Colombia. *Natural Histories* (April): 41–48.

Festinger, L. (1965). *A Theory of Cognitive Dissonance.* 3d ed. Stanford: Stanford University Press.

Flinn, W. L. (1968). The Process of Migration to a Shantytown in Bogotá, Colombia. *Inter American Economic Affairs,* 22 (2):77–88.

Fromm, E., and Maccoby, E. (1970). *Social Character in a Mexican Village.* Englewood Cliffs, N.J.: Prentice-Hall.

Gardiner, H. (1974). Human Figure Drawings as Indicators of Value Development among Thai Children. *Journal of Cross-cultural Psychology,* 5 (1):124–30.

Gaviria, J., and Guerrero, P. (1980). La Justicia y el loco [Justice and the insane]. *Revista Colombiana,* 7–27.

Gilligan, C. (1977). In a Different Voice: Women's Conceptions of the Self and Morality. *Harvard Educational Review,* 47 (4):481–517.

————. (1979). Woman's Place in a Man's Life Cycle. *Harvard Educational Review,* 49 (4):431–46.

Gloria, H. (1983). *Los Hijos de la calle* [The children of the street]. *El País,* November 12, 7.

Golden, C. (1979). *Clinical Interpretation of Objective Psychological Tests.* New York: Grune and Stratton.

Gutiérrez, J. (1972a). *Gamin: Un Ser Olvidado* [The gamine: The forgotten person]. Mexico City: McGraw-Hill.

————. (1972b). The Gamines. In Masserman, J., ed. *Science and Psychoanalysis,* vol. 21, pp. 45–61. New York: Grune and Stratton.

Harris, B. D. (1963). *Children's Drawings as Measures of Intellectual Maturity.* New York: Harcourt Brace and World.

Holinsteiner, M., and Tacon, P. (1983). Urban Migration in Developing Countries: Consequences for Families and Children. In Wagner, D., ed., *New Directions for Child Development,* pp. 5–25. San Francisco: Jossey-Bass.

Holtzman, W. (1980). Projective Techniques. In Triandis, H., and Berry, J. eds., *Handbook of Cross-cultural Methodology,* vol. 2, pp. 245–78. New York: Allyn and Bacon.

Hutt, M. (1985). *The Hutt Adaptation of the Bender-Gestalt Test.* 4th ed. New York: Grune and Stratton.

Interamerican Development Bank (1987). *Simulations of Labor Markets in Two Countries: Colombia and Mexico 1985–2000.* Economic and

Social Progress Report. Washington, D.C.: Interamerican Development Bank.

International Catholic Child Bureau (1984). *Programme on Street Children and Street Youth* (Project Profiles, Series no. 1). Geneva: International Catholic Child Bureau.

Jahoda, G. (1956). Assessment of Abstract Behavior in a Non-Western Culture. *Journal of Abnormal Social Psychology*, 53:237–43.

Jaquette, J. (1976). Female Participation in Latin America. In Iglitzin, L., and Ross, R., eds., *Women in the World*, pp. 55–74. Santa Barbara: Clio Books.

Jaramillo, O. (1976). El Sub-mundo de los Gamines [The subworld of the gamines]. *Nueva Frontera*, 73:5–16.

Jeri, F. R. (1976). Consumo de Drogas Peligrosas por miembros y familias de la Fuerza Armada y Fuerza Policial Peruana [The consumption of dangerous drugs in the Peruvian armed forces and police department]. *Revista de la Sanidad de las Fuerzas Policiales*, 37:104–12.

———. (1982). The Coca Paste Epidemic in South America. *Revista de la Sanidad de las Fuerzas Policiales*, 43 (2):170–79.

Jeri, F. R., Sanchez, C., Pozo, T., and Fernandez, M. (1978). Sindrome de la Pasta de Coca: Observaciones en un grupo de 158 pacientes del area de Lima [Coca paste syndrome: Observations of 158 patients in Lima]. *Revista Sanidad Ministerio Interior*, 39:1–18.

Jung, C. G. (1971). *The Portable Jung*. New York: Viking Press.

Kohlberg, L., and Kramer, R. (1969). Continuities and Discontinuities in Childhood to Adult Moral Development. *Human Development*, 12:93–120.

Kohs, S. C. (1923). *Intelligence Measurement: A Psychological and Statistical Study Based upon the Block-design Tests*. New York: Macmillan.

Koppitz, E. (1968). *Psychological Evaluation of Children's Human Figure Drawings*. New York: Grune and Stratton.

———. (1984). *Psychological Evaluation of Human Figure Drawings by Middle School Pupils*. New York: Grune and Stratton.

Koppitz, E., and Casullo, M. (1983). Exploring Cultural Influences on the Human Figure Drawings of Young Adolescents. *Perceptual Motor Skills*, 57:479–83.

Koppitz, E., and de Moreau, M. A. (1968). A Comparison of Emotional Indicators on Human Figure Drawings of Children from Mexico and from the United States. *Revista Interamericana de Psicologia*, 2:41–48.

Kvale, S. (1986). Interpretation of the Qualitative Research Interview. *Transformations*, 2 (1):32–42.

Laosa, L., Swartz, J., and Diaz-Guerrero, R. (1974). Perceptual-cognitive and Personality Development of Mexican and Anglo-American Children as Measured by Human Figure Drawings. *Developmental Psychology*, 10 (1):131–39.

Leeds, A. (1974). Housing Settlement Types, Arrangements for Living, Proletarianization, and the Social Structure of the City. In Cornelius, W., aand Trueblood, F. M., eds., *Latin America Urban Research*, vol.4, pp. 67–99. London: Sage Publications.

Lemay, M. (1975). *El Cabecillo: Los Grupos de Inadaptados* [The ringleader in unaccepted groups]. Paris: University Press of France.

Lewis, O. (1965). *La Vida*. New York: Random House.

Lindzey, G. (1961). *Projective Techniques and Cross-cultural Research*. New York: Appleton-Century-Crofts.

Lomnitz, L. (1974). The Social and Economic Organization of a Mexican Shantytown. In Cornelius, W., and Trueblood, F., eds., *Latin America Urban Research*, vol. 4, pp. 135–55. London: Sage Publications.

———. (1977). *Networks and Marginality: Life in a Mexican Shantytown*. New York: Academic Press.

Lopez, A., and Lopez, E. (1964). *Estudio Medico-Social de la Vagancia Infantil de Bogotá* [A social and medical study of child vagrants in Bogotá]. *Revista Colombiana de Psiquiatria*, 1 (1):37–44.

Machover, K. (1949). *Personality Projection in the Drawings of a Human Figure*. Springfield, Ill.: Charles Thomas.

Makarenko, A. (1973). *The Road to Life*. New York: Oriole Editions.

Mangin, W. (1967). Latin American Squatter Settlements: A Problem and a Solution. *Latin American Research Review*, 2:65–98.

Mead, M. (1954). Research on primitive children. In Carmichael, L. E., ed., *Handbook of Child Psychology*, pp. 735–80. New York: Wiley.

———. (1968). *Growing Up in New Guinea*. New York: Dell.

Meunier, J. (1977). *Les gamins de Bogotá* [The *gamines* of Bogotá]. Paris: J. C. Lattes.

Minturn, L., and Lambert, W. W. (1964). *Mothers of Six Cultures: Antecedents of Child Rearing*. New York: John Wiley and Sons.

Mintz, S. (1984). *Caribbean Transformations*. Baltimore: Johns Hopkins University Press.

Mohan, R. (1980). *The People of Bogotá: Who They Are, What They Earn, Where They Live* (World Bank Staff Working Paper no. 390). Washington, D.C.: World Bank.

Moynihan, D. P. (1965). *The Negro Family: The Case for National Action*. Washington, D.C.: U.S. Department of Labor.

Muñoz, V.C., and Pachón, X.C. (1980). *Gamines Testimonios* [Gamines' testimonies]. Bogotá: Carlos Valencia Editores.

Muñoz, V. C., and Palacios, M. V. (1980). *El Niño Trabajador* [The child worker]. Bogotá: Carlos Valencia Editores.

Nelson, J. M. (1969). Migrants, Urban Poverty, and Instability in Developing Countries. In Cornelius, W., and Trueblood, F., eds., *Latin America Urban Research*, vol. 4, p. 101. London: Sage Publications.

Nerlove, S., and Roberts, J. (1975). Natural Indicators of Cognitive

Development: An Observational Study of Rural Guatemalan Children. *Ethos*, 3:265–95.

Néron, G. (1953). *El Niño Vago* [The child vagabond]. Madrid: Impreso de España.

Nicolo, J. (1981). *Musaraños* [The vermin]. Bogotá: Servicio Juvenil.

Ochoa, M. (1979). *Consumo suboptimo de alimentos en paises subdesarrollados, un modelo microeconomico* [Suboptimal consumption of food in underdeveloped countries, a microeconomic model]. Ithaca: Cornell University Press.

Pardo, L. A., and Vergara, E. L. (1964). Estudio Medico-social de la Vagrancia Infantil de Bogotá [Social and Medical Study of Childhood Vagrancy in Bogotá]. *Revista Colombiana de Psychiatria*, 1 (1):37–67.

Pascal, G., and Suttell, M. (1951). *The Bender-Gestalt Test*. New York: Grune and Stratton.

Patiño, N. O. (1983). 600 de mil niños consumen "basuko" [600 out of a thousand children consume "basuko"]. *El Tiempo* (Bogotá), July 11, 11A.

Peatrie, L. R. (1968). *The View from the Barrio*. Ann Arbor: University of Michigan Press.

———. (1977). Concept of Marginality as Applied to Squatter Settlements. In Cornelius, W., and Trueblood, F., eds., *Latin America Urban Research*, vol. 4, pp. 101–9. London: Sage Publications.

Pineda, V. G., de Muñoz, E. I., Pineda, P. V., Echeverry, Y., and Arias, J. (1978). *El Gamin su Albergue Social y su Familia* [The gamine's social home and family], vol. 1. Bogotá: Instituto Colombiano de Bienestar Familiar.

Poole, E. (1903). Waifs of the Streets. *McClures*, 21:40–48.

Regan, R. (1966). *Uncompromising Heroes*. Berkeley: University of California Press.

Ricaurte, C. O. (1972). Aspectos Historicos y Linguisticos del Gamin Bogotano [Historical and linguistic aspects of the gamines of Bogotá]. *Revista de la Dirección de Divulgacion Cultural*, 10:7–73.

———. (1977). *Quienes Son los Gamines* [Who are the gamines]. Bogotá: Editorial Colombiana.

Roback, H. B. (1968). Human Figure Drawings: Their Utility in the Clinical Psychologist's Armamentarium for Personality Assessment. *Psychological Bulletin*, 70 (1):1–19.

Rohner, R. (1975). *They Love Me, They Love Me Not: A Worldwide Study of the Effects of Parental Acceptance and Rejection*. New Haven: Human Relations Area Files Press.

Rothenberg, R. E. (1983). The Orphan Archetype. *Psychological Perspectives*, 14 (2):181–94.

Rotter, B. (1967). *Psicopatologia del Gamin Bogotano* [Psychopathology of the Bogotá gamine]. Paper presented at the Meeting of the Seventh National Congress of Psychiatry, Bogotá, Colombia.

Samper, L. N. (1983). Cocaina [Cocaine]. El Tiempo (Bogotá), October 5.
———. (1984). Ressurge el "gaminismo" [The resurgence of gaminismo]. El Tiempo (Bogotá), September 13, 42.
Segall, M. H. (1983). On the Search for the Independent Variable in Cross-cultural Psychology. In Irvine, S. H., and Berry, L. W., eds., Human Assessment and Cultural Factors, pp. 122–37. New York: Plenum.
Siegal, J. (1969). The Rope of God. Berkeley: University of California Press.
Story, R. I. (1960). The Revised Bender-Gestalt Test and Male Alcoholics. Journal of Projective Techniques, 24:186–93.
Sullivan, H. S. (1953). Interpersonal Theory of Psychiatry. New York: Norton.
Swenson, C. H. (1968). Empirical Evaluation of Human Figure Drawings: 1957–1966. Psychological Bulletin, 70:20–44.
Tacon, P. (1981a). My Child Now: An Action Plan on Behalf of Children without Families. UNICEF document.
———. (1981b). My Child Minus One. UNICEF document.
———. (1981c). My Child Minus Two. UNICEF document.
———. (1983). Regional Program for Latin America and the Caribbean. UNICEF document.
Tanner, N. (1974). Matrifocality in Indonesia and Africa and among Black Americans. In Rosaldo, M., and Lamphere, L., eds., Women, Culture, and Society, pp. 129–56. Stanford: Stanford University Press.
Téllez, G. M. (1976). Gamines. Bogotá: Editorial Temis.
Tolar, A., and Brannigan, G. (1980). Research and Clinical Applications of the Bender-Gestalt Test. Springfield, Ill.: Charles C. Thomas.
Triandis, H. C., and Berry, J., eds. (1980). Handbook of Cross-cultural Psychology: Methodology, vol. 2. Boston: Allyn and Bacon.
Verjan, L. A., and de Lujo, L. M. (1982). Estudio Morfologico del Lexico Del Gamin [A study of the morphology of the gamine lexicon]. Unpublished Ph.D. dissertation, Universidad Nacional, Bogotá, Colombia.
Villar, G. (1978). Psicologia y clases sociales en Colombia [Psychology and social class in Colombia]. Bogotá: Ediciones Gepe.
Villota, R. (1979). Problematica de la niñez de la calle [The problem of the children of the streets]. Revista Javeriana, 91 (455):473–77.
Wagley, C. (1976). Amazon Town. London: Oxford University Press.
Weisner, T., and Gallimore, R. (1977). My Brother's Keeper: Child and Sibling Caretaking. Current Anthropology, 18 (2):169–90.
Whiting, J., and Whiting, B. (1975). Children in Six Cultures. Cambridge: Harvard University Press.
Witkin, H., and Berry, J. (1975). Psychological Differentiation in Cross-cultural Psychology. Journal of Cross-cultural Psychology, 6:4–87.

Index

About the Author

Lewis Aptekar is an Associate Professor of Counselor Education at San Jose State University. This book is a result of his work as a Fulbright Scholar in Colombia. He is currently a Partners of the Americas' Kellogg Fellow in International Development.

His publications, which have appeared in many professional journals, have reflected his clinical work as a licensed psychologist and his anthropological approach to studying the problems of Latin American and Mexican-American adolescents with a variety of mental health problems. He is currently studying the mental health of Third World children who are victims of disasters.